Perfect Fit

Also by Clare Gilmore

Love Interest

Perfect Fit

Fit

A Novel

Clare Gilmore

ST. MARTIN'S GRIFFIN
NEW YORK

First published in the United States by St. Martin's Griffin, an imprint of St. Martin's Publishing Group

PERFECT FIT. Copyright © 2024 by Clare Gilmore. All rights reserved. Printed in the United States of America. For information, address St. Martin's Publishing Group, 120 Broadway, New York, NY 10271.

www.stmartins.com

Designed by Jen Edwards
Needle illustration © puruan/Shutterstock

Library of Congress Cataloging-in-Publication Data

Names: Gilmore, Clare, author.
Title: Perfect fit : a novel / Clare Gilmore.
Description: First edition. | New York : St. Martin's Griffin, 2024.
Identifiers: LCCN 2024016785 | ISBN 9781250880567 (trade paperback) | ISBN 9781250880574 (ebook)
Subjects: LCGFT: Romance fiction. | Novels.
Classification: LCC PS3607.I452147 P47 2024 | DDC 813/.6—dc23/eng/20240415
LC record available at https://lccn.loc.gov/2024016785

Our books may be purchased in bulk for promotional, educational, or business use. Please contact your local bookseller or the Macmillan Corporate and Premium Sales Department at 1-800-221-7945, extension 5442, or by email at MacmillanSpecialMarkets@macmillan.com.

First Edition: 2024

10 9 8 7 6 5 4 3 2 1

For the triers, for the tired ones,
and for anyone who ever thought:
If I don't have the right outfit, I'm not going.

Perfect Fit

CHAPTER ONE

Do you ever wonder what happened to the girl who peaked in high school?

I think the answer depends on which version of her you're talking about. And in my theory, there are two versions:

1. The All-American Girl
2. The It Girl

I will elaborate on the difference.

The All-American Girl was a cheerleader. The All-American Girl was a good student. She was a good *person*, too, and everybody knew it. Charismatic and lovely and darling. Remember her? Or a version of her? Let's call her Annabelle.

In our archetypical example, Annabelle had a magnetic smile and cute freckles on her shoulders. She dated the quarterback, hosted the prom after-party on her family farm, organized bake sales, became the subject of several songs. After she got married, Annabelle got involved in a multilevel marketing scheme. You're pretty sure she's still doing that, but honestly, you had to unfollow her on principle a few years back. Even though you really, genuinely wish Annabelle and her entire downline the best.

You have nothing against Annabelle, and you never did.

The point is—

The point. Is.

You probably don't ever *wonder* about Annabelle.

But I think a lot of people wonder about the other girl who peaked in high school. The brief, time-capsule It Girl. She was your high school's female Icarus, a flawed teenager who flew too close to the sun and got burned, then fell from a great height and never recovered her hometown reputation. Archetypically.

Remember *her*?

Let's call her Josephine.

Josephine had hazel eyes with green specks you could only ever see in the sunlight. Long lashes, long legs, long everything. She was known for her fashion sense and her aloof personality—and, of course, her three-years-older boyfriend.

Nobody from high school remembers Josephine as tough, or thick-skinned, or smart, or kind, or impressionable. But everyone remembers the way she appeared to them. And *everyone* remembers how her It Girl era ended.

I do think people wonder where Josephine is now. What she's doing with her life. How she's been.

I *hope* they wonder if they were wrong about her all along.

Anyway. Completely unrelated, but she—*I*—just hit a cyclist with her car.

(Not on purpose!)

(And technically, *he* ran into *me*.)

A tiny squeak spills past my lips right as I feel the collision, my body rocking forward as I stomp on the brakes. I grip the worn leather of my steering wheel, panting, and crane my neck to peer in my rearview mirror. There's a small portion of the back window visible— about two useful inches—between the boxes piled in my trunk.

All I can see is a sliver of blue sky and a line of cars behind me.

I shift into park and unbuckle my seat belt. Outside, a driver honks, but I ignore it and move to the opposite back corner of my car—where I could've *sworn* I spotted a cyclist in my rearview about five seconds before I felt the bump.

Sure enough, a man in a clean-cut black suit and a backpack still strapped between his shoulder blades is rolling onto his knees, groaning as he palms the concrete. Beside him, his bike looks equally pummeled.

It's the Giant Escape 3, I note absently, one of the best commuter bikes out there. I know because I almost bought one.

"Are you okay?" I ask, crouching low beside his tabletop position.

I'm apprised only of this man's hunched-over profile at the moment, but even like this, I can tell he's made up of lean, trained muscle, broad shoulders, a rippling back. It's when he turns his head at the sound of my voice that I catch sight of his face full-on.

My stomach buckles when I *recognize* him.

Will Grant.

Large, hesitant eyes. The color makes me think his maker mixed a cloudy, marbled sky with the color of the Blue Ridge Mountains against a haze. Honey-brown hair, several inches long and in desperate need of taming after his crash. His face is clean-shaven and square-shaped, his chin very softly dimpled right in the middle. He's older now—but still my same age, so twenty-seven or twenty-eight?—with the beginnings of crow's feet forming in the corners of his eyes.

And look. Maybe he works on them, probably he doesn't. But I have a three-step lash routine, and Will Grant is outdoing me.

"Josie?" His voice is different, too. Deeper, and maybe less . . .

alive? It's like he's working very hard to say my name, which, sure, given the accident—

I snap out of my daze, give my head a brief shake, unlock every clenched muscle that seized in his presence. The *now* is more important than the *then*. "Are you hurt?"

"I'm fine," he groans, rolling out his neck.

"You don't *sound* fine," I say, panicked for a plethora of reasons. "You sound like something's broken."

Will half sighs, half grunts, eyes on the pavement. "Does *anybody* who says they're fine ever really mean it?"

His voice is coming out smoother now, more mellow, but the words are doing a better job of conveying a feeling than acting as a method of communication.

That feeling is: exasperated.

Already, after a grand total of twenty-eight words exchanged between us after *ten years without seeing each other,* Will Grant is *exasperated* with me.

"I guess what I mean is, are you imminently close to death?" I ask.

Will finally looks up again. He blinks at me twice. "I'm on my knees in the middle of an extremely busy road. That's relative."

"Do you need an ambulance?" I try again.

"No, I'm *fine.*" This time, one corner of his mouth ticks up, though it drops so quickly I might have imagined it. "Will be, anyway."

"I am *so* sorry," I mutter, hands fluttering helplessly over his form. I'm nervous to touch him. Nervous it'll hurt worse if I get too close.

"It's my fault, not yours. I hit you."

"Still—"

The driver behind us unleashes a long peal of their horn. We both turn and glare at the woman gesturing through her window.

"Let me pull over," I say. "Can you manage your bike?"

He nods, squeezing his eyes shut before pushing off the ground.

I jump back into my car, pulling onto the shoulder of South Lamar Boulevard. It's eight o'clock on a Wednesday morning. Traffic could not be worse heading into downtown Austin.

What's Will *doing* here?

Better question: What's Will doing *here*?

My abs still do not unclench, even as I slowly rationalize that yes, I probably *should have* expected a run-in like this one day.

Not like a *literal* run-in. But figuratively speaking.

I met the Grant twins when they moved to Nashville as high school seniors. According to my sources (read: my mother), they both live and work in Manhattan now, but their family is *from here.* Austin. My current city of residence. I couldn't have expected to build a whole-ass life in *their* hometown without seeing one of the twins eventually.

Though, between Will and Zoe . . . I think I'm relieved it's him and not her.

I *think.*

I mutter bountiful profanities under my breath. Today is a bad day to be late. It's a bad day to be distracted by high school memories *and* late.

I normally try to get an earlier start than this—and if I'm *really* early, I'll ride my own bike to work and get ready at the office—but I spent too much time in front of the mirror this morning, perfecting my makeup, my hair, my outfit, reciting my presentation until I had it memorized back to front.

I send up a prayer that this unwanted reunion isn't a bad omen.

When I turn off my ignition and climb out of my Ford Escape, Will is standing five feet from my bumper, frowning at it with his hands clenched around his mangled handlebars. Even the second time, it's a jump scare to see him in person.

"I dented your car," he says. "Sorry about that."

"You couldn't possibly have—" I cut myself off as I turn, eyes widening at the small dent on the bumper just below the rear door. "Wow."

"Yeah."

"How fast were you going?"

"Fast," he murmurs darkly. "I was running late, trying to sneak past the car traffic." After another moment he adds, "I was weaving."

"Weaving is dangerous," I say, like a rule-following dork.

"No shit." He winces as he taps at a quickly forming bruise on his face with two fingers.

Will's legs seem okay, but there's a tear in one pant leg near the knee, and his white shirt is covered in street tar. A small scrape on his upper left cheek is perforating his skin.

A nearly dominant part of me would like to finish assessing our collective damage and get out of Will Grant's presence as quickly as possible. My instincts are screaming at me to retreat. But, as is often the case, my people-pleasing personality wins out. I can't leave him now that we've broken this ten-year barrier until every wrinkle has been smoothed. Until every wound has been cleaned, sterilized, covered up, and hidden away.

"I have a first aid kit in my car. And I can drive you," I add. "To wherever and whatever it is you're late for."

Will tilts his head, his blue eyes locking on mine. *"I hit you."*

"I know that. But I still want to help."

After a beat of silence where Will openly stares at me, he asks, "Why on earth would you want to help *me*?"

I laugh, the sound burbling out of me like shaken-up fizzy water through the neck of a bottle. Too many feelings, nowhere to go but out. My skin is hot and tight. I search my lexicon for an adequate response before settling on "I don't know."

Will's gaze softens. I feel awkward. He probably (definitely) feels awkward. This entire situation is so damn awkward, and now my abs are starting to hurt.

I glance down at his bike, willing it to self-repair. "That doesn't look operational, I'm afraid. A ride is the least I can do. Where are you headed?"

I don't ask the other question—*What the fuck are you doing in town at all, and on the most important Wednesday I've had in a while???*—even though it's what I'm dying to know.

There isn't a family-oriented holiday coming up; it's early June. And anyway, I don't remember the Grants being close with the family they left behind in Austin when they moved away. Will's parents are in Nashville, and his career and personal life are in New York.

Why. Is. He. Here?

Traveling for work is my best guess, but the bike is throwing me off.

Will's lips tug up on one side again as he considers me more seriously. It's still not a smile, not even close. He completely ignores my previous question and says, "Thank you for the offer, but I'll be fine—"

"You were going fast enough to *put a dent in my car*," I interrupt. "Obviously, whatever you have going on this morning is important." For some reason, this makes his half-baked smile kick up another twenty degrees. "Calling an Uber or even a friend, if you've managed to acquire one of those since we knew each other"—he snorts softly—"is going to take forever in this traffic. Please let me help you?"

Will sighs and his expression gives. I've worn him down. "I can't show up to meet my client in these clothes."

"In that case," I say, "today is your lucky day."

"How on *earth*," Will says, "is today my lucky day?"

"Because you hit *me*. And I have an entire closet in my trunk."

He eyes my body, hands clenching the handlebars tighter. "I don't think you and I have the same style, Josie."

I open my trunk. When some of the boxes tumble out, I'm

prepared. (I have dealt with this five times already this week.) Sample testing is one of my favorite parts of my job. There's something endlessly satisfying about feeling the design beneath your fingertips, seeing it on a real person instead of a mannequin or a computer screen.

"You look like a thirty-two?" I guess, turning back to Will.

He nods, and now his amusement has caught fire, his smile begrudgingly holding around his eyes. Are those dimples on his cheeks? I don't remember them, but then again, Will didn't do much smiling when we were high school seniors. They match the divot in his chin.

"That's one of our men's sample sizes," I say. "We've got slacks in gray, black, forest green, navy blue. There are some white shirts around here, too. Different box, I think." I put three of them on the ground, riffling through the material. "Wait, those are women's blazers. Hang on."

"I nearly forgot," Will calls to me.

I stand back up, my gaze switching to him. "Forgot what?"

His voice comes out low and focused. "That you're the CEO of a clothing company."

I pause to consider the nuance of what he means. We're facing each other now as adults with real careers and fully developed brains. Two things neither of us had the last time we spoke.

To Will, I was Zoe's best friend. I once overheard him refer to me as a surface-level kind of girl. (I think it was his reaction to my girlish enthusiasm over an album release I was excited about, which enraged me to the point of mentally dismissing him.) To me, Will was Zoe's malcontent twin brother, hot as fuck, but strictly off-limits, and too moody besides.

Funny, considering now Will's looking at me like I hold a modicum of interest to him, and I'm looking at him noting he's still moody but can at least manage a dimpled smile.

I fiddle with the shirt cuffs of the blouse I'm wearing. Dusty blue, tucked into high-waisted cream balloon pants. "Yes," I say.

"I heard a couple years ago." He cocks his head to one side, a lock of hair falling between his eyes, just as my heart stalls out and revs back to life at the idea that I have come up in conversations he was part of. "Are these—" Will points at the clothes, still in boxes at my feet. "Are you suggesting I wear trade secrets to work today?"

"Trade secrets might be a *little* dramatic—"

"But these items aren't on sale yet, are they?"

"No, they're not."

Even though it's the height of summer and the Texas wind is warm, I shiver as the cars passing by push the air against us in rushes, over and over.

I can't tell if this is getting more or less awkward by the second. If I was aiming for polite, I'd ask about Zoe, but that's a can of worms I'm pretty sure I don't want to mentally open now, or maybe ever. Will isn't exactly being effusive, either.

He steps toward me, rolling his bike with him. He's taller than me but not by much, maybe just a few inches. Which means he'd be taller than most girls by a *lot* more than a few inches.

"I think we might be headed to the same place," he admits. "Your office is in that complex on North Congress, isn't it?"

I nod.

"So is the client I'm meeting this morning." His lips part just a smidge, eyes roving from the boxes at my feet to the additional boxes in the trunk of my car. "Do you think there's room for my bike in there?"

My shoulders perk up. He's accepting my help. It feels like a truce, or at least a mutual agreement to ignore the past. "Definitely! We can put the back seats down. Take off the front wheel. We'll make it work."

I spring into action, climbing into my trunk so I can push the boxes toward the front seats and neatly stack them. Part of me knows my ass is aimed at Will, and part of me hopes he's too busy taking off his bike wheel to notice. Before I climb out, I secure a pair of black pants and a white shirt that match what he's wearing.

As the owner of a fashion brand, I'll deny it to the day I crack open my retirement fund, but sometimes, the predictability of men's clothing comes in handy.

Will places the bike into the space I've cleared as if relocating a cherished feather and then grabs his front wheel off the ground, resting it on top of the bike. His arm stretches up, straining against dirty cotton to close the trunk.

He nods at the clothes in my hands, pulling the backpack off his shoulders. "I'll change into them in the Starbucks bathroom on the first floor. I promise not to ruin them, and I'll make sure they get back to you."

"Oh, don't worry about that. It'll get you through one day, but the inseam on these pants needs some work, and the material of the shirt feels wrong to me."

I hand over the clothes and our thumbs brush. My nervous system spirals. Will pushes the items neatly into the top of his backpack.

Finally, my curiosity cracks all the way open, igniting the coals of my interest. "Where do you work?" I ask, heading toward the driver's side door.

He mirrors me on the other side of the car. "I work at Ellis Consulting."

Well then.

I school my features from sour back to neutral before slipping inside.

Ellis is the firm I *wanted* to use for my business, but I couldn't afford their exorbitant rates and had to settle for a different consultant with a worse reputation.

If it were up to me, I wouldn't be using a consultant at all. But my primary investor is "highly recommending it."

"Nice," I say after both our doors close, sounding as salty as I feel. "I've heard of Ellis. Very fancy logo."

Cajolingly, Will says, "Revenant has a nice logo."

"Don't say it just to make me feel better."

"It's like you don't know me at all."

I snort. "Will Grant, I *don't* know you at all. Never did, even back then. You were a brick wall of pouting."

"I didn't pout."

"All you did was pout. You were Season One Conrad Fisher. You were Olivia Rodrigo's entire *Sour* album, on repeat. You were Ken when Barbie took away his mojo dojo casa house. You were—"

"At least four other references I won't understand?" he interrupts.

"Don't worry," I say. "All the other surface-level girls would get them."

Will either doesn't remember making that comment or he's making a show of confusion by knitting his brows together. I can't tell, because, as established, we never really got to know each other. Something seems to click, though, and his befuddlement shifts to embarrassment.

I pop open the console between us and shuffle around until my hands grip the first aid kit wedged between spare sunglasses, tissues, gum. Tampons, a sewing kit, hair clips—

"You don't happen to have four fives I could trade you for a twenty?"

"I do, actually—" My head snaps up. We're nose to nose.

He's smiling now—not just an almost-smile, a *real* smile, both his dimples completely fleshed out and bare to me—his blue eyes starker in the shadows of the car. My breath stutters on an inhale, swirling around in my lungs.

I have felt this feeling before, with him near, *causing it,* and it was a huge mistake. *Backpedal, immediately.*

"I was just kidding, Josie." There's a playfulness to his tone I'm pretty sure might be a rarity for Will. As if he's trying it on for size but isn't quite used to it.

"You're capable of that?"

"Only once my pouting phase ended."

I point at my supplies. "I like to be prepared."

He nods, biting the inside of his cheek. "Mm-hmm."

I can't tell if he's making fun of me or not—or if, perhaps, he's thinking about how I'm easily predictable with my hyper-organized car full of trend-right hand sanitizer and mini peanut butter protein bars—so I say nothing and pop open the kit, pulling out a couple of alcohol wipes, Neosporin, Band-Aids. When I pass the items from my hands to his, our skin grazes *again,* and it feels like a memory I don't want.

I pull off the shoulder of the boulevard, braiding my car back into the traffic headed downtown. My phone is still connected to Bluetooth, and Gracie Abrams starts to play. I turn down the volume and flick my eyes over to Will beside me, who has the visor mirror open and is fixing up the scrape on his cheek. He's careful and thorough, cleaning the wound, covering it.

"You don't live here, do you?" I ask.

He doesn't break focus from the mirror. "You know I lived here first, don't you?"

"I wasn't *claiming* Austin." Vocally.

"Good, because it's a claim you would've lost."

"I was just wondering."

There's a pause while Will balls up the Band-Aid scraps and pockets them. "No, I don't live here. I live in Manhattan, but I have clients in Austin."

"Your employer doesn't compensate your Ubers?"

"I *like* cycling to work," Will says, his tone indicating he doesn't expect me to understand the appeal. "And I chose a hotel in Zilker because it's where I grew up."

Okay, I will *not* be telling him I also live in Zilker. It would border on creepy, even though I had no idea that's where he and Zoe lived as kids.

"Where'd the bike come from?"

"It's a rental," Will clarifies, eyebrow lifting. "Is this an interrogation?"

I blush and shut up, focusing on the road. "Grumpy," I mumble. Beside me, Will's palms move up and down his thighs in slow slides.

"How can I make this up to you?" he asks a minute later.

"Buy Revenant products," I joke.

"I already do that." I glance over to see if he's kidding, my focus catching on the tiny Band-Aid stuck to his cheekbone. But his eyes are serious and warm on mine. "I like Revenant clothes," he murmurs. "I like the way they . . . feel."

That face, coupled with the praise falling off his tongue, is flipping my stomach. It's not even a direct compliment, and I'm still pretty sure it's the nicest thing Will Grant has ever said to me. Which isn't a grand assumption. It's just factual.

"Yeah?" I ask.

He faces forward, obviously uncomfortable repeating himself. "Besides. Revenant is the Austin cult classic."

I snort. "Did you just quote that *Bite the Hand* profile?"

Will laughs deeply. It reverberates around the car, spreading out like it plans to stay once he's gone. "I did."

"You obsessed with me or something?"

"I'm *professionally* intrigued by your business model," he counters.

"That's what all the men say to me."

"Are you insinuating," Will says, "that a man has *actually* tried to pick you up by hitting on your company?"

"Every year, at the CEO summit I go to."

After a few seconds of silent thinking he says, "I don't know how to respond to that," which makes me laugh out loud.

"Exactly how much do you know about Revenant?" I ask.

He looks back over. Our eyes hold one heartbeat too long. "About as much as was written in that profile. I read it twice."

Twice. He read it twice. He just *admitted* to me he read it twice.

The profile in question was a lengthy piece published by a New York digital media start-up after the editor in chief reached out to me, saying he'd gotten a tip I was one to watch, and could he interview me for a digital spread?

I'd barely had the courage to say yes. Ever since I accepted the fact that I *cannot* use social media in a healthy way—the same way others can't have only two drinks, or go window-shopping but *not* spend any (all) of their money—press isn't something I *ever* look forward to. I become obsessed with my public perception, put too much worth into other people's opinions of me.

But that editor had seemed intentional. Plus, he never once referred to me as a girl boss (a term and concept I *loathe*) in our first phone call. I liked him instantly, and when we set up a call, the conversation flowed.

That was a year and a half ago, right at the cusp of Revenant's rapid growth. Before, I was doing only drops, making every sale to order with a handful of employees and one manufacturer. But *after* it published—and especially after the TikTok fashion girls covered the highlights in a bunch of viral videos I've never personally seen—Revenant exploded.

I grip the steering wheel, daring myself to keep my gaze forward. Every time I glance over, I'm worried I'm going to wreck for how distracting Will's focus on me feels.

I change the subject back to him. "What kind of companies do you work with?"

"Lots," he admits after a second. "But usually start-ups." Will shifts next to me, adjusting in his seat, and changes the subject right back. "The CEO isn't worried about being late?"

"Cut me some slack. I was at the office until two in the morning yesterday."

Will whistles. "More trade secrets, or can I ask?"

"Just finalizing a presentation."

"On what?"

"Is this an interrogation?" I parrot.

"Cute."

I throw him a good-natured eye roll. "Actually, I'm pitching a strategy to a consulting firm today. We're probably going to hire them."

There's a pause. "Not Ellis, though." He doesn't phrase it as a question, as if Will already knows I'm not working with his employer.

"No. I can't afford Ellis."

The tall buildings of the city loom before us as we cross the bridge over the Colorado River. I turn, heading toward North Congress Avenue and the building where my company rents a floor. Downtown is alive right now, people crossing the street with lattes in hand, wearing everything from streetwear to last night's college date-party costume. I spot a thirty-something woman in a Revenant blazer. It sends a zip of happiness from my head to my toes.

"Where should I drop you off?"

"I usually lock up at the bike rack in the garage."

We head in that direction. Will's presence in my car seems to grow, like he's filling up the space just before he leaves it. He shifts again, one elbow leaning on my console. I finally catch his scent—which hits my memory in the same instant. He smells like warm cedar logs baked in sunlight. There's something sweet but almost earthy about it, too.

He also smells a bit like pavement. That's probably circumstantial.

I pull over by the bike rack and pop the trunk. We climb out and meet around back.

"Do you need help getting back to your hotel later?" I ask. "Or the bike shop?"

Belatedly, I realize that if Will says yes, I'll have to see him *again*. Stupid, stupid. But I can't seem to help myself.

Will picks up his bike. There's not a hint of strain in his voice when he speaks, which I find biologically fascinating. "You know, for a corporate exec, you're not making me feel like I'm wasting your time just by breathing near you."

"Is that your general experience with my kind?"

"Mostly."

"Guess I can be different after all," I snark.

His face takes on an expression I can't interpret. "Thanks for the help, Josie. Really. But I'll take care of myself from here."

"Okay." Relief and regret flood me in equal doses. I rub the heel of my palm against my hip bone. "It was . . . good . . . to see you."

Will snorts. "Sounds like you really meant that."

I throw him a look. Will smirks—which I take as his parting sentiment—before he bends over, unzipping his backpack and pulling out a bike lock.

Only once I start my car and strap in is there a knock on the window that makes me jump.

Will stares at me through the glass, gesturing for me to roll the window down. I do.

"I didn't mean to scare you," he says, leaning his forearm along the gap in the door. He's close enough that I can smell peppermint on his breath.

"I'm not scared of you," I manage.

"What time is your presentation?"

"Um." I blink. "Eleven thirty."

He nods, and his eyes go distant. "Okay."

Okay?

"I . . ." Will trails off, then shakes his head slightly. He pulls his weight off my car and takes a step back. "It was good to see you, too." He rubs his lips together. "Josie." My name comes off his tongue like he's tasting the way it sounds. "I'll be seeing you."

"You will?" My voice sounds horrified.

Dimples. Both of them. "Of course. I'm going to fix your car."

I shake my head. "No need. It's just a tiny scratch—"

"Josephine," he scolds, voice low, and my whole body violently erupts, hearing my full name from *him* after all this time. "I am *going* to fix your car."

"Mkay," I manage, then locate the cognizance to add, "Least you can do, honestly."

"There she is." Will taps twice on the hood and starts backing away, slinging his backpack over his shoulder. "I have to go."

"Yes. That was the whole point of the ride."

He bites on a smile. We're finding our groove. Still, thank God this is almost over. My abs are exhausted.

"I'll find you," he says. "Somehow."

I nod. "Do that."

Will keeps staring at me until he turns away, picking up his pace as he heads for the ground entrance of the building. I'm halfway tempted to shout after him, to ask if he'd mind fixing me, too, because I think the way he just slammed into me broke open a wound I thought I'd closed for good ten years back.

CHAPTER TWO

have this rule.

(I have a lot of rules.)

But I've got this one specific rule about how my workday begins. It's ritualistic, refined over time, and nonnegotiable.

If I break the rule, chaos ensues.

The rule is: I *have* to start the day with an iced caramel oat milk latte. Doesn't matter if I'm traveling, at the office, or working from home. ICOML (pronounced *EYE-com-ul*) has to be involved or I break down due to inconsistency.

The other nonnegotiable start to my morning is Camila San-chez, my best friend. She's also Revenant's chief brand officer and the only person besides me who has been with this company from almost the very start.

When I walk into the office, Cami approaches with an ICOML in hand, her luscious dark hair pulled into a low pony wrapped in a Revenant bow, eyes heavily lined in a muted purple color. She passes the iced coffee from her palm to mine and unleashes her monologue.

"Asset Protection is swearing up and down we've got a case of organized crime on our hands, and Hailey Bieber wore *this* bow"—she points at the back of her head—"in a YouTube video that came out yesterday. So, obviously, we're out of stock online. Also, the college interns start in five days, don't forget. Did you approve the samples yet for the new men's line?"

"Organized crime," I say. "Why does that feel like an impressive achievement?"

"Oh, I agree," Cami says. "I acted upset when they told me about it, but secretly I was thinking we've made it."

"The Hailey Bieber thing scares me," I admit, shuddering as we pass by the retail team's desk area. "You know how much I hate—"

"Trending," Cami finishes. "Yep, I know."

Revenant's office space is open-floor concept, its windows swallowing the walls to showcase views of the city. Our desks stand, sit, even hover near the floor if you feel like getting horizontal. Visually, the space is neutral and clean-cut, much like the clothes we sell. On one wall, a string of gray letter decals spells out our tagline: *Fill your closet once.*

"I haven't forgotten about the interns," I say. "I blocked off that whole Monday morning for a get-to-know-you breakfast. And about the samples—"

Most other companies would have green-lit those samples by now, but that's not how Revenant operates. We mean what we say about filling your closet once. That's Revenant's whole thing: a well-made capsule wardrobe you build over time.

My mind careens back to Will. I picture him buttoning the sample shirt across his chest with his scraped-up, calloused fingers in a nearby Starbucks bathroom, then heading for the elevators while he drinks something surly, like a drip coffee with no cream or sugar.

Should I ask him his opinion on the samples when he *finds me, somehow*?

It's not like I have other men in my life to poll. I haven't dated in more than four years, and my older brother, Robbie—who lives in North Carolina—shops exclusively on Amazon. My dad supports Revenant, but he lives back home in Nashville. We usually pool feedback from the men in the office, but something about getting Will's opinion has my stomach somersaulting.

"I need two days to gather my thoughts," I tell Cami.

"Great!" We land in front of her office, and Cami halts, turning to face me straight on. "Now that all the boring stuff is out of the way—"

"Nice try—"

"Maybe you could give me a status update on—"

"No." I'm already shaking my head when I say it. We've done this every morning for two weeks. "Cami, don't you trust me?"

Her hands clench into tiny, dramatic fists between our faces. "To run a fashion brand? Sure, Josie. To plan my bachelorette party? Less and less by the day."

"*Don't let me get involved, even when I start begging*. Remember saying that? Remember telling me those exact words after you got so wrapped up in David's proposal plan that you found the ring"—I gesture down to her left hand, where her princess-cut engagement ring sparkles—"in his parents' house with your spare key?"

Cami rolls her eyes. "You act like they'd hidden it well."

"It was in his mother's underwear drawer!"

"Which is *weird*!" Cami exclaims, pointing an accusatory finger in the air as she backs toward her office. Behind her, I catch a glimpse of her messy desk littered with trinkets, empty cups, six or seven lipsticks. "That's fucking *weird*, right?"

I laugh despite myself. It is pretty weird, but I refuse to give her the satisfaction of admitting it. "Could've gone your whole life never knowing. But you meddled."

"I had to bathe it in jewelry cleaner for hours after the proposal."

"Which you had on hand because you meddled."

"Just give me *one* hint about the bachelorette."

"It's in Nashville."

Cami groans. She's only five-two, but when she gets worked up, her personality feels big enough to fill our whole office. "I already *knew* that, asshole!"

It was one of the only things she picked: the location. I'm not thrilled about it, considering Nashville is where I'm from and I typically avoid it apart from family holidays. But as any good bridesmaid knows *and* recites to herself on repeat throughout the wedding festivities—when the gown looks horrible on their body type, when there's nothing vegetarian on the rehearsal dinner menu, when the bride asks them to take out every orange flower from the bouquets because *they're not really orange they're peach, and I hate peach!*—"It's not about me."

Cami kerplunks into her chair, and I smirk as I keep walking, heading to my own office four doors down. It's neat and organized, with pastel highlighters jammed in a cup and Revenant's first designs framed in white birchwood on the wall. Beneath my desk is a walking pad, and in one corner is a Zen garden I sometimes play with when I need to think.

I've barely sat down when Derrick appears in my doorway.

Derrick Lovell: a Dennis Quaid look-alike in his late fifties with salt-and-pepper hair and a grandfatherly voice, who's known for having a Midas-like business touch, as well as dozens of plaid shirts from the nineties prep craze. He's Revenant's biggest investor, and not a bad guy, as far as I can tell, but I'd wager he didn't become the CEO of five (five!) retail giants by only being nice.

"Josie." He nods in greeting. Today he's wearing a flimsy blue-and-yellow plaid shirt tucked into plain khakis, and old shoes with literal holes. This outfit, from a bona fide billionaire.

"Derrick."

"I heard a rumor from security you were here until two in the morning."

I wince. "Yeah, well, I came in late today, didn't I?"

"It's eight forty-five."

I stare at him. He stares at me. Sometimes, I swear I catch glimpses of fatherly care on Derrick's face when he looks at me. I know he's got a daughter around my age. She's twenty-three, maybe?

"Can you email me that presentation?" he asks.

"You bet."

His hand doesn't unclench from the door handle. "Can you also give me an overview?"

I recline in my chair, grabbing a highlighter to fiddle with. "Sustainable"—Derrick winces—"sourcing," I finish.

"I was afraid you were going to say that."

"It gets worse."

Derrick's face pales. "How."

"I want to get B Corp Certified."

I may as well have told him I'm interested in flushing money down the toilet. Still, Derrick's expression is a *little* dramatic right now.

He points it skyward, releases a weary sigh. "You are bleeding me dry, Davis."

"That's simply untrue."

"Remind me of the *point* of a B Corp Certification?" he asks.

"It basically means our company has been verified to have high standards."

Derrick glowers. "So, you would like to raise this company's standards?"

I smirk. "I'd like everyone to raise their standards, but yes, I'll start with Revenant."

He pinches the bridge of his nose. "And what standards are we raising?"

"Accountability, transparency, charitable giving, and supply-chain best practices."

Derrick nods, staring sideways. "High standards are expensive, no doubt."

I stand up, coming around the corner of my desk to face him. "This is a good thing, Derrick. I promise."

He points a finger at me. "You'd better make us believe it today, Josie. If the consultant isn't on board, neither am I."

I nod and say, "I'm not worried."

I am *so* worried.

I am *constantly* worried.

I work myself into spirals, worrying. I pace my kitchen at four a.m., worrying. Every time Revenant hits a goal, outperforms a plan, *trends* on social media, I worry, waiting for the other shoe to drop. Because it feels inevitable. Nothing this good can last. The tide of public opinion will turn; the customers will revolt.

They will take their final measure of me and determine I'm unworthy.

Still, amidst these fears, I *desperately* want everything about the little business I started in my dorm room with my grandmother's old sewing machine to stay absolutely perfect.

Unlike me, I hope Revenant never needs a second wind.

CHAPTER THREE

The consultant we're planning to hire is the Carlisle Group. Today is our first in-person meeting, and if all goes well, we'll sign the contracts. The guy I've been emailing with is named Kyle. (In my head, I've been calling him Carlisle Kyle.)

"Josephine," Kyle says, shaking my hand as he and his two co-workers enter our boardroom. His hand softens around mine but doesn't let go, almost like he's just . . . holding it. Immediate ick. "Good to meet you in person."

"Likewise," I say brightly, taking my hand back. I point at three chairs near the front of the long table. "Saved you the best seats in the house."

One of the others—perhaps Carlisle Lyle—winks as he passes. I roll out my neck, shutting the glass door to the boardroom, and exchange a goofy, unserious look with Cami as I make my way to the front.

Most of the eyes in this room are warm and encouraging. These people *know* me. It's only the Carlisles I need to impress.

I take a sip of my water as the chatter softens. Then I hear a knock on the glass door.

I turn my head, squinting, and make out the outline of a man beyond the wall. It takes me a second to place him from this distance, but yep—

That's Will fucking Grant, all right.

He has one palm pushed flat against the glass, one leg hooked behind the other. When our eyes lock, his face turns just enough to paint itself in the colors of my presentation theme, reflecting onto his skin. Orange and pink and soft, dusty blue.

His face conveys nothing. He just leans there, waiting for me.

What time is your presentation?

"Um." I blink, shaking my head, and then address the room. Only half of them hear me, the other half still making introductions. "One moment, please."

My heels click back over to the door. I feel dizzier and dizzier the more Will comes into focus. A clarity rocks me as I register the clothes he's dressed in; he's wearing the samples like they were made for him.

And the tiny Band-Aid is still stuck to his upper cheekbone.

I pull open the door, step outside into the deserted hallway.

"I'm gonna talk really fast, okay?" he says.

I gape at him, stunned. "Okay."

I don't know whether to feel angry or confused or bewildered or all three. Will *knew* I was busy right now. Exactly right now. Unless this is an emergency—

"I'm the reason you were quoted such a high rate when you approached Ellis about working together."

His words make me immediately nauseous.

"Why?" I bite out.

His face contorts. His voice comes out hollow. "They wanted me for the job since I'm the newest and often work with start-ups your size. But I told my boss we knew each other, and I didn't think it was . . ." He blushes and drops eye contact. "I told my boss it was not a good idea. So, they offered your business to a different consultant who charges more because of his experience level."

I should be angry—I should be *so* angry—but instead I'm just embarrassed, ashamed.

Not a good idea. You, Josie, are not a good idea.

"You needed to get that off your chest *right this minute*?" I hiss.

Will's expression is urgency swirled up in a cocktail of regret. "The best way I know how to apologize is to fix it, Josie."

"How," I ask, "are you planning to fix this?"

He swallows thickly. "I spent the last three hours studying Revenant in between my other meetings. I know every public detail about your business back to front. I would have done this later, but my flight back to New York is in a few hours, and I knew your other consultant option was here, so I figured it was now or never." He nods at the room. "I also had a feeling it was Carlisle, and I can't in good conscience let you settle for them."

"Oh, *now* your conscience has something to say?"

"I am *so* sorry, Josie. You have no idea how sorry I am." He pauses, then inhales to go on, his voice scraping out of him fast and urgent. "I'll sign a nondisclosure if you let me listen to your presentation, even if you turn me down afterward. But I hope you choose me. Not because you owe me anything, but because you'll get Ellis on your payroll for cheaper. And I will work harder for you than I have ever worked on anything to make up for this."

It's impossible not to hear the earnestness in his voice, impossible not to see the twist in his face. As frustrated and blindsided as I am—this, I can revel in.

"What do you say?" Will asks.

My lips part in a desperate attempt to form a coherent response. "We were going to sign contracts with Carlisle today."

"Don't," Will says, his voice low. "Trust me, Josie. *Don't.*"

He sounds like he's speaking from experience. I want to ask more questions about that, but there's no time. I can already feel the stares of everyone in the boardroom on my back, their curiosity growing.

"You don't have to answer me right this instant," he says. "But Josie, I think this could work. You and me."

He first thought it was not a good idea. And now he thinks it could work?

My mind is swirling, and my abs have reclenched. Nothing about today is making sense.

From a business perspective, it's a no-brainer. Ellis is the superior firm. At an affordable rate, it's the clear winner. But what exactly did I say this morning that changed his mind about working with me? And why didn't he admit the truth then?

"I'm so frustrated right now," I mutter.

For whatever reason, this relaxes him. "Yeah. You have every right to be."

"I'm not doing this to ease your conscience," I say. "I'm doing it because it's a smart business decision."

He nods gently. "I know."

"You'd better not be bluffing about how hard you're willing to work."

Will shakes his head. "Not bluffing."

I shoot him one last glare. "Follow me."

Will's blue-gray eyes dance with victory.

I pull open the door and summon all the authority I possess. "We've got one more," I say, addressing no one in particular. "Can someone pull up an extra chair?"

Spite is what gets me through that presentation. The urge to prove to Will I'm competent, I'm easy to work with, I'm *good* at this. I speak mostly just to him, keeping his eyes, holding his gaze. The desire to make him regret turning me down in the first place is the pulse racing beneath my skin. It's the breeze in my hair on the weekend. My frustration transforms into an even voice, a series of smart words I don't trip over. Will, for his part, looks thoughtful. Like he might genuinely be entertaining the B Corp idea, and that's also infuriating, for no reason.

He asks a question about my sustainability ideas; I offer a calm, collected answer. Carlisle Kyle's head whips back at the sound of Will's voice, and his expression changes from bored to sharp. Kyle doesn't look away from Will until the rest of the room is dismissed.

"What the fuck is *he* doing here?" Kyle asks.

"You'll watch your language," Derrick warns.

It's just us now. The consultants, me, Derrick. I'm tempted to take one of the vacated seats (these heels are a bitch), but I'm the CEO. I stay standing so everybody remembers it.

"Josie." Derrick threads his fingers and sets them on the table in front of him. Slowly, his head turns in my direction. "Explain?"

I gulp, second-guessing myself now. If I follow through with this, it'll be the most madcap scheme I've agreed to in years. My most spontaneous decision since . . . since *that* one. The big, bad, friendship-ruining decision I made when I was seventeen. And funny enough, Will Grant was involved then, too.

Apparently, he brings out my impulsivity.

But when I look across the table at him, a levelheaded patience shines back at me, the emotion stretching across every foot separating us. I can *feel* Will's intent.

It feels honest.

Hopeful.

When I look at Kyle and the others, I can't feel anything.

"This is Will Grant, from Ellis," I say. "Revenant's consultant of choice."

There's a brief, stunned silence as my words land, followed by two scoffs from the Carlisle team and one wince from Derrick.

"We had a handshake agreement," Kyle says.

"I changed my mind," I say.

Another scoff. "*You changed your mind?*" Kyle throws a hand in Will's direction. "Don't fall for him, Josephine. He doesn't care about you. He's only doing this to get at me."

"Josie, that's *not* true," Will says. "I didn't even know Kyle was here until I showed up."

I try to care, try to focus on the conversation unfolding, but the animosity in this room isn't coming from me at this point, nor is it directed my way. I didn't sleep last night, and I don't have time for this, and I *didn't even want a consultant in the first place,* and when was the last time I ate something? Every useless, hypermasculine word Kyle says pushes on my skull with sharp edges. My vision starts to dance.

"I need a minute."

My feet carry me toward the glass door, heels echoing now that the room is silent. When I pass by Will, he stands, but I don't stop. Can't. Not when I'm feeling this woozy.

Lucky for me, there's a ritual for this, too.

CHAPTER FOUR

I adore the UT Austin campus. In particular, Whitis Court. Knobby, ancient trees that stretch out overhead and blanket the space in dappled shade. A constantly overstuffed bike rack, concrete picnic tables, old grills. The whole thing is enclosed by buildings I used to frequent. Six years out of college and I still find excuses to visit once a month.

I swear the chain restaurants around campus taste better, too. When I need to decompress, I'll go by the nearest sandwich shop and bring my lunch here, unrolling the blanket I keep in my car to have a picnic at my old stomping grounds.

I like people-watching the students—especially the freshmen. I wish I could bottle the looks on their faces, figure out how to feel their peace. Walking to class, gazing into the eyes of their crush, lounging in the grass reading a textbook. Since it's summer, campus is mostly deserted right now, but still. This is how I keep that period of life in my pocket, how I uncork the peaceful memories when I'm feeling some type of way.

"The problem," my mother says, the sound of her chipper voice wrapping around my heart through my AirPods, across three states and eight hundred and fifty miles, "is that Mindy Meyer is already bringing red velvet *cookies*. So, I can't exactly bring my red velvet cupcakes with cream cheese swirl."

"Fuck Mindy Meyer," I tell her, my hands wrapping around the sandwich in my lap. I'm sitting cross-legged, my picnic adjacent to the dorm I lived in almost ten years ago when I first moved to Austin. The dorm where I got to know Camila. "Your red velvet cupcakes are orgasmic."

"Darling, I don't care to know what inanimate objects give you an orgasm."

"I've never even heard of a red velvet cookie."

"Right?" Mom screeches. "It's diabolically brilliant!"

"What's the occasion?" I ask before taking another bite of my lunch.

"Oh, her daughter Ellen is getting married. We've been gently asked to throw her an engagement shower. Which reminds me. As far away as you are from receiving a proposal, I hope you don't mind I put a large chunk of your wedding fund into the stock market."

"Mom, *what?*"

"But all's well that ends well, because I doubled it just yesterday."

I smirk and shake my head, standing up and grabbing the blanket. "Does Dad know?"

A pause. "He does *now.*"

My mother, God love her, has never worked a traditional job a day in her life. When I was fifteen, she used to call me in the middle of the school day and ask if I needed anything. Tampon, brownies for chemistry class, fresh underwear?

There were years—many years, after Robbie went to college and I got my driver's license alongside my independence—when Mom fell into a depression born from the absence of being needed. But now she has hobbies, and one of them is the stock market.

"And look, we both know I adore your sister-in-law. But I don't think her parents put more than fifty thousand into that wedding, and I just want *more* for you—"

"I'm getting married at Lake Como," I announce, walking back to my car.

"You're very funny, darling, but Grandma Jean *cannot* travel to Italy at her age."

"Grandma Jean is not invited."

"JoJo."

"Mother."

I reach my car and unlock it, eyeing the boxes of samples in the backseat. My mind is at work again, reviewing everything I need to accomplish this afternoon.

"I gotta go, Mom."

"Fine, but one more thing. Would you mind raising the price of your purses online? I'm interested in gifting one to Georgie Halstead, but I just *know* she's going to look up how much I spent, and frankly, it won't be enough."

"No. Try Chloé."

"This is what I get for supporting your endeavors!"

"Give Dad kisses for me."

"Wait!"

I roll my eyes, strapping in. "Yes?"

There's a pause as I pull back onto Guadalupe Street. "You okay, JoJo?"

I grip the steering wheel. "Fine. Just wanted to hear your voice, that's all."

She sighs. "I'm going to squeeze you extra tight when you're in Nashville for Camila's bachelorette."

"That'll be a busy weekend," I say.

"You'll make the time for your parents."

I smile softly. "I will."

We hang up, and I pull my AirPods out of my ears. What is it about talking to my mother that's a simultaneous choke hold and a breath of fresh air? I overcorrected *so hard* trying to differentiate myself from her that I wound up the CEO of my own fashion brand. But in carefully measured doses, I adore her, and in some ways, Harriet Davis is my idol.

Back in the office, I head straight for the boardroom. The Carlisle guys have vanished at this point, but Will is still there with Derrick, their heads bent low over paperwork with our company lawyer, Ilya.

"Sorry about that," I say, like I was gone for three minutes rather than fifty-seven.

Will stands again. His eyes rove over me. "Hey," he says, his voice oddly warm.

"Hi."

Derrick stands, too. "We've ironed out the details, Josie. You picked an impressive young man as a business partner. I wasn't sure about the impulsivity of this, but Mr. Grant has sold me already."

Will's face reveals nothing, but he rubs his neck, uncomfortable with the compliment—his tell. I remember it from before. He'd always rub his neck around *me*.

"Great!" I chime in, my voice shrill. Somehow, I knew Will would win over Derrick without breaking a sweat. "And the contracts?"

"All taken care of," Ilya confirms, stacking his documents.

"We'll let you two talk." Derrick and Ilya head for the door. Derrick calls over his shoulder, "Maybe the three of us could get dinner one night this week before I head back to California."

"Anytime," Will says. He fiddles with the collar of his—my—Revenant's—shirt while his eyes track the others leaving the room. Only once the door closes behind them does he whip his head back and settle his full attention on me.

I let my focus linger over the shape of his shoulders beneath that crisp white shirt, the way his smooth wrists peek out from each cuff. The thicker material of the fabric glides over the planes of his chest and stomach, and when Will slips his hands into his pockets, I track that, too.

"You're wearing it well," I say. "How is the feel?"

"It feels . . . good," he finishes, looking down at himself.

I tamp down the urge to be more gracious with him after that compliment. I'm still sort of heartbroken over what he admitted— Will initially thinking our proximity was *not a good idea*—but these days, my personal feelings fall to the wayside when it comes to my business. I'll have to inspect them later. When I'm lying in bed and sleep won't come.

"Will, I need you to explain yourself. From the beginning."

His lips push into a flat line. "Like I said this morning, my clients are start-ups. I was in the meeting when we got word you were looking for a consultant."

My brain sighs, long and deep. "You told them you'd known me in high school."

He nods, his blue eyes glass-like. His expression is tortured, hesitant. "I implied to my boss that there were unrelated circumstances that might make it hard for us to work together."

Will clears his throat. Sighs. "But the truth is I had a feeling we could work together perfectly amicably. I just selfishly didn't want to see you."

It stings like hydrogen peroxide on a fresh cut.

Sure, I never wanted to see Will Grant again either, but I can't *imagine* a scenario in which I would have impacted his career to avoid it. I wouldn't even be this frustrated if Will had offered up an alternative solution a few months ago. But instead, he'd left me to go seek out a competitor he obviously thinks the worst of.

"If that was supposed to make me feel better, it didn't," I say.

Will rubs his forehead. "This isn't coming out right."

"You *think*?"

"Look," he says, running his fingers through his wavy hair before he shoves his hand back in his pocket. His voice is deep but gentle. "I was wrong. It was selfish and unfair of me. It was a moment of extreme weakness. The truth is, I was nervous. The idea of seeing you again made me really fucking nervous."

"Why? Because the two of us working together would've pissed off Zoe?"

"No." Will shakes his head, eyes earnest. "It had nothing to do with Zoe. I felt nervous to see you because I've never been proud of the way I left things with you."

I bristle just as he winces. "Let's *not* talk about it," I say.

"Fine," Will murmurs. "But for the record, there are things I regret."

"Well, *same,* obviously," I nearly spit.

Will groans. "No, Josie, not *that,* I regret what happened *after—*"

"I don't want to talk about it!" I shriek.

Our bodies are less than a foot apart. I take a step back, chest heaving. "You and I were never more than acquaintances who made one mutual error and learned from it. Now and forevermore, we'll only have a business relationship. I can move on from the personal stuff if you can, too. I can forgive you for wanting to avoid me if you promise to help me get B Corp Certified."

"I promise," Will says, "to help you get B Corp Certified."

"Then it's settled," I say.

"Wait. I have one more groveling explanation to give you."

Despite myself, I smirk. "Go on."

Will clears his throat, gesturing at the room. "I'm not normally like this. I know how presumptuous all of it was. How rude of me to show up like that, just as you were about to start your presentation. I swear I would have avoided it if I'd felt like there was another option I could have figured out in time. I also want you to know I'm not in the habit of asking anyone to take unfounded chances on me.

So, if you want a referral from another client, I'm happy to provide one. And lastly, I didn't come here to goad Kyle, despite what he said. I swear to you."

I absorb his speech, feeling simultaneously impressed and relieved.

"You used to work at Carlisle?" I ask.

Will nods. "I left that job for this one."

I nod and say, "Okay. What will it be like?"

Will stares. "Hmm?"

"Between you and me." I gesture between us. "You said you're not normally like this, but I want to know what to expect. What will it be like?"

His eyes hold mine. "You're in charge of everything. I'm only here to support your endgame. That's what it will be like between you and me. You telling me what to do, and me doing it. You telling me where to go, and me going."

My face flushes at the notion, but I say, "Good. That's good."

"Anything else?" he asks, blinking twice, eyelashes thick and long and dark.

"How long will you be in town for?"

"I can cancel my flight home and stay all week. I still have to fix your car, after all."

I nod. "And yes, for the record, I *would* like a client referral."

"No problem. Just one more thing." Will takes another step forward, and my head tilts back to keep hold of his eyes. "I'm really big on communication."

"Me, too," I say. "Constant communication."

"It eliminates misunderstandings and helps us get to the point."

"Agreed," I breathe.

"Great." His eyes flash to my neck and move up again. "In that case, let me get your phone number."

CHAPTER FIVE

When I get home early that evening, I collapse on the couch and google Zoe Grant.

I've done this a handful of times since graduating college, but never in the last few years. I gave up when I began to feel like a stalker with nothing to show for my efforts. I always thought it was odd Zoe didn't have LinkedIn, but who was I to judge? I haven't been on true social media since my senior year of high school—when I deleted Instagram, Twitter, and Facebook in one fell swoop.

But this time, the search results pull up something new: feature articles Zoe has written for *The New York Times Book Review*.

I make a small noise of shock.

Zoe works for *The New York Times*. Zoe's a *writer* for *The New York Times*.

It makes absolute perfect sense.

I pull myself off the couch and meander to the kitchen, reading her reviews. They're smart, witty, incisive. She's mostly kind, but occasionally, I come across a sharp line of criticism that gives me full-body shivers, and my empathetic heart stretches out to those authors. I can relate; I've *been* on the other side of a Zoe Grant criticism, and it's usually so poignant, all you can do is bow your head and accept it while thanking her for thinking of you at all.

I pour a soda over ice and head back to the couch, still reading. The more I read, the easier it is to call forth what she was like.

My friendship with Zoe made absolutely *no sense* on paper. She wrote short stories during study hall, had blue streaks in her brown hair but wouldn't indulge in a manicure. I, by comparison, hadn't shown a naked fingernail in public since age twelve and spent my study halls organizing my Pinterest fashion boards. During the first month of senior year, I remember Zoe—the new girl—scribbling furiously in a notepad all the time, like she was beholden to some sort of ticking clock. It wasn't until I caught the word *princess* on her notepad followed by something like *Elthior* that I realized she wasn't doing homework; she was writing fiction.

I pondered this all day and night, obsessing over what this princess of Elthior might dress like. Was she a utilitarian, warrior-type princess? Or did she prefer feminine ball gowns? What was the culture of fashion in Elthior? How expansive was the princess's closet?

The next day, I worked up the courage to talk to Zoe for the first time. I asked if I could read her story—while her face bloomed tomato red—and then explained why. So I could draw the characters' outfits.

Oh my gosh, Zoe said, clutching her notebook to her chest. *You're secretly weird too!* Which might have been the first time I'd ever felt seen by someone my age.

I didn't have any close friends and hadn't for the duration of high school. My family spent every moment I wasn't in school at Sea Island—a luxury beach resort in Georgia—where I kept the company of college-aged staff and wealthy adults who mostly talked about their real estate portfolios. During the summer between eighth grade and freshman year, friend groups formed, and I wasn't invited to become part of one. I didn't love sports, or drama, or band, and it didn't help that freshman year, I started dating a senior (who took a shine to me because he'd known my older brother from the lacrosse team). I hung out with his friends until they all graduated, and he subsequently dumped me.

By the time sophomore year rolled around, I'd established an aura of *aloof, distant, other*. Social media was being piloted that decade; I focused on my online persona instead. Crafting it, curating it. Which was addicting, and rewarding in doses, but it didn't solve my truest dilemma: nobody actually wanted to be my friend in real life.

On the handful of occasions I got invited to something, there were so many inside jokes I didn't understand. I was never good at making people laugh, voicing an opinion, getting others to open up. I'd usually just clam up and leave early, then go home and watch the fun play out online instead. It was social anxiety, through and through, but back then, I couldn't name it so easily. Interacting with followers who liked me online was better. I could take the time to consider my words, analyze every detail of what I showed to the world.

I could *curate* myself in a way people responded to positively.

By the time Zoe appeared at Woodmont High, I'd given up on finding a best friend in high school, and certainly didn't expect one in her. But she *did* let me read the short story, and I *did* draw designs for the Princess of Elthior that night. When I showed them to Zoe during our next study hall, she loved them, even put them on her Tumblr feed with the story itself.

After that, Zoe Grant became my best friend. We'd go to Friday night football games together covered in red paint. We'd gossip over our English teacher's toupee. She'd write stories; I'd illustrate the characters' outfits.

And eventually, Zoe told me what happened between her best

friend in Austin and her twin brother, Will—whom I tolerated but
didn't often speak to directly. Mainly because he was sullen and
unfriendly, but also because he'd hurt Zoe's feelings by stealing away
her best friend and he hadn't even realized.

I invited her to Sea Island with my family over fall break. When
we started applying to colleges, Zoe informed me I'd love the University of Texas. I didn't think I'd get in, but Zoe convinced me to
apply anyway. She wanted to go somewhere more prestigious but
never made me feel dumb for not being as smart as her, for not
having a chance at the places she was applying. (In return, I never
offered opinions on Zoe's outfit choices, even though I wanted to.)

It was my favorite year of high school. My parents even released
me from the usual Sea Island obligation over spring break so I could
go on the senior trip with the rest of my class. I was determined for
it to be the best trip ever. I wanted to finally feel like I had become
part of the group, to make memories and remember high school
fondly.

And then Will Grant and I kissed on the beach, and the only
thing I became was another villain in Zoe's story.

A sharp *rap* startles me enough to drop my phone on my face.

"Ow," I grunt, my nose scrunching.

"Josie!"

I turn my head sideways. My friends Giovanna and Leonie are
in the middle of my rosebushes, their faces pressed up to my living
room window. Behind them, the sun is dropping. Gio points at it
emphatically and taps her wrist three times.

"Coming!" I shout, launching off the couch. As quickly as possible, I change into shorts, a tank top, and my tennis shoes, and then
I'm at the kitchen sink, filling up a water bottle. They meet me by
my garage door. I strap on my helmet and check my tire pressure.

Giovanna is a slender, gorgeous Italian woman with dark hair
and olive skin. I met her during cycling class—a single-hour PE

credit we took when we were college sophomores, which we proceeded to make our entire personality. Her girlfriend is Leonie, a naturally blond and waiflike full-time yoga instructor who met Giovanna a couple years ago during a one-on-one yoga class that ended *unprofessionally,* as the story goes. They have a combined following of one hundred thousand people on Instagram and are considered the lesbian darlings of Austin.

"Let's get going before we lose the sunlight," Leonie says when I'm ready. "I still want to get in twenty miles if we can."

"You lead," I say, and Leonie takes off.

"Everything okay?" Gio throws me a concerned glance as she hooks her leg over the bike and straightens her handlebars.

"I'm fine." I climb onto my own black-and-pink Liv bicycle. "Just distracted. This will help."

"Did you get hydrangeas?"

I follow her gaze to the flower beds that line the left side of my place. Four giant hydrangea bushes are in bloom, the petals shifting in an ombré from pearl white to baby blue. Beneath them, a fresh bed of mulch has been laid.

"Huh." I stare at this addition to my foliage for the first time.

"When did your landscaper come?"

I think on it. "Two weeks ago?"

"Josie," Gio says.

"Gio," I say.

"And you only just noticed?" She rolls her eyes and starts pedaling. "Does your brain ever turn off?"

"Honestly? No."

I look back at the hydrangeas one last time, pleased now that I've taken the time to notice them. My landscaper has been servicing this house since Cami and I were just renters and the property belonged to our landlord. We moved in first thing after college graduation. Cami lives with her fiancé now, but I grew so attached to the house that when our landlord put it on the market four years later, I made sure to offer.

I pedal behind my friends, settling into the rhythm as we cruise down one street, then the next. With the sun creeping lower and the wind slipping past my skin, the scent of barbecue in the air, the feel of the rubber beneath my grip, I'm back in the present. Here. Now. I'm twenty-seven years old, with a mortgage and a business and a best friend who's getting married soon and a *biker gang*.

Today was an off day, but everyone has those. Tomorrow, I'll refocus. No more spite, no more vulnerability. Or shame, or self-consciousness, or doubt. My reunion with Will Grant is just a means to an end, and that end is: B Corp Certification.

We ride hard, making up for the twenty minutes of lost time by pushing ourselves against the sunset, but it's exactly the workout I need. At 8:26, we climb off our bikes at the Austin Beer Garden and lock up, ordering beers and wedging our salt-kissed bodies onto the end of a family-style picnic bench outside.

"Should I be worried my older brother's teenage son wants to do his own laundry?" Leonie asks with no preamble.

Gio turns sideways to face her girlfriend. "*Why* do you know this about him?"

"Remember when I house-sat last week? I watched his kids and their dog? Well, I thought doing the laundry would be a kind gesture, and the girl was nice about it, but the boy, like, *freaked out* when I went to grab his laundry hamper."

"Why are you calling them *the girl* and *the boy*?" I ask.

"Because I can't remember their names." Leonie's eyes widen comically. "It's either Steven and Taylor or Stephanie and Tyler. We didn't speak much, it wasn't written anywhere, and we never directly addressed each other." She takes a sip of her pilsner. "If it wasn't obvious, my brother and I aren't close."

"Josie, do *you* know your niece's and nephew's names?" Gio asks.

I frown. "Meyer and . . ."

"Ha!" Leonie points at me. "It's *hard*!"

"My brother lives in North Carolina," I retort. "I hardly ever see his family. And anyway, I remembered. The girl's name is Poppy. Their names combined sound like a lemon poppy-seed muffin. It's a memory trick."

"The fact that you *both* need a memory trick to remember your older brothers' children's names." Gio rolls her eyes.

"I'll have to come up with one for Thanksgiving," Leonie says.

"Anyway." Gio traces the rim of her beer glass. "He's a teenager. That math is totally mathing for Tyler-slash-Steven."

"To show your support of his sexual exploration, you should buy him some new socks for Christmas," I say with a grin.

"Revenant has *great* socks." Gio winks at me. "And *we* have a discount code."

"Don't you dare," I mutter, my voice darkening with an empty threat, "let Leonie's older brother's teenage son masturbate for twenty percent off in this economy."

"Gosh, sometimes I forget about the CEO thing." As soon as she says it, Leonie immediately pops her head up and glances around. As if she's worried she spoke too loud and now I'm about to get swamped by paparazzi. (Which does not happen, now or ever. People are more likely to want a picture with the two of them than with me.)

"Sometimes I forget, too," I say. Which isn't true, but I suppose I'm trying to make Leonie feel better about the fact that she doesn't look at me and think *chief executive officer*. "To be honest, founding Revenant was mostly an accident."

Giovanna watches me, her expression thoughtful. "I know that's what you always say, J, but I don't buy it and I never have. You can act nonchalant when you've got helmet hair and sweat around your crotch—"

"So, every other day," Leonie interjects.

"—but you don't become a CEO by accident. You care, and you try, and you *want*. Just like the rest of us." Gio winks at me again, this time like she's in on a secret I'm hiding.

Maybe she's right, but none of this felt intentional when I started out. The first few designs I posted on Instagram when I was a junior in college—on a secret account—took off right away. Before I knew it, I wasn't posting only my illustrated designs anymore, but the actual clothing I'd sewn on a machine. Then I was doing drops, making money. Nervously answering questions, showing my face on stories: *Where do I get my fabric? How did I learn how to sew? How old am I, and what contour do I use, and what do I study in school?*

After a whole year, I finally let the followers know my name. They could see that it was *me* behind Revenant. Me, Josephine Davis. A twenty-one-year-old college senior with a lucrative side hustle ballooning by the day. It was *me* they wanted to see modeling the clothes, testing the designs. Revenant was me, and I was Revenant, and together we were a *brand,* something new and exciting and wholly different from the half-baked, aloof It Girl I became in high school.

But as soon as I realized what was happening—that people's opinions of *me* were also their opinions of my *designs,* and vice versa—I took myself out of the spotlight, where I've stayed ever since. It was the only way I knew how to protect myself from criticism. To carry on, to believe I wasn't a doomed failure, even when a design I loved didn't sell or a perfectly legitimate business critique put me in a spiral about my self-worth.

But at that point, it didn't matter. Everyone knew my face and my name. I became another archetype: female founder. And throughout my twenties, I watched as the media caricatured me.

I've never been anyone's real-life inspiration. That, I firmly believe. But one thing I've always been is everyone's favorite stranger to follow.

"How's the bachelorette planning going?" Gio unclips her silver helmet as we climb off our bikes. It's nine thirty now and the two of us are back at my house.

"That question needs a content warning," I mutter.

She laughs. "I'm here to help, aren't I?"

"Everything's been ordered," I say, passing through my kitchen to the main area of the house.

My table is an array of pink and white, stacked with cowboy hats, plastic straws, feather boas, shot glass necklaces, a white sash, iced sugar cookies shaped like tequila bottles with *Down the hatch, down the aisle!* carefully scripted in frosting by a local bakery. On my couch, I've lined up the hangover kits: mini packs of Advil, Liquid I.V. supplements, Band-Aids, eye masks, individually wrapped makeup wipes. On the coffee table: tote bags I custom ordered with each bridesmaid's name. On the floor: a bachelorette sign I'm only halfway finished painting, outlined on a piece of butcher paper I got from an art supply store.

"When it's my turn for this shit," Giovanna breathes, "I want to go to a spa here in town with, like, four local friends, and then get cocktails before we fall asleep in our own beds."

"When it's *my* turn for this shit," I reply, "I want to spend the day on Lake Travis with no bachelorette props and exclusively drink Corona."

"Deal."

"Do you want to paint the sign or stuff the tote bags?" I magnanimously offer.

"I'll paint," Gio says. "You stuff."

We get to work, and Gio selects a Spotify playlist to keep us company. "This one's called 'Country Pop Hits—Singers Not Yet Canceled,'" she says.

"Sounds promising."

"So, about those hydrangeas." Gio dips a paintbrush into the pink paint and eyes the faint pencil tracings I marked on the butcher paper. She's kneeling over the sign, elbows on the carpet. "How many household tasks are you currently outsourcing?"

"All of them." I grab a tote bag. This one's for Mariana, Cami's cousin. "I have a landscaper, a house cleaner, a pest guy, *and* someone helping me with minor renovations."

"Like what?"

"A garbage disposal!" I announce enthusiastically, stuffing Mariana's tote bag with a shot glass necklace. "Now I won't have to use a plunger in my kitchen sink!"

"Remind me why you *didn't* buy a house from a decade more recent than the thirties?"

"I like this place." I look around at the sunny yellow walls, the old hardwood floors. "It's homey."

Gio makes a *humph* noise and keeps painting. "Have you furnished Cami's old room yet?"

"I will, as soon as I have a guest. But I never have guests."

"Not even *male* guests?" Gio asks.

"Why would a *male* guest stay in the guest room?"

"He wouldn't, ideally."

"Then what's the problem?"

"The *problem*, Josie," Gio says, her voice exasperated, "is you own a house you've lived in for six years and a company you've been heading up for seven. Those are very impressive facts. But you haven't dated anyone since you and Clay broke up after college—which is just fucking absurd, because you are gorgeous and also accidentally hilarious. I mean, as long as you aren't talking about inventory. You bore me to tears when you talk about inventory. But, like, even back in college, I don't think I ever saw you get drunk enough to take a man home from the bar. You've never made a *single* impulsive decision in my presence."

I flinch and briefly squeeze my eyes shut.

Gio doesn't know about the impulsive decision I made in high school that sort of ruined the concept for me. The only person I met after high school whom I told about that is Camila.

"What exactly are you getting at?" I ask.

"Don't you ever wish you were living a little bit more like a twenty-something with a tasteless wardrobe and a perpetual hangover who doesn't have it all figured out?"

"First of all, wardrobes are personal. There's no such thing as tasteless, in my opinion."

"Okay, Grace Kelly."

"And second, I do *not* have it all figured out," I retort, shoving the sparkly cowboy hat into the tote bag. It doesn't fit.

"Could've fooled me."

"You're the one in a stable relationship."

"You should try it. Codependence is sexy." She turns and shoots me a wink.

"Do you know the look I get from most men when they find out who I am?" I tie the string of the cowboy hat to the strap and put Mariana's party bag in a corner. "It's like . . ." I look at the ceiling, thinking back on all the occasions over the course of my singledom in which a man has hit on me. "It's like the fact that I have a CEO title instantly emasculates them. I can *see* the change on their face when I say it, and any flirtation is squashed from there."

"That's a *them* problem. Besides. I can't believe I'm the one saying this, but not all men are like that. You have to find someone so secure in their manhood that your professional authority is just part of your charm."

Instantly, and against my will, my thoughts draw back to Will Grant. How he'd admitted he was *professionally intrigued* by my business model. The way he stood up when I walked in or out of a room. Like a modern man and an eighteenth-century English viscount combined.

"What's got you so focused on my love life?" I ask.

"We're going to be twenty-eight next year. That's, like, officially our *late twenties*."

"The horror," I deadpan.

"Camila's getting *married*, J!" She gesticulates, and a splotch of pink paint flicks off her brush and onto my carpet. "Fucking married! And your little social media fashion brand is about to open its first physical store, and Leonie's talking about taking out a loan so she can open her own yoga studio! What am *I* doing?"

"Single-handedly carrying the Rare Beauty PR list on your back?"

"And delivering groceries!" she reminds me. "I'm the poster child for the gig economy. By the way, is this sign supposed to say *Cami Gets Slammied*?"

"She picked that out, not me," I grumble.

"Frankly, I'm surprised Camila Sanchez is letting you plan a single thing."

"The whole itinerary is a secret," I remind her, starting on my third bag. "Just not the coordinated outfits, or the slogans, or the props."

"So, the branding, Camila controlled." She throws me a grin, a smudge of paint already drying on her cheek. "Makes sense."

"And yet you claim," I say, pointing a flamingo-pink penis straw at Gio's face while her expression contorts in lesbian horror, "that *I'm* the one who can't leave work at the office."

"Prove me wrong," she challenges. "Do something reckless and youthful and emotional and impulsive."

"Maybe I will."

CHAPTER SIX

Later that night, after I've showered and crawled into bed, my bones tired, my mind disassociating, I check my phone one last time before muting it and see a new text from Will.

I saved his number after he sent me a message at the office with his full name, as if I didn't know it: Will Grant. But for some reason, I saved the contact as only **Will**.

> **Will:** I extended my trip through Sunday
>> **Josie:** ok. Why sunday?
> **Will:** I can't meet with you tomorrow because of my other client but if you have time Friday, I want to pick your brain about B Corp strategies. And Saturday, I'm going to fix your car.
>> **Josie:** You want to pick my brain?
> **Will:** Don't fall over
>> **Josie:** You know it's mostly girl pop lyrics and glitter up there, right?

Will: We both know that's not true

    Josie: Did you get Derrick's dinner invitation?

Will: Yep. Eberly at eight thirty tomorrow night. I'll be there.

    Josie: Great

Will: Can I pick you up on the way?

    Josie: why on earth would you want to?

Will: To take pictures of your car. I need to show my cousin.

    Josie: What does your cousin have to do with literally anything?

Will: Just give me your address, Josephine

    Josie: 154 marmot Lane

Will: See you tomorrow night

I push my phone onto the bedside table and force my eyes shut, trying to block out everything, let sleep steal me away. But I drift off imagining versions of him between seventeen and twenty-seven. Will at twenty. Twenty-two. Twenty-five. I imagine the divot in his chin sharpening with age, his shoulders broadening, his voice dropping lower. And I fall asleep to the sound of him saying, *You and me.*

Thursday is my favorite day of the workweek. Objectively, worst to best, the list goes like this: Tuesday, Monday, Wednesday, Friday, Thursday.

I'm not taking questions on the list.

But Thursday is the best because it's my creative day. I get to mess around with the design team, gossip with Camila on brand strategies, watch the social team shoot content, and do the other fun, sparkly things. Plus, I have Pilates on Thursdays and the entire soundtrack is female rappers. It fills up my well, and on my way home after the day, just as the summer sunshine is fading to a purplish hue behind the far tree line, I'm still in a great mood. Not even dinner with Derrick Lovell and Will Grant tonight, as off-kilter as *that's* going to be, will sour this day.

Until I find him waiting on my doorstep.

Which is a problem because it's not even eight o'clock yet, and I'm wearing a neon-pink athletic bra and very tight bike shorts. My hair is in a matted blond knot on top of my head. I'm still glistening.

Will Grant, by contrast, is sitting on my front porch in a suit, looking like James Bond or maybe Harvey Specter, his brown hair combed back, hands behind him on the concrete to support his upper body weight. When he sees me pull into the driveway, he stands.

Of course he stands.

I get out of my car, hauling a backpack in one arm and a shoulder bag in the other, and head toward him with a tense face. If this was a *Bachelor* clip, I would plainly and simply not be getting the first impression rose.

His eyes flick up and down me, then flash back up to my face. Is that a red flush beneath his chin?

Will clears his throat. "I take it you're struggling with the dress code as well?"

"He jokes," I say.

Will's dimples grow larger and larger with every passing second. "Did I get the reservation time wrong?"

"No." I move past him on the steps, fiddling with my keys. "I just expected you to be here five minutes before the reservation, considering I live *five minutes from the restaurant.*"

"How was I supposed to know that?"

"Because you're *from* here?"

Will gives me a look. "When I lived in Austin, my family didn't go to dinner at restaurants like this one."

It's a subtle way of saying his family doesn't come from money—like mine does, to a degree, and like Derrick's kids will, to a *much* larger degree.

"Give me twenty minutes," I say. "Make yourself comfortable."

"Um." Will eyes the bachelorette paraphernalia scattered literally *everywhere.* "Okay."

I'm in too much of a rush now to explain, so I barricade myself in my bedroom and turn on the shower, imagining what he's thinking about only a few walls away. *So much pink. So many sparkles. All those cardboard boxes piled by the door.*

After I scrub my body down with soap under the warm spray and dry off, I throw on a simple green smock dress and strap my feet into a pair of low nude heels. I slap on a few makeup necessities and dry-shampoo my hair, then swirl Listerine. The longer I leave Will alone in my home, the more insecure I become. Forget picking my brain tomorrow at the office. He's going to take one look around and say, *You know what? I think I already get the gist of who Josephine Davis is these days, thanks.*

"You have three sewing machines in this room," Will informs me when I make it back to him, slightly breathless. He's absent-mindedly rubbing a thumb over his full bottom lip as he turns to look at me.

"Four," I correct, knocking on a vintage piece of rolltop furniture. "This one was passed down from my oma. It's a foldaway, and it doesn't work."

"What's in progress over there?" He points at the Brother, which I use for embroidery. It's set up on the table in the midst of the props.

"Oh. My best friend is getting married. Camila Sanchez, maybe you met her in the boardroom? I'm embroidering her bachelorette sash with her new last name."

"What about"—he turns ninety degrees, points at the Singer on the kitchen countertop—"*that* one?"

"Making some pajamas out of this buttery fabric I got."

"In the kitchen?"

"I don't cook much."

"Okay." He smirks. "And that one?" Will nods to the corner of the room, where the small mint-green desktop machine is currently presiding over a pile of hardbacks.

"Terrible quality, but it was cheap and looked cute in Instagram photos, back when I was the one taking them. Now I just use it as an artistic bookend."

Will nods, his eyes finally pulling over to mine. Another scan up and down my body, quick as a flash of light, but his expression doesn't change. "All set?"

"Wait a minute." I put my hands on my hips. "No snarky comment on the glitter blanketing the grooves in the floor? The pile of returns ready to ship out?"

"All that tells me," Will says, eyes narrowing, "is you're a dedicated friend and you shop online—which, let's face it, could be a write-off in your case. Besides, I like this house. I'll admit I pictured you somewhere fancier, but now that I've seen your home, I think it suits you."

I bristle at the positive, calming note to his voice. "Well, thank you."

His blue eyes dance. He knows he's thrown me. "Shall we?"

"Yep." I head for the door. "Did you get the pictures of my car you needed for your cousin?"

He holds it open and lets me exit first. "I did. He owns a repair shop. He says it'll only take the day, since he preordered the part when I first called on Wednesday morning."

"I'll be in town," I say, "but Revenant has its first pop-up on Saturday. I'll ride my bicycle there, so you can have the car."

We head down the cobblestoned side path to Will's rental car, parked on the darkening street. "You have a bicycle?" he asks.

"Yes."

"A road bike?"

"It's a hybrid."

After a minute where I can *feel* Will's mental gymnastics—his attempt to digest this hobby we have in common even amidst his notions of me—he says, "Cool."

When we reach his car, he opens the passenger door. I slide into the seat without making eye contact but grumble a *thanks* under my breath, my body heating.

After he climbs in, he says, "So. You've apparently got exactly five minutes to tell me what you think of Derrick."

I burst into a short laugh, then cover my mouth with both hands. He looks amused at my amusement, his dimples poking through.

"What?"

"Nothing." I shake my head. "It's just, Derrick has probably been in a million situations where someone asked him what he thinks of me. This is the first time it's happened the other way around."

Will frowns as he pulls onto the road. "Nobody's ever asked your opinion of him?"

"I think most people were so thrilled with his investment that personal opinions didn't matter. But for the record, I like Derrick. He respects me."

Will's grip on the steering wheel tightens as he takes a right turn. "He listens to you?"

"He always listens. And he almost always argues back. But I don't see that as a bad thing. Derrick pushes me, exposes my limitations. I'm young and I lack experience. That's just a fact there's no getting around." After a beat I add, "He's making me take online CEO classes."

Will smirks. "How's that going?"

"Don't tell him I said so, but it was a good idea."

As the air-conditioning circulates, I'm hit again with Will's scent. Cedar in sunlight. I peek at his profile and let myself watch him while he focuses on the road. There's a tenseness to the set of his jaw, but his posture is almost forcibly relaxed. I wouldn't have guessed he felt out of place with me unless I'd known to look for it.

Has Will told Zoe about this yet? That we ran into each other after all this time, that he signed a contract with my company? I wonder what their relationship is like these days. Are they closer than they were as teenagers? More estranged than ever?

"How do you like Austin?" Will asks.

"I never want to leave."

"Yeah." He sighs. "I remember that feeling."

"What about New York?" I ask.

"New York is great. It's always been great." He shifts in his seat, eyes darting over to me briefly. "I'm just tired, I think. I sleep better here, away from the noise of Manhattan. This is my favorite place to visit clients."

"So *that's* why you changed your mind about Revenant," I joke.

"No," Will says. "I changed my mind because I was in the wrong, and you deserve better." When I don't immediately reply, he adds, voice going soft, "You've always deserved better from me, Josie."

My voice catches in my throat. "Yeah, well, Zoe deserved better from both of us."

After a moment he says, "I leaned in first."

"We leaned in at the exact same time," I say, while goose bumps erupt over every inch of my skin. "Don't rewrite history to ease my conscience. It was perfectly mutual."

We pull up to the restaurant parking lot thirty seconds later, but neither of us makes a move to immediately vacate the car. I'm envisioning his lips on my skin. His fingers in my hair. His voice, urgent and broken, murmuring *You feel perfect* on a deserted stretch of beach.

He's thinking of it, too. I can tell.

Will turns to me in his seat, his eyes as dark as the water that night. "I can't change what happened in the past, or the way I wasn't there for you afterward. All I can do is give you my absolute best from this point on. You haven't seen me at my best—not then, and not yesterday—but that changes starting tonight."

I bite my lower lip in amusement. "Did you practice that?"

"Three times. How did I do?"

"Pretty good," I say, laughing.

Will offers me a small smile. "Shall we go swindle the most notorious retail shark on the West Coast out of a four-hundred-dollar bottle of wine?"

"Five hundred," I counter. "He's got property outside Napa."

Derrick ends up surpassing both our guesses, and I think it's because he's pleased with this turn of events—buddying up with Ellis Consulting, and at a discount. I've discovered that Derrick Lovell wines and dines people only when he thinks he's getting the better end of a deal, and tonight, he's pulling out all the stops on Will. But after the appetizer plates are cleared away, Derrick takes a phone call and comes back to our table in a rush.

"I have to get back to SF." He pulls his coat off his chair, nodding at us once with no further explanation. "I'll flag down our waiter and pay the bill. See you both soon."

With that, he's gone. Will turns to me, his brow hitched.

"He's like that," I explain. "It's either his wife, his kids, or another one of his investments that needs tending to."

"He flies private, I assume?"

I nod. "I was on that jet once. The pilot's name is Gerald. He likes to joke about maintenance issues."

Will blanches.

Our entrées arrive, and as we tuck in, I make a calculated ploy to turn the conversation on him.

"Tell me about your time in New York."

Will sneaks a look at me, cutting into his roast chicken with careful, meticulous precision. He looks . . . anxious, all of a sudden. I can tell by the way his eyebrows are drawn together, like he's rehearsing his lines before he speaks them aloud. "I went to NYU for college and studied finance. After I graduated, I accepted a job on Wall Street at an investment bank—"

"No." I cut him off. "You were a *finance bro?*"

I'm mostly joking, but Will blushes, caught out. "Reformed," he corrects me, with emphasis, and quite a bit of self-awareness. "Don't look at me like that, Josephine."

"Like what?"

"Like I crush dreams. Like I'm thirty seconds away from lecturing you about diversifying your portfolio."

"How bad is the itch?"

He glares, leaning an elbow on the table between us. "I left that job after three years," he goes on, "and moved to the Carlisle Group. Which was fine until I got assigned to this company that was doing some shady stuff with privileged information."

"Think I heard about that."

"Everybody heard about that," Will grumbles. "I couldn't move past it, even though everyone else did, and fairly quickly. I'd reached a . . ." His head does a small tic. "Crisis of conscience, of sorts. I needed out."

"Which leads us here," I say.

Will nods. "Now I mostly work with start-ups in a variety of industries, but I try to avoid New York– or Silicon Valley–based companies."

"Why?"

He frowns. "They more often cut corners I'm not interested in cutting. So, instead, I spend a lot of time in Austin, Boulder, and Miami when I travel, which suits me much better."

"You really are reformed."

"Don't sound so disappointed."

The ambience of this restaurant—the low lighting, sultry music, overpriced wine warming my ears—is doing its level best to shrink the distance between us. Our voices drop lower, conspiring as well, and our shoulders droop in, magnetic.

I shake off the feeling, turn my attention to my plate. Will does the same, a quietness expanding as we start to eat. He refills both of our wineglasses wordlessly. Pours me water from the carafe.

"Can I ask you something?" I grab my wineglass by the stem, swirl it a couple times as I watch Will over the rim. He nods at me, taking a bite of his chicken. My eyes flick away from the sight of his jaw working, back to the deep red in my glass. "Did you tell your boss it wasn't a good idea for Revenant to be your client because of Zoe or because of yourself?"

"Myself," he answers immediately. "Zoe wouldn't have cared."

I frown. "You honestly don't think so?"

"I *know* she wouldn't. Zoe and I . . ." He looks beyond me. "There were other things going on that had nothing to do with you that drove us apart during high school. But we're as close now as we were when we lived in Austin. So no, I can say with confidence that when I tell her we're working together, Zoe's not going to mind. She may even think it's some kind of cosmic fate. She's like that."

He smiles, and I do, too. "I remember. Obsessed with the zodiac, with destiny. All that."

It eases my mind, knowing Zoe isn't going to be furious when she discovers this. I should give all three of us more credit for how much we've grown up.

"Now can I ask *you* a question?" Will counters.

Something about the flash in his eyes gives me pause, as if the question coming my way has far more depth than I'm prepared for.

But fair's fair.

"Sure," I say.

"What is it," he says, voice impossibly low, "that you want more than anything?"

Fuck.

"That's rather broad," I deflect. "And ambiguous."

"*That's* a cheap answer."

"What do my personal desires have to do with Revenant?"

"Everything, Josie. They have *everything* to do with the creation that fell out of your head and now exists in the real world, perceivable and consumable by friends and strangers alike."

"You're freaking me out."

"Good. Nobody ever gets anywhere interesting when things are comfortable."

"To be clear, are you asking me to contort myself into an uncomfortable position as a means of keeping you interested? Here I thought you were a *reformed* finance bro."

"Stop avoiding the question. I answered yours, didn't I?"

He waits patiently, letting me summon the courage to articulate something that no one—and I mean *no one*—has ever asked me before.

What do I want more than anything?

My brain runs through a list of obvious responses: *to get B Corp Certified, to make our customers happy and confident with the way they look, to be the best friend to Camila I can possibly be, to be a daughter and sister my family is proud of.* But something tells me Will's not going to accept any of those. They're all associated with somebody else. They're all desires built on *perception.* Which maybe says something all on its own about my fatal flaw.

What do I want, just for me?

"I want my existence to be meaningful," I all but whisper. My eyes are trained on the bottle of wine, but I force them up to Will's. He's watching me with singular, patient attention, with the same focus he gave me in that presentation yesterday. "I want to add value to my community and still be true to myself. A girl who's into clothes and self-care and pretty things and riding my bicycle, but also environmental conservation and positive social change. I have a fear of being a waste of space. So I guess my biggest desire is . . . the opposite of that? I want to have to *try,* but not just for the sake of it. I want the focus of my efforts to be good, and deep, and meaningful. Does that make any sense at all?"

I press my lips together, a blush collecting on my cheeks as the full weight of my speech settles over Will Grant. His eyes are roving my face, searching for something.

"Makes perfect sense," he says, his voice scraping out. "And for the record, I know exactly how you feel."

This, I wasn't expecting. The fact that we both love cycling is one thing, but connecting on an emotional level is . . . uncharted.

"Really?" I ask, my tone soft.

Will nods, his stormy eyes still locked on mine. I wonder if he's planning to elaborate—to give me a morsel of history that explains his own insecurity over the depth of humanity he doesn't know if he can personally accomplish—and for a moment, it seems like he just might. But then our waiter comes back holding a to-go box with Derrick's untouched meal, and the moment passes.

Still. I leave dinner that night feeling a little bit less alone.

On our drive home after the meal, Will asks me about my bike. When I tell him it's mostly pink, he emits a bitten-off laugh and says, "I bet that suits you." He walks me up to my front porch, bids me good night, his eyes lingering on mine until the door clicks shut between us.

On Friday, after our meeting when Will "picks my brain"—which is mostly him asking questions about my company vision and me going on a passionate tangent—he leaves me with not one, but five reference letters from his other clients.

They're glowing, every one of them.

CHAPTER SEVEN

The Saturday pop-up was Camila's idea. Soft launch a physical store before you actually open one.

(Camila's a genius.)

We're hosting the all-day event in an airy rental space in the Warehouse District of downtown Austin. I arrive hopeful, optimistic. But when I say it goes from bad to worse, I mean it like this: what started as a controllable dumpster fire devolves into the gaping, smoking crater where a fiery meteor hit the earth.

It's a gorgeous day, the smallest breeze carrying a hint of daisies and early summer grass across the Austin sky. I left my keys on my front car tire for Will and rode my bike here instead. Cami is by my side, strapped up in her signature weekend athleisure, an iPad cinched to her waist. I head next door to buy a carafe of coffee for us and the other staff who are coming to help later. Then we get to work. We spread out racks of clothes on hangers, organize sweaters on the shelves. Cami and I spend the morning hanging, folding, staging.

The new director, Margaret—who, before coming to Revenant, managed a handful of fashion stores for a large brand in Dallas— does not show up as early as we do. I can see the confusion grow on Cami's face the later it gets. Finally, Margaret arrives at ten thirty, looking pleasantly surprised we've already staged the place.

The event is supposed to start at eleven a.m. sharp. By this point, we have a small line of customers waiting outside the event space. It becomes clear Margaret has not trained herself—or any of the other staff pitching in today—on the checkout devices. (At ten forty-five, we're watching YouTube videos on how to accept card payments.) And that's just the beginning of our problems.

Once the doors open (late) and customers begin browsing, the lack of fitting rooms becomes apparent. (One! And it's also the only bathroom!)

I go into problem-solving mode: call my spray tan girl, offer her hundreds of dollars if she can quickly wipe down her spray tents and bring them by for the day. Then I send a staff member to Target to buy every college-dorm floor-length mirror.

Cami shoots me guilty looks while all this is going on, but I can't pause to talk about it. My brain has never worked like that. You have to get through something, come out on the other side of it, before you're allowed to admit how bad things got. And anyway, she's stuck behind a line of customers waiting to check out (one of the devices bugged out two hours in; we're down to two, and frankly, three wasn't enough to begin with).

In the middle of the afternoon, we run completely out of sizes small, medium, and large. Maybe that sounds like sales are going well, and sure, they're not going terribly, but the racks are still more than half full. I've never seen so many extra-smalls in my life. I make a mental note to politely ask Margaret how she determined the product mix.

Margaret, who has spent most of the day over by the photo wall, snapping pictures of influencers. It's the one aspect of the event she put together the night before. The wall's got the *Fill your closet once* tagline, pink streamers, silver balloons. Not even our brand colors, which are navy blue and ivory.

When Gio comes through around three o'clock, she gives me a pitying look.

"Brace yourself for some social media backlash," she warns me. "There are videos going around talking about the poor execution."

I nod at her, busying myself with folding and refolding sweaters that are too small for most human beings to wear, especially since sweaters tend to be oversized anyway. "How bad are we talking?"

"People who aren't even in Austin are joining the conversation. It's becoming about . . ." I glance up. Gio winces. "Age, and experience. People are saying Revenant is an unsustainable press darling."

I bite into my tongue, glancing over at Margaret again. She'd been a great employee for a company with a huge brick-and-mortar footprint. But I guess the problem is she's never worked for a start-up.

"Also," Gio goes on, "I heard someone say they need a discount on a shirt because it has spray tan smudges on it."

I'm holding it together all right until a beautiful blond plus-sized woman with a Parisian fashion sense finds me toward the end of the event and—very gently, very quietly—tells me she's disappointed in the size inclusivity at this pop-up. Our XL sizes and our XXLs are gone at this point, too.

"It's inexcusable," I tell her. She's wearing the Revenant bow around her softly curled ponytail. "And I'm personally going to make sure it doesn't happen again. Not online, and not in any store we ever open."

She sighs, evaluating me. Like she's wondering how sincere a person I am. If she can hold me to my word. "I love your clothes. I love the way they look on me, and I've never had a problem online.

I just hope when your Austin store opens, I'll be able to try something on."

Five minutes later, I get a text from Derrick with a TikTok attached. It's an Austin influencer who posted about the pop-up, detailing everything that went wrong. Talking about problems I haven't even heard of yet: that the discount codes we advertised weren't reflected on the receipts, that a few items were priced differently online.

Who planned this?

Director of retail experience. She's new, I explain, as if that will appease him, my fingers shaking as I type. Been with Revenant two months.

I've barely replied when Derrick shoots back another text: Fire her.

That's not even what sends me to the back parking lot in tears moments later. It's an email that hits my inbox mere seconds after Derrick's command.

> Miss Davis,
>
> We're deeply sorry for the mix-up, but it looks like your table at Andalo was double-booked for next Saturday. Since the other bachelorette party booked first, we've had to cancel your reservation. You will be fully refunded. Again, our sincerest apologies. Below is a list of alternative clubs in the Nashville area that may accept a group your size.
>
> Best,
> Andalo

That's when the meteor makes contact, the words *fire her* repeating on a brutal loop in my mind, only it's not Derrick saying them about Margaret. It's Cami saying them about me.

You messed up. You did a bad job. You ruined something important. You weren't a good enough maid of honor, and you're also a bad fucking friend. Fire her, fire her, fire her.

I heave breaths in and out of my nose, slowing as my vision blurs from tears.

That club was the thing Cami was looking forward to *most* about her whole bachelorette weekend. She wanted to dance on a table with bottle service included, all her favorite women in a circle around her, shrieking the lyrics to Jason Derulo songs played at a sped-up tempo. She wanted to feel sexy and confident and in the middle of it all, the center of attention for once, everybody doting on her, just for that one night. I promised her we would do it all.

Camila Sanchez has six sisters, two cousins that are basically sisters, two more future sisters-in-law. But out of all those women, she chose *me* to be her maid of honor.

Fire her, my brain supplies cruelly, as I push out of the doors and bolt around the corner, choking back a sob. I rush to the back of the building.

You're doing a bad job. Not just at this wedding. Everything. You're bad at your job. You're bad at life. No one wants to be with you. Everyone who works for you secretly hates you. You're so bad at all of it. Who do you think you are? You can't be in charge of all these people. You aren't good enough. You aren't worthy. You're only going to keep disappointing—

"Josie?"

I slam into something hard and warm. Another body, whose scent I know immediately. Will grabs me by each elbow, steadying me. I try to focus on his face, but he's blurry.

"I think I lost a c-contact!" I cry.

"It's on your cheek. Hold still." One of his hands cups the back of my neck, warm and heavy, while three of his knuckles settle on my cheek. "Got it," he breathes, sending minty breath over my skin. "I have contact solution in my car. Come here."

The hand on my neck drops to wrap around mine. Will pulls

me deeper into the parking lot. I'm crying harder now, squeezing both of my eyes tightly shut as he leads me. Finally, he pulls me to a stop and unlocks his car.

"Here." Will transfers the rogue contact from his fingertip to mine and douses it with saline.

I crouch in front of his side mirror, carefully securing the contact back in place. But once it's fixed up, my tears keep coming. My body is heaving with sobs. Will doesn't move away, but he doesn't make a move to touch me again, either.

I am really, *really* crying. Not cute, dainty crying. Not soft, silent crying. I'm hacking sobs, sniffing like I've got a runny nose, hiccuping, gulping for small sips of air. I see Will's hand flinch down by his side, like he's tempted to comfort me but decides against it.

"W-What are you doing here?" I ask.

"I saw the press. Came to see if I could help."

This admission does absolutely nothing to curb my tears. "We're ab-bout to close," I tell him.

"Probably for the best," he admits darkly. "Truth be told, that's the help I was going to offer. Or strongly suggest."

I sob-laugh. "It was tragic."

"That all? I've been hearing adjectives like understaffed, incompetent, and—brace yourself, this one's going to sting—*bad lighting.*"

"All of the above."

"May I say," Will murmurs, "it's unlike you to get eviscerated for bad lighting?"

"You may. It's a factual statement."

My tears ebb, and the blue in his eyes concentrates. "Why are you crying? Did something specific happen, or was it just . . . everything?"

I shake my head, pushing hair out of my face so I can see him more clearly. He's dressed simply in light jeans and a plain gray T-shirt, his brown hair mussed. "No. I mean, yes, it was everything. But I've dealt with shit hitting the fan more times than I can remember without crying. It was about Camila."

Will looks down at me, his frown deepening. "Your CBO?"

"She's also my best friend. And her bachelorette party, which I planned, is next Saturday. We're going to Nashville, and she wanted to visit this club, only they double-booked us, and now I don't know what we're supposed to do that night that feels special for her. And I really want it to feel special," I say, pushing down another sob, "because Camila has been this rock for her family almost her whole life. When she was sixteen, her mom died, and she was basically in charge of all her sisters and little cousins. Her grandma was Camila's legal guardian, but she was ill. Anyway, Cami's done a lot for her family, and for once, it's *her* turn to have everybody care about her and love on her and celebrate her. Out of all that family, she picked me to be her maid of honor, and I don't want to fuck it up." I finish in a whisper.

I didn't notice until now, but my mascara is smudged over the collar of his T-shirt. I must have really bumped him earlier. "Fuck, I stained your shirt."

He glances down. "It's no big deal. What's the name of the club? In Nashville?"

"Andalo. They sent a list of other places I can call, so at least that's something."

"But Camila specifically wanted to go there," Will clarifies.

I nod. "They do a whole shebang for bachelorette groups. Fireworks that come out of champagne, disposable cameras, special songs from the DJ, bottle service. I booked the table months ago. I don't know what happened."

Will's hands dip into his pockets. "How about this. You forward me that email. I'll call the other clubs and see what can be done. You head inside and close that shit show down for good."

"Will, that's not part of your job."

"I know it's not. Let me help anyway."

"Why?"

He frowns. "Because you need help, that's why."

I don't have the bandwidth to decode his expression right now, so instead, I forward him the email from the club and say a quick thank-you before heading back inside.

The last of our frustrated customers are straggling out the door, empty-handed. The balloons over by the photo wall have lost half their helium, but Margaret's as chipper as she was when she walked in at ten thirty.

"I think that went great!" she announces, tucking her cell phone into her back pocket. "How about you guys?"

Cami's already folding leftover inventory back into boxes. She doesn't say a word but offers a tight smile. I can see doubt settle into Margaret's expression the longer the silence stretches out—especially when she catches the uneasy looks from the other staff and, worst of all, the smudged mascara under my eyes.

"Everybody can head out," I jump in. "Thanks for all your hard work, especially on a Saturday. Camila and I will load the rental truck."

Mark offers me a weak smile, and Brandi rubs my shoulder as they grab their things and make for the door. Margaret lingers, approaching Camila.

"Hey, I can take care of that. Since I didn't show up in time this morn—"

"It's okay." Cami lifts her head and shoots Margaret a lukewarm smile. "I appreciate the offer, but I already grabbed the keys to the truck. My fiancé is on his way to help us load. We'll manage."

The air in the room grows tight as Margaret grabs her belongings, muttering that she'll see us both Monday morning. I stay quiet and unmoving, my hands loosely resting on my hips until she's gone.

Camila walks over to her oversized purse and riffles around inside until she pulls out a lunch box. The same one she used to carry

Jell-O shots on our way to date parties in college. (It was her party trick.) Nestled into a bed of slushy ice are two mini bottles of La Marca prosecco.

"This was supposed to be a celebratory drink." She scoops up the bottles and stares at their necks wedged between her fingertips.

"Well," I say, "we don't have to tell the mini alcohols about that."

"That their identity has been stolen? That we're now drinking in mourning?"

"I need it more desperately now than I would've if today had gone off without a hitch."

She sighs, dropping to the floor. She crosses her legs and sets both bottles in front of her. I walk over and sit down opposite, unscrewing each cap.

"I asked Margaret if we needed to hire an event management company," Cami admits, taking a swig. "She said we didn't."

"We probably needed one," I agree.

"Am I going to have to fire her?" Cami asks. "I've never fired anyone before."

"Firing people sucks," I say, thinking back on the handful of people I've had to let go over the years. "But if this was her first flop, maybe not?"

"It wasn't her first flop."

"Oh."

After a minute Cami asks, "I know Derrick has an opinion."

"Derrick says to fire her."

Cami barks out a laugh. "Derrick is ruthless."

"She's your employee," I say. "It's your call."

She bites her lip, looking sideways. "I didn't really call David. But I can."

"No need. Will Grant is here. He can help us load the truck."

Her brown eyes lock back on mine, narrowing. "I know we've both been busy over the last couple of days—"

"*Days?*"

"Years," she amends. "But at some point, J, I need you to explain why you signed a contract with a man who looks like a young Henry Cavill and writes sonnets at you with his eyes in *public*."

"He does not," I say staunchly. "It's a completely different look, I swear. I need to give you the full story later. Will and I know each other from high school."

"Okay, well, that's cool, but whatever he's doing with his eyes when he looks at you is indecent all the same. More indecent than Jason Lorcan adjusting his pants every time we talk about expanding into intimates."

I laugh. "Jason Lorcan can dream on. We're not expanding into intimates."

"What is this, a dictatorship?" Cami scoffs in mock outrage. "Jason and I would like to renegotiate."

"Bras are out anyway." I take another sip of my mourning alcohol, wondering if Will's made any progress on the phone with another club. "Hey, Cami?"

"Hey."

"Andalo double-booked us and then canceled on me."

She nods, burbles out a small laugh, and takes another sip, draining her bottle. She sets it down and reclines all the way against the floor. "Clubs are out anyway."

CHAPTER EIGHT

The three of us load the truck, sweating in the setting sun as we work.

"What does a consultant even *do*?" Cami asks, passing a plastic bin over to Will. "Okay, wait, I know that sounded accusatory—"

"No, it's fine," Will says, looking like he'd laugh if he wasn't weighed down by a box of jeans. "It's a valid question. The best way to describe my job is I'm a fixer, or a troubleshooter. You could come to me with any problem you don't have time to solve, and it would be my job to help you figure out a solution."

"So, anything goes." Cami pops a hip and rests her hand on it, gazing up at Will in the truck.

"Within reason," he says, warily.

Cami smirks. "Are you billing us for this manual labor?"

"No." Will stacks the box, then turns back to grab the next one I offer him. "We can call this a free bonus service."

"What about for calling the Nashville clubs?" I ask.

"That," Will says, lifting my box of hangers, "was just because I'm nice." He throws me a look, challenging me to refute it.

"And?" I ask.

"*And* I booked you a new reservation on Broadway. It's at this place called Wagon Wheel. Based on the website, it looks like a rootin' tootin' good time."

"But really," Cami says, "how high-class were we hoping to get on this stereotypical bachelorette trip, anyway?"

"I'll be in Nashville next weekend, too," Will says, his voice strained as he pulls down the overhead truck door. "Visiting my mom."

I frown. Just his mom? Not his dad, too?

"Be honest, Will Grant," Cami says. "Are you the double-booking that got our first reservation canceled?"

"You caught me."

"Maybe we'll see you around the mechanical bull." She winks at him.

Will turns to me, looking disturbed. "Make sure every bridesmaid wears pants that night."

"You sound like you're giving advice from a traumatic past experience," I say.

His face stays neutral. "Yes."

"Let's go to Agricole," Cami says. "I want free food."

Will shakes his head. "I've been trying to eat at that restaurant for months, every time I visit Austin. It's impossible to get in without a reservation. Also, it's impossible to get a reservation."

"My fiancé is the sous chef." Cami snags the truck keys from Will's hand. "We'll get in."

He stares at her. "Your fiancé is David Ortega?"

Cami grins. "The one and only. Are you a foodie?"

Will blinks. "In a sense."

"In what sense?"

He rubs the back of his neck. That tell again. "I like . . . to cook."

She laughs. "Him, too. Want to meet us there?"

Will nods, his stoic, surly masculine aura temporarily deserting him, replaced with a boyish curiosity. He disappears to his car. I smile and take my final swig of prosecco, then shove the empty bottle into my purse. Cami and I climb into the high seats of the rental truck and thunder our way down the road toward Agricole in East Austin. It's just about the only meal in the world that could make this terrible day any better.

David's been working here for five years—about the same length of time he and Camila have been together. They met during his first month on the job when he was fresh out of culinary school and newly returned to the Austin restaurant scene from New York.

When the three of us walk in, Cami makes pleading eyes at the host. He throws her a stern look and a muttered *Could've warned me,* but then he sets us up at the chef's bar on stools that materialize out of a secret closet. We've got a view of half the kitchen—the salsa station, the garnishing station, a wood-fired oven for meats and breads.

Cami leans over me to shout at Will above the clank of hot pans. "This is the best seat in the house!"

"Camila!" One of the staging chefs blinks at her. "What the fuck you doing here?"

"I had a bad day."

"David!" the chef shouts toward the back of the kitchen.

"WHAT!"

"Your fiancée is here!"

"Did she have a bad day?"

"David!" Cami shouts, leaning onto the bar top. "I'm up here!"

David Ortega materializes from around the corner in his chef whites, eyes locked on his fiancée. In Spanish he says to her, "You're still so pretty even when you're sad."

"Make me happy again."

He smirks, something romantic and *just for them* behind his eyes, and then turns to me and Will. "Hey, J."

"Hey," I say. "This is Will Grant."

David reaches across the bar to shake Will's hand, just as the chef at the garnish station shouts, "Will fucking Grant?!" He's a man roughly our age with a very petite beer belly and short red hair.

"Brooks?" Will says.

"Yeah, it's fucking Brooks!" says fucking Brooks. He's holding a pair of tongs toward the sky, a stem of cilantro still in its claws. "We went to high school together!" Brooks says to David. Then to Will: "You still living in New York, man?"

"Yep. It's great to see you."

The staging chef sets warm tortillas, mole, and corn salsa in front of us. Will looks overwhelmed. His eyes are darting between the food, his old friend, David, and me.

"Eat," Brooks says. "We'll catch up later!" He turns back to his garnishes, smiling to himself as he shakes his head. "Will fucking Grant!"

David leans his elbows against the bar. "Any dietary restrictions?" he asks Will.

"I'll eat anything you put in front of me."

David grins. "My kind of customer." He slides down toward Camila, and the two of them switch back to Spanish again, their voices dropping low.

"Were you and Brooks close?" I ask Will.

His voice goes soft as he watches Brooks's back. "We were best friends in high school."

"You didn't keep in touch?"

Will shakes his head. He says nothing for several seconds. Then he rubs a thumb over his lower lip and murmurs, "He's the one my high school girlfriend dumped me for."

My eyebrows jump into my hairline. "The girlfriend you

long-distance dated when we were seniors? The girlfriend who kept you so damn moody all the time?"

Will shoots me a look. "I wasn't moody all the time."

"You *were*. Do you want me to break out the references you won't understand again?"

He shrugs, lips quirking. "Sure, why not."

"You were James from *folklore*. You were Kylo Ren when he could see Rey through the force bond but couldn't touch her. You were Zayn right before he left One Direction. You were—"

"I changed my mind," Will interrupts.

I move on without a hitch. "I wonder if she and Brooks are still together."

"They're not," Will says.

"You know this . . ."

"Because I have Instagram, Josie, you should try it sometime. It's the perfect way to sate your curiosity about a person without having to speak to them."

"I sometimes *like* speaking to people," I inform him.

"From high school?" He shoots me a disbelieving look.

I ignore this and shift the conversation back to him. "So does that mean you've forgiven Brooks? For making a move on your girlfriend once you went to Nashville?"

"Of course I forgive him." Will grabs a tortilla. "It's been ten years since we were seventeen-year-olds. And anyway, it would be good to catch up with Brooks. I'm trying to . . ." He drifts off, ripping the tortilla in half.

"What?" I probe. Will aims a wary look at me. I flush. "Sorry. You don't have to—"

Quickly, he says, voice ragged, "I'm trying to get back to the man I used to be. Actively trying. Every day, all the time."

The man I used to be. It implies he wants to get away from the man he became.

I have so many follow-up questions, all of which, I'm pretty sure, are too personal for the relationship we've established.

Yesterday, while Will was "picking my brain" in one of the Revenant conference rooms, we buried our admissions from the Eberly dinner the night before and focused on work. On strategy. On Will becoming my professional *fixer*. But now, two nights later, we're right back to it. Big questions with vulnerable answers.

"Is it working?" I ask softly. "Getting back to your old self?"

His blue eyes slant in my direction, cascading up and down my face. "Yes and no. I feel more centered than I have in a long time. But I don't think it's possible to go back. You have to grab the pieces of yourself you want to hang on to and let go of the rest of it, then move forward anyway, the best you can."

My lips pull up as his wisdom settles over me. "Will Grant," I say. "You're nothing at all like the other finance bros of my acquaintance."

He smiles back, dimples flashing, eyes dancing. "That's the point, Josie." He turns back to the food in front of us, dipping his tortilla into the mole. "That's the whole entire point."

When we finish dinner, Cami heads home in our U-Haul to her and David's house in North Loop after we relocate my bike to Will's rental car. He drives me home, where my newly repaired SUV waits in the driveway.

"It's like you were never there," I joke, gesturing at the bumper. "I can't believe you wanted to *get rid of* the imprint of your face on my car's ass."

I can tell Will's fighting a smirk as he gets out to help with my bike. Every time I make him battle a smile, I add a tally mark in my head.

I meet him in the driveway and grab the handlebars from him. "You're headed back to Manhattan in the morning?"

Will clears his throat in a semblance of a confirmation, backing away. "First thing."

The question launches out of me before I can rethink it: "What are you going to tell Zoe?"

"The truth," he says. I dig my fingernails into the handlebar tape. "Did you want me to pass on a message?"

"No," I say quickly.

Will frowns. "She'd be happy to hear from you."

He says it the way two people often promise to get together for lunch but never do. Like he means well but isn't positive on the follow-through.

"Zoe made it clear she didn't want to hear from me," I say. "It may have been a long time ago, but I want to respect her boundaries."

His frown deepens.

"You'll be back in two weeks?" I hate the anxious note in my voice. *He signed a contract. He's not going to abandon me.*

Will's frown lapses into a gentle smile. "Next time you see me, I'll be the walking encyclopedia of B Corp."

I tilt my head. "Was that a joke?"

"No," he clarifies.

"Oh, good. It wasn't funny."

Will laughs. Out loud.

"Did I just get you to *laugh*?" I ask. "By saying you aren't funny?"

"I've never claimed to be funny."

"Just moody."

"I've never claimed to be moody, either. And anyway, it's not exactly a fair comparison, you to me." He gestures between us.

"Why not?" I ask.

"Because anyone compared to you would seem moody. You're . . ."

"Chipper?"

"I was going to go with *uplifting*."

"Madison Greenberg once told me I was aloof."

"You can't be aloof *and* uplifting?"

"Now or then?" I ask.

"What do you mean?"

"Did you think I was uplifting then, or do you think I'm up-lifting now?"

"Why not always?" he asks.

I shrug. "So you think I'm the same as I used to be."

Will considers, scratching at his elbow. "To be honest, I've never known *what* to think of you, Josephine. You've always been a riddle to me."

His words land like warm rays on my skin, easing my senses from head to toe. Here I'd thought Will had found some sort of key to figuring me out. That years ago, he'd unlocked the answer and decided it wasn't very interesting.

"I could never figure you out either," I say.

Will sighs, backing toward his car. "It's a shame neither of us tried very hard. Until now."

CHAPTER NINE

S tart from the beginning," Camila says.

I pull my mimosa closer, eyeing the fizzing bubbles as they tame. Beyond our little airport restaurant, Camila's sisters and cousins are lined up outside the gate even though we still have forty-five minutes until boarding starts. Giovanna isn't even here yet.

I look Cami directly in her large, warm brown eyes. "You remember when we were freshmen and I told you about my high school best friend, Zoe?"

Camila nods. "She excommunicated you after you made out with her twin brother on senior spring break."

I wince.

"Wait. That's *Will*? *Will's* the twin brother? Will Grant, our new consultant?"

My wince winces. "Yeah."

She points at me, her sparkly pink fingernail flickering. "I knew something was going on between you two."

"There's nothing going on between us," I assure her. "There never *was* anything going on between us. What happened that night when we were seventeen was just a random, drunken encounter that blew up in our faces—"

Cami holds up a hand, indicating I pause. "Backpedal. Walk me through it."

I sigh, glancing at the ceiling. Telling my best friend of nine years about a seven-month friend I couldn't stay on good terms with is cannonballing my anxiety.

"The issue started between Zoe and Will before they moved to Nashville," I begin. "Zoe had this friend, Amber, whom she'd gotten close with in Austin. Apparently, Amber and Will were interested in each other and started dating. Zoe didn't mind at first, even supported it, but eventually, it became obvious Amber had never cared about her friendship with Zoe."

"Became obvious how?" Cami asks.

I tilt my head, remembering the story. "Zoe had never been included by other girls—they thought she was weird—and then Amber started being nice to her out of the blue. Since Amber was also spending more time with Will as a result of her friendship with Zoe, they got together. But then Amber told Zoe to stop being clingy? That they needed to redefine their friendship? Basically, Amber didn't want to be around Zoe unless Will was also there."

"Ouch," Cami says.

I nod in agreement. "So, you can imagine the chip Zoe had on her shoulder when she moved to Nashville and tried to make new friends."

"Did you know?" Cami asks. "Did Zoe *tell* you about that experience before you and Will . . ." She makes a kissy face, tilting her head back and forth with her eyes closed.

I wrinkle my nose. "I knew," I admit, cheeks flushing. "Zoe told me what happened, and I understood her side of it, completely. She felt like she'd been used and then dropped." I pause. Take a sip of my mimosa. "I felt so bad for her. I could see how hurt Zoe had been by it. Not just by Amber, but by Will, too, who was ignorant of the entire situation. I'd hardly spoken more than a *greeting* to Will Grant at that point, and frankly, I couldn't understand what *any girl* would see in him other than his obvious good looks."

"Such a shame girls never go for obvious good looks," Cami intones.

"*Anyway,*" I go on, ignoring her. "There was this one night on the beach, the last night of senior spring break. We'd all been drinking heavily. There was music, a bonfire, drinking games. I got this call from my mom—about Oma." I swallow thickly, and Cami reaches across the table for my hand.

"She passed away that night," Cami guesses.

I nod, clearing my throat, training my brain away from the news my mom had given me on the phone. Oma had died alone in her home. It was an accident, a bad fall. No one was there to help her.

Camila smiles warmly. "I remember you telling me how close you were when you were growing up."

It's true; for years, I'd been closer with Oma than I'd been with my own mother. Oma was, for all intents and purposes, the fun relative and the love bomber. Oma is the reason I know anything about fashion. She explained the history of Ralph Lauren to me, showed me old photos of Coco Chanel and Jackie Kennedy. She used to say all the time: *Men invest in real estate. Women invest in jewelry.* She would tell me to look at the tennis wives, not the football wives, for fashion inspiration, and don't trust any magazine but *Vogue.* Such a character. So thoughtful, and simultaneously vain at her core, but I loved her desperately. My whole family did.

"I was drunk and heartbroken," I say. "I wanted a moment away from the bonfire crowd, and I spotted Will Grant down at the far end of the beach."

I can still see the image of him that night so vividly: his knees pointed at the sky, hands behind him fisting the sand, hair flapping with the breeze coming off the waves. Something had pulled me closer. I'd stumbled my way over and sat down beside him, offering the last dregs of my Blue Raspberry Lemonade Smirnoff. He drank it in one pull as I let the salty air fill up my lungs. Then I exhaled a liquor-soaked breath over his profile.

My girlfriend dumped me this morning, he told me, his gaze not breaking from the ocean.

I was down in Rosemary Beach as a guest of the Grant family, so I'd borne witness to Will's *extra* grumpy mood that whole day. Zoe had joked earlier by the pool he'd probably had another scary dream—she assured me he was a sleep talker and woke up often from night frights—but I thought maybe he'd gotten a rejection email from a college he'd applied to. A breakup, I hadn't been expecting.

I don't remember asking Will why Amber dumped him. I don't remember caring, too swallowed by my own grief in that moment.

Good riddance, I said bitterly, choking back tears that would have alarmed him without context. *Amber sucks.*

You never even met Amber, Will said.

Zoe told me about Amber. She sucks.

Will had laughed at that, finally casting his head my way. The laugh was scratchy, scorching, and his eyes had the first drip of mirth I'd ever seen from him aimed at me.

I ruined it by saying *My grandmother just died. Or, I mean, she's been dead for a couple hours. But my mom just told me. And I really loved her, a lot.*

Will said nothing, though I saw his eyes dampen. After five seconds, he pulled me against his side. Impossibly, it felt like the only right thing for him to do. I rested my head on his shoulder. We were not friends. We were not enemies. We were just two people with nothing in common except for Zoe and, right then, a sadness the other person could match.

Do you want to tell me about her? he asked.

No. It'll make me cry.

You can cry if you want to.

We don't know each other well enough for that, I said with emphasis.

I could go get Zoe, he offered.

No, Zoe is flirting with Forrest, and she has a crush on Forrest, so I don't want to ruin their moment, I explained.

His focus on my face seemed to concentrate. There was a divot between his eyebrows. Sand on one temple. *But your grandmother just died, and Zoe is your best friend.*

Yes, Zoe is my best friend, and Zoe deserves a best friend who doesn't put their own needs above hers all the time, I retort. More bitingly than I probably should have, given the girl I was referencing had just dumped Will anyway.

His gaze went past mine, as if searching the bonfire for Zoe.

How is she? he asked. *Not tonight. But in general, the whole year?*

You're the one who lives with her, I said, my voice constantly on the brink of wobbling. But whether Will knew what he was doing or not, he was a good distraction from the weight of sadness pressing on my chest.

Zoe and I haven't talked much the past year, he admitted.

Well, she's happy, I think, I told him. *It's hard moving to a new city as a senior. I'm sure you know.* He nodded, blue eyes on mine. One of his arms was still around me. The other dug into the sand, gripping it.

We were quiet for a few seconds, looking at each other for what felt like the first time.

I started dating Amber, Will said, *because I trust Zoe's judgment more than anyone's.*

The words felt like his defense.

If that were true, you would have warmed up to me by now, I argued.

What, like you've warmed up to me? he snarked back, though his tone was playful.

Somehow, our knees had fallen against each other. Our faces were still tilted in. Will's gaze landed on my lips for a second time.

You're hard to read, he said.

False. I'm actually incredibly easy to read. Everybody thinks so.

Will shook his head, and the distance between us narrowed. *Not me, Josephine. The more of you I see, the more I discover I don't have a clue.*

I didn't realize you were looking.

I was, and I wasn't. After another moment he added, *I was. While I told myself I wasn't.*

Our noses grazed, and my skin felt like it was caramelizing. My joints were unbolting, my body going limp. The hand Will had dug into the sand came to my knee.

Kissing, Will said, voice like gravel, *when we're both drunk, a couple hours after your grandmother died and my girlfriend dumped me, would be an incredibly stupid thing for us to do. Right?* He did not sound at all confident in his own theory.

I don't know, I said. *I just want to feel less horrible right now.*

Fair enough, Will concluded, and his lips met mine.

I'd kissed exactly two boys before: my first boyfriend, when I was fourteen and dating a seventeen-year-old senior, and then a Sea Island fling last summer.

None of those kisses felt like *this*. Intense, desperate, greedy, emotional.

When our mouths slid together, Will made an immediate noise, halfway between a groan and a growl, that elicited an immediate noise from *me*, halfway between a gasp and a sigh. His lips were warm. They tasted perfectly salty and sweet, like an Ocean Spray candy. We kissed *so gently,* nervous but highly eager, two drunk teenagers who wanted to dive into each other's skin. Will breathed softly as he broke from my lips. His cool raspberry breath danced along my eyelashes. His mouth traveled down the side of my face, hovering and then sucking on the place where my jaw met my neck. I climbed onto his lap and his sandy palms went straight to my exposed lower back.

Slowly, we were developing a language. *Kiss here. Touch here. That feels good. This feels better.*

Wolf whistles from the bonfire were what broke us apart.

We turned toward the sound, our chests heaving. And even from that distance, we could see Zoe's furious gaze dancing in the firelight. She had no context. She didn't know Will was single. She didn't know I was heartbroken, desperate not to feel my emotions, desperate to replace them with something tactile. All she knew was she'd confided her deepest insecurity to me—that girls used her to get to her brother—and I'd thrown it right back in her face.

"Soooo yeah," I conclude, downing the rest of my mimosa. Cami is looking at me with alarmed eyes from across the table, her whole body leaned in. "That was pretty much the stupidest conversation I've ever had, followed up by the stupidest decision Will Grant and I collectively ever made. Followed by the stupidest drunk three-way fight I've ever partaken in. Zoe was equally intoxicated and screamed at both of us for like ten minutes straight before we got a word in edgewise. Obviously, it ended badly."

"Josie, *oh my God,*" Cami says.

"I know. I'd claimed to be such a good friend. But in that moment, I didn't even *consider* how much what we did would hurt Zoe's feelings."

I'm flustered just remembering the aftermath. A silent car ride back to Tennessee in the morning. Confused parents. Sobbing and crying and feeling like the world was ending, like I was getting hit from all sides. Oma's funeral, then two tense months of school lead-ing up to graduation. I was devastated by the universe, disappointed in myself, for losing my oma and Zoe in one night.

Cami calls the waiter over and we order two more mimosas.

"Josie, baby." Cami tilts her head. "I'm sorry you had to find out in those circumstances about your oma. That was a bad situation waiting to happen. Did Zoe not come around and understand it was a drunken mistake?"

"The last thing she said to me was that I shouldn't speak to her again," I admit. "I wrote her a letter apologizing and delivered it to her mailbox the Sunday before we started back at school. I tried to explain that I cared about her friendship more than anything and what happened between Will and me was simply because our emo-tions were running high. I didn't tell her about my oma, though. I remember thinking it would have been a guilt trip. But the next day in study hall, Zoe kneeled by my desk to say *I'm really sorry about your oma.* Which means Will told her. But she didn't say anything else, then walked off quick as a whip. I got the message. My letter didn't change Zoe's mind about our friendship."

"What about Will?" Cami asks. "Did you ever talk to him again?"

"I avoided him at school. He tried to talk to me the next week, but I told him it wasn't a good idea." I can still recall the confusion on Will's face when I'd walked away.

Not a good idea.

Oh my God. *I'm* the one who said it first. He simply repeated the sentiment to his boss ten years later.

"Maybe this reunion is fate," Cami says. "Maybe Zoe wishes things had evolved differently."

"She's had ten years to reach out," I say.

"And you?" Cami asks.

"And me what?"

"Other than the letter, how hard did you work to reach out?"

"What do you mean?" I ask.

Cami throws me a *come on* look. "I mean—and please don't take this the wrong way, J, I know you were grieving, but—it kind of sounds like you threw in the towel and gave up on your friendship with Zoe without putting up too much of a fight? You didn't have a real, honest conversation with her in person. Instead, you wrote her a letter. Even years later, you could have checked in, but you didn't. The reason I think that's so odd is because I *know* you, Josie, and you never give up. You're a fighter."

Cami's right about one thing. I *didn't* fight for my friendship with Zoe. I accepted it was over, then crawled into a corner and cowered there. Partially because I couldn't make sense of why she'd allowed me to be her friend in the first place. We were so different. Not in a cute, opposites-attract way, but in a make-it-make-sense way. I'd packed three suitcases for that beach trip and Zoe had brought a carry-on. I took photos of my outfits for Instagram; Zoe was a short-story Tumblr girl. I was the one doing the hurting; she was the one getting hurt.

"She deserved to find a better friend than me," I say.

"Josephine," Cami says, reaching for my hand again. "Trust me. There's no such thing."

CHAPTER TEN

We have to be the most-hated group of women in a one-hundred-mile radius at the moment. Thirteen of us, dressed in denim and cowboy boots, hair teased, makeup slathered, a picture of David Ortega's face tattooed on our cheeks and shoulders and wrists.

I've owned a business for seven years now, but I've *never* had to be as authoritative as I was thirty minutes ago, corralling a dozen drunks onto this party wagon (which I reserved by calling 615-GID-DYUP several months back). The trailer is hitched to a cherry-red tractor with wheels so tall they reach my shoulders, driven by a man who announced himself as Farmer Bob and who was, frankly, a little too cavalier with the safety instructions.

I definitely prefer the morose disposition of our bartender, Wylie: a mid-thirties jock type with a muscle tee and a man bun. I know his name only due to the name tag, and not because he's offered up a single word yet, despite taking our consistent drink orders from behind the small bar in the corner ever since we climbed aboard. Something tells me if a member of our bridal party is hanging by one boot over the side of the wagon at any point this afternoon, Wylie, and *not* Farmer Bob, will be the one to intervene.

"How do people hold a job in this town?" Giovanna asks, leaning both elbows on the wagon's edge as she gazes out at Broadway. It's four o'clock and lines are already forming outside the four-story bars down by the Cumberland River.

I point at the masses. "Bold of you to assume any of these people are going to be in Nashville come Monday."

"Where *do* the locals go?"

"How should I know?" I take a sip of my seltzer. "I haven't been local in ten years."

"Is that a woman wearing a dinosaur costume?" Gio raises a cool eyebrow at a walking mascot missing her headpiece. "Carrying a *bow and arrow*?"

"I'm sure it's fake."

(I'm not.)

"GET THE FUCK OUT OF NASHVILLE!" a dude in a University of Tennessee baseball cap shouts at us.

"Oh! There's a local!" Gio exclaims, pointing at him like he's a starfish and she's a small child in an aquarium.

"Don't be so sure. He's got a guitar," I note, "strapped to his back."

"AUSTIN IS THE REAL UT!" Cami's younger sister Patricia shouts at the guy from the other end of the wagon.

"Oh, *that's* crossing a line!" he rallies back, cupping both hands around his mouth. "Can I get your number?"

We're in such standstill traffic that Patricia nods, giggling, while the guy comes into the street and passes his phone up to her. Gio and I watch in rapt amusement as he stands below us, hands on his hips, and proceeds to flirt.

In the middle of the wagon, Cami is in a dance circle popping her booty while everyone gasses her up, screaming at the top of their lungs in unison with the blaring Fergie tracks. When she spots me watching her, she bursts through the circle and grabs me.

"Dance!" she commands.

I toss my drink into the garbage can. We hold hands and spin in a ridiculous circle, jumping and dancing, until I'm bodychecked by Mariana. Half her margarita seeps down the front of my overalls.

"Nobody will know!" she tells me seriously, cupping my cheek. "They'll never know!"

"Mariana, I don't think *we'll* know."

"Another!" she announces, cementing this fate. She links arms with me and steers us toward Wylie—who looks more and more horrified by the second.

Hours later, I'm wedged into the corner of a honky-tonk booth as every Sanchez sister belts Shania Twain to a roomful of strangers, most of whom have taken it upon themselves to roundly ignore the drunk women onstage.

"Let's go, girls," Camila repeats into the mic for maybe the fifth time, just before she accidentally drops it. Her sisters rush to pick it up, two of them bonking heads.

"Lights on, nobody's home," Gio says.

We call Ubers soon after, and the Sanchez women stumble off-stage, piling into the rides with lyrics still humming between their lips.

"Are you even drunk?" Cami whines as I pull her up the stairs of our Airbnb. The two of us are sharing a room, which is already destroyed with clothes and makeup and jade rollers. Back when we lived together, we could hardly keep the place in order given how many *belongings* we each needed to function.

"Tomorrow," I promise her.

"Can you tell Will Grant I said thank you again for getting us a reservation tomorrow night?" she mumbles. "Even if it is at *Wagon Wheel*."

"Beggars can't be choosers," I sing. "How much water have you had tonight?"

Cami laughs maniacally. I push her onto the bed and take off her shoes, then head to the bathroom and fill up a glass. When I come back, Cami is in tears, slumped on her stomach across the whole bed.

I'm not *that* alarmed—she's a drunk crier—but still, I rush over and kneel in front of her, pushing the glass against her cheek.

"Hey, we're going to *bring the party* to Wagon Wheel."

"That's not why I'm crying!" she wails, wiping at her eyes, smearing mascara across both her face and the bedspread. Her forehead thunks down.

"Then why are you crying?"

Muffled, she says, "Josie. I have to tell you something."

My stomach drops.

Here it comes. Part of me was expecting this.

I'm having second thoughts about the bridal party.

Actually, I want Patricia as my maid of honor.

David has never liked you.

Every villainous thing they say about you in the press is true.

But it's none of those fears.

It's worse.

"I'm leaving Revenant," she says to the bedspread, and my heart cracks right in half.

I met Camila during freshman orientation.

My first impression of her was how short she was. Camila had a bob back then, dark hair that was almost black, messy curtain bangs. (These days, every time she gets stressed, she threatens to cut them again. Only it's not the threat she thinks it is, because David and I have both agreed Cami looked great with bangs.) That day, she was wearing the coolest earrings I'd ever seen in my life. They were gold, Egyptian-looking, and they wrapped up and down her ears. Once we became friends, I borrowed them all the time.

Cami and I got paired up during a breakout discussion. I remember her telling me, completely unprompted, that she wanted to do marketing for a fashion brand when she graduated college. Maybe Anthro, maybe Reformation, or maybe a company that didn't exist yet.

Here's a truth I've never admitted, even to myself: part of the reason I had the balls to turn Revenant into what it is today is because I knew it fit into Camila Sanchez's plan.

I was fragile my freshman year of college, and Cami, very quickly, figured that out. She didn't know *everything*. Not at first. But she knew I didn't have social media, and she knew I didn't go to many parties. I think she was drawn to me because I made her feel like she wasn't the only person missing out.

We became friends slowly. Migrating toward each other in lecture halls, eating together in the cafeteria. Neither of us was an open book at first, but that changed one afternoon in the library—when we accidentally spotted a couple going at it in the stacks. We ran away giggling loudly in tandem, and it was like the frost melted. We were in on a secret, together.

I don't know that I ever thought of Cami as fragile, but she *was* cracking. As the year went on, it became more and more obvious. Her grandma was getting sicker. Her younger sisters had been reliant on Cami and her cousin Mariana for years by the time Cami went to college. She was struggling with a full course load, trying to balance it with her responsibilities as a caretaker. Her family lived forty-five minutes away. She spent a lot of time driving back and forth between campus and their place.

Sometimes, she'd come by my dorm room well after midnight when my roommate was out at a party. I could always tell she'd just gotten back to campus based on the weary look on her face. She would jump on my bed and watch me sew something or draw a design at my desk while *New Girl* played on my TV in the background, and we'd talk.

Am I a bad person, she asked me one night, *because I'd rather be here, staying up too late and wasting time with you, than saving money and living at home?*

I think you're the least bad person I know, I told her. *And also, what you want makes you exactly the same as every other freshman.*

Another night, when we were practicing our speeches for Public Speaking 101, Cami asked me why I didn't have social media.

I had an unhealthy relationship with it, I said. Completely honestly.

In what way? she asked.

I shrugged, marking a note in the margin of my printed speech, and mumbled out a response without looking her in the eye. *Like, I was obsessed with posting pictures of my outfits. And I was obsessed with following fashion bloggers, but I couldn't separate what was real from what was staged. It messed with my head. To be honest, I would have gone on letting it, but in April, pretty much my entire grade unfollowed me and some people were even trolling me a little bit and it hurt my feelings and I just decided a clean break from the whole thing was what I needed not to hate myself every morning when I woke up.*

When I finally glanced up, Cami was watching me with a confused look, and I knew exactly what she saw.

A healthy, able-bodied, tall, blond-haired, hazel-eyed girl with smooth skin and just enough freckles to look airbrushed, and, of course, *money.* I knew when Cami looked at me, she saw money. Money in the handbags I had lined up on the top shelf of my closet, money in my skin care, money in the fabric, money in the sewing machine, money in the full cost of out-of-state tuition, because lord knows I didn't study enough in high school to manage a scholarship.

What on earth, Cami asked me, her voice deadening, *were you trolled for in high school that prompted you to delete all of your social media?*

And I just—told her: *I had a public make-out with my best friend's twin brother in front of, like, fifty of our classmates, on a beach during senior spring break. People sort of slut-shamed me after that. Plus, it also hurt my best friend's feelings because she thought I had been using her just to get close to her hot brother.*

Cami considered my admission. *Well, did you* like *him?*

No? I said. *Yes?*

You aren't sure? she asked.

I shook my head. *We were warming up to each other. But still, it was a stupid, impulsive mistake, and it hurt Zoe's feelings.*

Chalk it up to a learning experience, Cami said. *Nobody's perfect. I'm not. Carry the lesson forward and move on.*

You don't think I'm a bad person? I asked.

If you were a bad person, Cami said, throwing me a look, *you wouldn't be feeling any remorse. But I can tell you're swallowed by it, Josie, even though I'm not sure you should be. I get that Zoe was hurt, but you didn't make out with her* boyfriend. *You kissed her brother. Do you think he feels as guilty as you do?*

I have no idea, I admitted.

Cami crossed her arms over her chest, peering at me through her bangs. *If you ever hurt my feelings, I'll tell you, and we'll have a conversation about it. Same goes for you if I hurt yours. And we do our best not to hurt each other in the first place. Deal?*

She was so pragmatic. I've always loved that about Camila. Where I'm highly emotional, she's logic and reason. Where I'm overly dramatic, she pulls me back to earth.

Deal, I said, and over the course of nine years, we always, *always* abided by it.

CHAPTER ELEVEN

C ami doesn't remember a thing.

Or at least, she's acting like she doesn't, and Camila Sanchez has never been one to play coy. She calls it like it is, doesn't beat around the bush.

Which means she doesn't remember a thing.

This morning I found her with her head bent over the toilet, a Liquid I.V. packet clutched in one palm. After I got her a glass of water and asked if she was okay, Cami hushed me aggressively (she was not) and mumbled in Spanish for half an hour.

Luckily her sister Jane had some weed, which Cami smoked after swallowing one of Mariana's anti-nausea pills. After that, it was a hot shower and a rallying pep talk from David (I got him to record it, then I played it on the Airbnb's sound system for the whole house to hear; it started with "Pick yourself up by your bootstraps" and finished with "If you're not ruining a local's day in three hours you're failing").

One shot of tequila for the bride, and now we're here.

Here being a swanky restaurant in the 12 South neighborhood at a long wooden table laden with white and pink flowers—and airplane bottles of Tito's vodka spread out between the bouquets like confetti. Nobody's touched them; we're all still nursing espresso martinis, our first sips of alcohol of the day.

At the opposite end of the table, Cami peruses her menu. Her sisters are lined up on either side of her, bickering over what to order.

"Josie?"

I rip my gaze off Camila and look at Gio.

"Hmm?" I mumble.

She gives me a knowing look. "You've been in your head all morning."

I wince. "Sorry."

"Work stuff?"

"Kind of," I admit, trying to keep my eyes off Cami.

Gio nods. "I'm sort of amazed you pulled this off." She gestures around.

It was a huge time suck; I won't deny it. I felt more and more guilty with every hour I spent planning *this* instead of doing productive work to bolster Revenant's bottom line.

Maybe that should tell me something. It probably *would* tell me something if I paused long enough to let it.

"Do you think it's weird," I ask, "that she wants *me* to be her maid of honor? Over all six of her sisters? And the cousins?"

Gio leans toward me, lowering her voice. "She picked you to be her maid of honor because other than David, she's closest with *you*. You're the one who supported Camila when she was stressed out of her mind back in college. Remember all those times you took her clicker to classes *you weren't even registered for,* just so Cami could get attendance points while she was dealing with some new brand of family drama?"

"It wasn't *that* often."

She gives me a look. "You're a different kind of family to her, Jo."

Cami certainly feels like family to *me*. She feels so much like family I don't know how to manage without her.

How the *fuck* am I going to manage without her?

Where is she going? Why is she leaving? Is there a widespread corporate problem I've overlooked? I've made the most conscious effort I can possibly imagine to keep her happy. To make her stay. Camila's happiness is my pulse check. If she hasn't lost her faith in me, in Revenant, I'm still doing all right.

But if she *has*—lost her faith, that is—what do I need to do to restore it?

For the twentieth time today, I rack my brain, looking for some explanation as to why she'd want to leave. And for the twentieth time, I come up short.

I push down the tears threatening my eyes and take a glug of my espresso martini, polishing it off. Then I twist open one of the airplane shots, swallow that, too.

I hail our waiter and say, "I'll have a margarita next, and can you make it a double?" And when he brings it, I suck it down in record time.

The other women follow my lead, and before I know it, I'm halfway to drunk, and we're done with lunch, heading to midtown to find some live music.

There's a rooftop we've rented—a surprise for Camila. When we show it to her, dousing her in a champagne shower, she comes up and hugs me, screams, "Best MOH ever!" before she proceeds to twerk down at all the ordinary bar-goers on the floor below us.

"Plebians!" Mariana shouts.

"You wish you were us!" Jane shouts.

"Hey, those are the girls from the party wagon!" someone shouts.

There is an exact relation between the way the sun is slipping into the horizon beyond us and the feeling of my veins loosening, of my inhibitions letting go. Who cares about Revenant? Who cares about work? What if we all stayed drunk *all the time*?

Cami invites the band upstairs to drink with us during a break in their set. The guitar player—a tall, slender guy with a lazy grin that feels practiced in the mirror—latches onto me the second our eyes lock.

"You look familiar. Are you a model?"

I shrug. "You've probably seen my face in a fashion magazine."

He puts a hand on my arm. "That's so hot."

Eighteen-year-old me would be reciprocating his flirtation at this point. Hell, even twenty-two-year-old me would've leaned in. But even though I can note objectively that 1) he smells nice, 2) he's not the worst to look at, and 3) he plays guitar in a band, I can't summon the energy to care. It's been a common theme of my singledom over the past four years, ever since Clay and I cut things off a couple years after college graduation. Hardly any man catches my attention, and *nobody* holds it.

My phone vibrates in my back pocket. I slip past the guitar player, muttering that I'll be right back.

When I look at the screen, my throat closes.

Will.

Who might be the singular exception to the nobody-holds-my-attention rule.

I haven't forgotten he's in town this weekend visiting his mother, but I've *also* been fairly confident we won't bump into him (unless Mrs. Grant has developed a sudden penchant for rowdy cowboys and downtown honky-tonks).

I take a deep breath and walk to the opposite edge of the patio, holding onto the railing as I answer the phone.

"Hello?"

"Hey." It's such a casual hey. That's a *hey* you'd use to greet a longtime best friend. That's the *hey* David gives Camila when he calls her, I just know it. "You're going to Andalo tonight. I just forwarded you the new reservation confirmation."

For several drunken moments, I say nothing and stare at the gray beginnings of night folding into the sky. The crowd below is starting to fill out at the corners, and the volume of the whole city is on its way to all the way up.

"What?" I ask numbly.

"Thirteen, right?" Will asks. He sounds like he's walking somewhere. "That's what I said for the reservation. Thirteen of you."

"Y-Yeah," I manage. "How did you—"

"Don't worry about that. Just check your email for the details. You need to be there at eight. I'll cancel the Wagon Wheel reservation for you, okay?"

"Will."

"Josephine." There's a touch of humor in his voice, as if he's indulging me. Do I sound as drunk as I am? Can he tell?

"This isn't what consultants do for their clients," I half whisper.

On the other end of the line, a stretch of silence. A sigh. And then, in a voice that strips me of every bit of my sanity, he says, "I know, Josie. But it's what friends do. And I think we could be friends. I think maybe we already are."

It's a bold claim. We've been back in each other's lives for less than two weeks. Still, in that time, I've gained more ground with Will than I did our entire senior year.

It's a shame neither of us tried very hard. Until now.

I white-knuckle the railing, feel the alcohol pulse and zip through my body. I want to say something—anything—but I'm terrified the words will come out wrong. Or maybe my true fear is they'll come out honest. I can't even *think* straight. Not when he's saying *those* words in *that* voice while I'm *this* drunk.

After this weekend is over, thoughts of him will become my

primary distraction, I can already tell. He wants to be friends, so why does it feel like there's kindling in my stomach waiting patiently for a wisp of flame?

"Is that . . . What do you think about that?" he finally asks, like he's holding out a friendship bracelet, waiting to see if I'll put it on.

I nod my head, belatedly realizing he can't see me. "Good," I say, settling on that single monosyllabic word as the full extent of my abilities. "Being friends would be good."

It's a lie.

I'm pretty sure being friends with Will Grant would be really, *really* bad, but only because he's the first man in four years to make me fumble with my words, to make me reach for my lip gloss, to put my heart in my throat.

Sure, maybe part of that is based on the history of us, but something tells me if I'd met him from scratch the day he hit my car, I'd feel just the same.

"Okay then." On the other end of the line, Will opens a door. "What time do you have to be at Andalo?"

"Eight," I repeat.

"Have a good time."

"Sometime soon, I'm going to do something nice for *you*."

"You already did," Will says. "I got to eat an award-winning dinner at Agricole."

"That was Cami," I say. "I still owe you."

"That's not how friendships work."

"You're right. We need to make a blood pact first."

I can hear his smile. "Bye, Josephine."

"Bye," I say back, already missing him. "And thank you, really."

When I turn around to look for Cami, the guitar player is waiting for me. He approaches when I pocket my phone, crowds me against the railing. "Baby," he coos.

"No."

Brushing past, I search our crowd for a flash of white and grab hold of Cami's arm when I see her. Her hangover is either long gone or buried deep. There's a beer in one of her hands, a champagne flute in the other. She smells like wheat and body spray.

"Andalo!" I shout.

Her eyes brighten. "Andalo?"

"Tonight! Eight p.m. We've got a new reservation!"

Cami shrieks and jumps into my arms, pecking me on the forehead. "You! Are! My Best Fucking Friend!"

I laugh and spin her in a circle before her weight shifts and she topples out of my grasp, landing against one of her cousins. "Isn't Josephine the best?" Cami asks her.

"The best!" the cousin concurs.

Cami shoots me one more glassy-eyed look of happiness before she runs off to tell every other bridesmaid. I watch her spread the news, pulling up my email to find the confirmation, just as Will promised.

Part of me knows it's a ridiculous thought. But I wonder—briefly, and with the full understanding that Camila Sanchez would *never* make a life decision that impulsively—if a perfect night at Andalo might change her mind about leaving.

CHAPTER TWELVE

Here's the secret to making other people happy: you accept that what makes them happy is what makes them happy, and you don't question it.

You don't question it as you're led into a red-hued, darkly lit club that smells like sweat and incense. You don't question it when dinner is served on breakable plates even though halfway through the meal someone's bare feet are going to be on the table. You don't question why some people *keep eating* after that kind of abhorrent foot proximity.

You don't question the music. You don't question the *volume* of the music. You don't even question why the guys serving your table keep glancing at the massive clock on the wall, waiting for their cue to begin clapping in tandem with the beat dropping.

You take a couple bites of dinner until hygiene compels you to stop, and then you stack the plates in one corner. You tell the bridesmaids to stand up in their seats, make sure anyone wearing precarious heels removes them. You take pictures and dance and sing at the top of your lungs even though no one can hear themselves *think* in here—genuinely, you might have to type out the next round of drink orders on your Notes app and hand it over—and you just let the person you're doing all this for be happy.

I stumble to the bathroom a while later, vodka soda clutched in one hand. Past the roped-off areas and massive tables in the main club room is a narrow hallway that does a decent job of blocking sound. My ears enjoy the relative quiet as I rattle the women's room doorknob.

A bouncer covered in tattoos comes up to me and gives me a nod, then tries the door. "You've got a boyfriend," he says. Not a question.

The sureness of it throws me off long enough to study him. He's maybe seven years older than me but has warm eyes I can tell he leads with when he flirts. He's employing them right now, offering me unsevered eye contact.

A rumpled man and woman leave the bathroom a few seconds later. Avoiding our eyes, avoiding each other's eyes. The bouncer and I watch them head down the hallway and depart in opposite directions.

"I don't have a boyfriend," I say. Not because I care one way or the other if the bouncer is interested. I just don't like lying.

His lips pinch, though I can't tell if it's because he's pleased or confused. "Then who was that guy who came by this afternoon and waited around for three hours to get you a reservation?"

My stomach floods with cold shock.

"He came here in person," I repeat, "and waited for hours?"

The bouncer nods. "I mean, yeah, he kept going back and forth between here and Valhalla, the sports bar next door, but when a cancellation came through this afternoon, we gave the reservation to him. And he said it was for you. Josephine Davis. That's the name you gave at the door when your group came in."

Warmth gathers in my heart like a whirling dervish, growing stronger, more powerful every moment. Then my heart beats with emphasis—once, twice, three times—and the white-hot feeling floods my veins in tiny sparks.

"Excuse me," I mutter.

I quickly use the bathroom and wash my hands, my mind careening. Instinct carries me across the main room. I swerve past clubbers on the dance floor and make a beeline for the front door. Outside in the alley, the air is smoky and damp. In the direction of Valhalla, a large sign glows bright, and shiny windows display the bar's bread-and-butter sports fanatics inside.

What are the odds he's still in there?

I push open the door as a cheer erupts in the direction of the TV screens. It's crowded in here, the music still loud and in direct competition with the sports announcers. The bar is strung in fairy lights that give the place a foggy glow.

I scan faces. My body feels as heavy as a bowling ball as I plow through groups, searching for him. If I don't find Will on a first pass, I tell myself, I'll go back to Andalo and let it go. Text him instead, thank him, ask him what on earth possessed him to—

"What are you doing here?" His deep, smooth voice stills me right in my tracks.

My eyes jerk up to his. The blue flecks wink silver at me.

"That's my line!" I push a finger into his chest, my gaze catching on the Predators T-shirt he's wearing.

Will's holding a frosty draft beer in one hand, but his other arm scoops around my waist. In an effortless movement, he pulls me against his chest just as I feel the brush of someone trying to sneak past me from behind.

"Thanks, man," the passerby says to Will, who nods, his chin catching on the crown of my head. I feel the rough stubble of his five-o'clock shadow before he releases me.

"Is something wrong with the reservation?" Will asks.

"Oh, you mean the reservation you apparently waited around all day for? That one?"

"What are you wearing?" A grin tugs at his lips as his gaze catches on my crop top, the word *PARTY* printed in all caps, bright pink across the front.

I glance down at myself. "We were supposed to go home and change before dinner, but you said to be there at eight and time got away from us."

"That," he says, his grin widening, a lock of hair creeping down across one temple, "is not even a remotely sufficient answer."

"Camila's shirt says *Wife of the Party,*" I explain. "Party, Wife of the Party. It's a pun."

"On a scale of one to ten, how much do you hate that shirt?"

"On a scale of one to ten, how much it's about what *I* think is a zero."

A dimple pops out. The left one. "Something tells me the list of people you'd let tell you what to wear is short."

"Short? It's microscopic. It was painful agreeing to the brides-maid dress. Orange is not my color."

Will laughs out loud, the sound like a cool breeze.

"It's weird I can amuse you now."

"You always amused me," he says. "I'm just comfortable enough to show it now."

I brush past the honesty of this and ask, tongue in cheek, "Come here often?"

Another person is trying to sneak behind me; we're stopped right in the aisle of traffic leading to the bar. This time I close the distance to Will on my own, stepping into his personal space while that same arm curls around my waist again.

"I know it's a weird coincidence," he allows, raising his glass to take a sip of his beer. I track the movement as he swallows, my

eyesight in line with his throat. "But this is the Preds bar, and my
mom is married to one of the old coaches."

He says it like it's nothing, which to him it must be, even though
Will just confirmed what I first suspected when he mentioned visiting only his mother: Will's parents aren't together anymore. My
chest pinches for him and Zoe, for their whole family, and I can't
help but wonder what happened. Back then, I'd never have guessed
they'd end up divorced.

My palms land on Will's chest, unsure where else to go while
more people pass behind me. "Were you planning to tell me you
were next door?"

"No." His eyes break from mine, traveling down to my *PARTY*
shirt. "I knew you had a full itinerary."

Something about that admission shoots affection up my spine.
The notion that he was near, and I didn't need to know because I
was busy. That Will would simply take care of things for me in the
background, no thanks necessary.

"Want to say hi?" Will asks.

I flinch. "To your mom?"

He nods.

"Does she hate me?"

"Viciously. I'm just offering you up as a meal for my own enter-
tainment, to be honest." I cast him a look. His grin settles but
doesn't drop. "No, of course she doesn't hate you, Josie. Come on."
He turns and leads me, his hand still loose on my lower back, toward a table in a corner of the bar. Mrs. Grant and a white-haired
man sit at a high-top watching the hockey game. When she spots
me, her eyes brighten, and she springs up from her seat.

"Josie Davis! Oh *my*!" Will's mother wraps me up in a hug, making motherly noises in the back of her throat. "Will mentioned you
were nearby. It's so lovely to see you!"

"You, too!" I say. "You look amazing!"

It's true. Mrs. Grant was always stunning, but now she has a glow. A professional-hockey-coach glow?

We do the usual catch-up and introductions, dancing around several elephants in the room, and then she says, "I'm so happy you're back in Will's and Zoe's lives."

I don't correct her about Zoe. All I say is "Me, too."

She looks back and forth between Will and me, curiosity at our situation plain as day on her face. I nip it in the bud by saying I need to get back to the bridal party.

"I'll walk you out," Will says.

Mrs. Grant grabs my hand, eyes warm and content. "I hope I see you again soon."

I return her sentiment, but my chest eases with every exhale as we leave the bar. Outside, the temperature has dropped in only twenty minutes. The night feels nearly cool. Will falls into step beside me as we head toward the Andalo entrance.

"Your mother remarried," I say.

"Yes."

"Your mother got divorced," I say.

He clears his throat. "Yes."

When I look over and up, Will's expression is relaxed, his eyes soft on mine. "It's a long story. Longer than you have time for right now. But I'll tell you another day if you want. TL;DR: Dad cheated, Mom left him."

I sigh, impossibly disappointed.

Will nods and looks away. "You never think it's going to happen to *your* family," he says quietly. "Secret girlfriends, double lives— that's the kind of thing that glamorous, absent fathers in television shows would do, not salesmen from Texas. But then it *does* happen to your family, and you learn clichés exist for a reason."

"I'm so sorry, Will."

"Thank you," he says, voice gruff but kind. His mouth shapes

into a wan smile. "And I'm sorry to bring you down on a trip cele-
brating the start of your best friend's marriage."

"I'd argue we're partway mourning the end of her singledom,
but anyway."

Will's smile turns genuine, bolstered by an easy, knowing fond-
ness. A dimple on his left cheek, half a dimple on his right. Suddenly there are one million questions I want to ask him. More pieces
of his life I'm dying to know. Plenty about the past, but I want to
know about Will's present. Where he eats out for dinner, how often
he rides his bike in the city, the order he'd rank the five boroughs
in, what his apartment looks like.

I push it all down, tell myself those facts aren't mine to know.

"How'd the bull riding go?" Will asks.

"Oh, tragic. The longest any of us lasted was six seconds, but at
least we all wore pants."

"Perverts everywhere are wiping their eyes."

I burst into a laugh, and Will's eyes flash triumphant. I settle
against the brick wall ten feet from the dark club door.

Will moves in front of me. "Well," he says.

"Well. I'd better head in."

His eyes jump around my face. "You'd better."

I do not move a muscle.

"Your mom was really nice to me," I say.

He bites the inside of his cheek. "That's because you were always
really nice to her. She simply treated you the way you deserve to be
treated."

After a moment I whisper, "I'm not positive that's true."

His head tilts. "Why do you think that?"

"I don't know," I say.

He studies me with a frown, something clicking behind his eyes.
"I owe you so many apologies, Josephine."

I laugh brittlely to push past the ache of his words. "What now?"

Will looks sideways. His jaw rolls. "It would be okay if you resented me."

My stomach lurches. "For what?"

"Exactly. For what?" he parrots, a challenge in his eyes.

With his permission, I say what we're both thinking. "For calling me a surface-level girl that one time?"

He nods. "You'd be justified in resenting me for that. I resent myself for saying it. I hated myself when I realized you'd heard it."

I pause and consider my next course of action. "It would be okay if you resented me, too. You tried to clear the air after we kissed, but I told you it wasn't a good idea for us to speak."

"I understood why you felt that way," Will says. "I was just trying to help. I could have tried harder, but I was . . ." He closes his eyes, gulping. "Wanting you. And that confused my priorities. I didn't know how to help you repair your friendship with Zoe without acknowledging how much I . . ." Again, he drifts off.

Every pore across my skin tightens. My breath locks inside my lungs. "Why?" I ask. "Why on earth did you want me?"

His voice slips out of him, the words seamless. "Because you are not and never have been a surface-level girl, Josephine. You're just a girl who loves things you have every right to love. And if I'm the boy who once convinced you that can't be true, then I will become the man who convinces you it absolutely is."

My heart seems to skitter instead of beating.

"You deserve to be treated with kindness," Will goes on, "because you are kind to everyone. You made yourself late to give me a ride when you could have left me on the side of that road and been totally grounded in doing so. You worked yourself into a fit when Andalo double-booked you because you wanted to make Camila happy." He laughs lowly. "You complimented my mom's necklace even though you would never wear it yourself."

"How did you know that?" I cry.

"You've got a tell," he says.

I noticed his tell; he noticed mine.

One of Will's hands comes to my temple, his thumb brushing my skin, just barely. My body overreacts, my muscles locking still.

"A tell?" I whisper.

He nods, looking entranced, and murmurs, "You blink three times in a row when you don't like an outfit. I noticed it earlier tonight when you were explaining the *PARTY* shirt to me. And I used to notice it with Zoe, all the time."

I glance away, feeling deeply ashamed he used to notice that. "Zoe had a unique fashion taste," I say neutrally, with the full understanding that fashion choices are ultimately a personal preference. Not to mention limited by finances, time, culture, geography.

"She came into her taste more once she met you," Will replies.

"I'll have to trust you on that."

"You don't trust anyone's taste but yours," Will muses, smiling gently. "And for the record, that doesn't make you self-absorbed or surface-level. It makes you iconic, but only to the people who don't know you well enough. The people who *do* know you . . ." He smirks. "Well, *they're* the ones who get to see you in the *PARTY* shirt."

"So, what you're saying is, the internet can't see me in this *PARTY* shirt, or they'll take away my It Girl status."

"I don't claim to know what the internet wants." His voice is like a quiet forest before everything wakes up. "And what I'm saying is, you deserve to be treated respectfully by everyone all the time, full stop. Including my mother. Including me. Including strangers on the internet who will never see you in the *PARTY* shirt."

His praise is like helium, slipping out of his mouth on a breath and under my limbs. I feel buoyed. I feel more intoxicated now than I've felt all night. Being understood by this man—even partly—is enough to send me to the moon and back. It's miraculous to be understood, and then to be wanted anyway.

It occurs to me Will's fingers are still resting against my temple. I see the thought occur to him in the same instant.

Which is notable, mainly because it's the first time in a *long* time that something physical regarding a man has occurred to me at all.

I exhale, breathing softly.

The pad of his thumb grazes my temple again, then the rest of his knuckles skate across the plane of my cheek. It's a light touch, gentle and unsure, but I don't make a sound.

My body is *awake*. His touch has aroused some long-dormant part of me.

I'm not exaggerating when I say I haven't been attracted to anyone in years. And if I'm *really* honest with myself, I stopped feeling attracted to my ex-boyfriend (a hockey player, for fuck's sake!) *months* before we ended things four years ago. Which has been great for my productivity, don't get me wrong.

I am the *blueprint* for productivity.

What other twenty-seven-year-old CEO do *you* know who also cycled fifty miles in a local charity race last month and never misses a grooming appointment (of which there are many)? All while taking CEO classes online that are frankly more intriguing to me than a vibrator.

Productivity at its finest!

I guess I've spent the past four years assuming I was just . . . growing out of it? Attraction, that is. Or—yes, okay—*maybe* part of me was expecting a queer awakening any year now. But no, not the case, and believe me when I say I've wondered about it enough. How my sexual drive could actively exist in high school and college and then simply vanish like that.

Back when Camila and I lived together, I spent many a midnight hour unwillingly listening to her and David make love to a Janis Joplin soundtrack while I quietly contemplated all the places my sex drive could have gone. While I wondered if I'd ever rediscover it.

But my sexual drive didn't disappear, not at all. It was stolen. And now Will Grant is wearing it around his neck.

I was wanting you, he'd said.

His hand settles against my collarbone while his eyes watch mine for a single sign of hesitation. I offer him none, my breath growing ragged, my pulse jumping beneath his palm.

I gulp, and his thumb traces the path of my throat as I swallow. My hands rest against his stomach, and I feel his abs clench underneath his shirt. I grip the fabric.

"What are you doing?" I ask.

He shakes his head, focus narrowed on my neck. "You smell like orange slices. And cinnamon sugar."

Oddly specific, but at least I know he means it.

"It's Jo Malone," I explain.

"No," he mumbles. "It's you."

My whole body hums. Will leans closer, nearly tipping into me. But he doesn't make a move to kiss me. Instead, he swallows thickly and closes his eyes, gathering himself. I stare at his eyelashes, at the scrunch of his nose, the wet on his lips.

He pushes off the brick wall and steps away.

It's not relief I feel—even though it should be. Relief is the *only* thing I *should* be feeling. I want him and he wants me, but at least this time both of us had the wherewithal to see past the alcohol thinning our blood and make the smarter choice.

Don't give in to it.

We resist the urge ten years too late.

Still, part of me thrills I can make him come this close to an impulsive decision.

"It's not that I don't want to," Will says, voice weak. There's a conflict in his eyes.

"Want to what?" I ask innocently.

He shakes his head at me, huffing out a laugh. "Nothing, I guess."

"Right. Nothing. Because I couldn't possibly be a good person if I never learned from my past mistakes," I say.

His eyebrows launch upward. "That so?"

"And you couldn't possibly be a good brother if you willingly engaged with a person your sister excommunicated without talking to her about it first."

He stares. "Who says I never talked to her about it first?"

My head tilts. He's got me there. "You spoke to Zoe about me?"

Will doesn't answer and takes another step back. "Good night, Josie."

"Wait."

"Not now." He nods toward the club door. "Your best friend needs you."

He's right. I've lapsed in my maid of honor duties for more than thirty minutes now. I head for the door, but I toss one last look at Will over my shoulder.

"I meant to say thank you," I call out. "That's the whole reason I came over to Valhalla. So I could thank you."

"You're welcome." He stands there, his smile small but star-bright, and waits for me to disappear.

CHAPTER THIRTEEN

My parents' house is in an old part of the city where the streets have manicured medians and every mailbox is adorned with the family surname. The house I grew up in is an expansive white-brick structure, vines creeping up the outside walls near a three-door garage and trees limned with sunlight all hours of the day. When my Uber pulls into the driveway, I spot the old swing Robbie used to push me on hanging from a tree branch in the front yard.

I thank my Uber driver and send him a tip before wheeling my suitcase—full-sized, every cubic inch utilized—up the driveway to the front door.

It's strange being here in early summer given I normally make an appearance only during holiday season. Honeysuckle on the wind, the grass plush and overgrown.

I'm just about to ring the doorbell when the navy-blue door swings open, revealing my mother. A tight bun, Dior slingback pumps, higher cheekbones than are strictly natural.

"I know, I know. The grass. But your father has been on a business trip all week, and now he's golfing with that horrid man from the club."

"Don't you hire a landscaping team?" I ask. "They could probably mow as well."

"He bought the mower, he wants to use the mower," Mom says, rolling her eyes.

"He bought the mower twenty years ago."

"Might you debate this with *him*?" She steps two heeled feet over the threshold, pulling me against her body as the scent of the perfume she's worn every day of my life washes over me in a cloud. "Did you go to church this morning?"

"Did *you*?"

Mom pulls back, evaluating the state of me. "No, I had a brunch."

"Same."

She narrows her eyes. I narrow mine back. Then she smirks and turns, making a gesture with her red-manicured fingers to usher me inside.

"Do you want some coffee? I've been playing around with one of those pour-overs."

I leave my suitcase in the hallway and shut the door behind me, following her into the house. I glance sideways and briefly note she's updated the dayroom. Every time I come home something's been remodeled.

"I'd love some coffee," I call to her. "Do you have anything baked?"

"Of course, darling, I went to Brightside Bakeshop and picked you up one of those stratas you love. What time is your flight?"

In the kitchen, I take a seat at a barstool. "Eight."

She perks up. "So you can stay for dinner?"

"If it's an early dinner."

I catch her smile as she turns and reaches into a cabinet for two mugs. "Lovely. Now, tell me *all* about the bachelorette party."

I do; I tell her every detail. Where we went, what we ordered, who fell over and scraped their knee. It took me a long time to understand this is how she wants it: a vicarious experience. When I was in high school, I'd shut her out. Give her a disgruntled *Fine, great, pretty, boring*. But at some point during my freshman year of college, I realized she wasn't being nosy. Hearing the little details of other people's lives is what makes my mother happy.

"Did you have fun?" Mom asks.

I sip on my coffee as I contemplate.

"I don't know," I answer honestly.

Even *before* Camila had drunkenly admitted she was leaving, I'd been stressed about corralling the girls and then paranoid someone would fall off the party wagon. After Cami's admission, my mood the whole next day had been fraught with anxiety and drunken inner monologue until Will Grant had—for lack of better phrasing—quieted me.

He'd taken my anxiety and soothed it. Listened to my best attempt at articulating that inner monologue and offered counterpoints. He stole my stress away, replaced it with a sense of ease. Even as heated as I'd been following our proximity, I'd gone back to Andalo and danced until my feet were numb, then sang karaoke at our Airbnb until I passed out.

It wasn't that I'd forgotten even for a moment about Cami's admission. It was that I stopped letting it infect every other thought I had.

"Toward the end of the weekend," I amend for Mom. "That's when I found my groove."

"Who helped you find it?" she asks.

I feed her a bland line, but I swear to God, there's a knowing, motherly glint in her eye. "Did the trip give you wedding fever?" she asks.

"*Mom.*"

She throws up her hands. "Just asking! You know Oma would roll over in her grave if she knew you were still single."

"Oma was married three times," I retort. "She would have understood me waiting for the right man."

Dad gets home forty-five minutes later—just moments after Mom mutters something under her breath to the effect of *If only men could make sex last as long as golf.* He kisses my forehead and gives my shoulders a squeeze.

"Have you checked your retirement fund recently?" he asks.

"No."

"Are you still making more money than me?"

"Yes."

Dad releases a jolly laugh. "Did you know the average age of a farmer in the United States is fifty-eight? We need to bolster the next generation of farmers."

"If you say so."

He grabs the remote, sits on the couch, and puts his feet up. "Want to watch *Suits*?"

The day vanishes as I watch TV with my parents. We order kung pao broccoli for dinner and talk about the stocks Mom's been trading. We drink lavender iced tea on the muggy back porch and FaceTime Robbie, plus his lemon-poppy-seed-muffin kids. When it's almost time for my flight to San Francisco (my next pressing work obligation to schmooze investors), my parents drive me to the airport together. They squeeze me in tight hugs outside the departures gate, tell me they love me, remind me how proud they are of the woman I've grown into.

And for some reason, I think I have Will Grant to thank for the quiet of this day, too.

CHAPTER FOURTEEN

After three days in San Francisco pitching VC firms, I touch down in Austin on Thursday morning and drive straight to the warehouse to observe some new tech. By the time I get home that night, my flowers have dried up and my fridge smells like bad dairy. I pull an Indian meal out of the freezer and heat it up, tossing the last of Camila's bachelorette props into a trash bag. After I eat, clean out the fridge, and take the trash to the curb, I finally collapse in front of my television. *Farmer Wants a Wife* is playing in the background while I scan emails on my phone.

I have a meeting with Will late tomorrow morning (I assigned his contact color Pantone Royal Blue). This meeting is just the two of us again. It's a notification I've been checking day in and day out, imagining he cancels it, postpones, invites Camila or another executive to attend. But none of those scenarios have occurred.

There's a familiar pull at my stomach, like the organ itself is rioting. It's been rioting every time I think his name.

I have an impossible number of questions about his life over the past ten years, and *that,* I tell myself, is the root of my fascination. Not the swirl of ocean blue in his otherwise crystalline eyes. Not the soft patches of brown hair that disobey his comb in the morning. Not the smooth, low, calming tone of his voice, or the sculpt of his shoulders, and definitely, absolutely *not* the way he says the word *good.*

So what if Zoe has decided she doesn't care anymore if I'm interested in Will? So what if that's actually true (and for the record, I'm still not sure it is)? Will Grant is technically a contract hire. On top of that, he lives in New York City, and I live in Austin. I'm pretty sure the differences in the lives we lead would be stark if you lined them up for review. He probably spends his weekends at swanky, dimly lit speakeasies he got invited to by a "New York ten"—a term Camila taught me—and meanwhile, I'm mostly bumming around breweries no more than five road miles from my home, wiping away the sweat from my bike ride with a paper towel.

And even *if* we could ignore all that, push past it for the sake of a good fling whenever one of us found ourselves in the other's city, and we could ignore the emotional turmoil from our past, and we could ignore the fact that we don't now and never have belonged in each other's circles—I have *no time.* None. Even when I'm traveling, I'm answering emails or taking CEO classes at night, or on the phone with someone in Asia at eight p.m.

And even if, by some miracle, we found ourselves in a situation where *none* of the aforementioned concerns mattered—

I haven't been intimate with a man in *years.* They say you can't unlearn how to ride a bike, but frankly, I think I might've forgotten how to fuck.

Will Grant is a no-fly zone.

Do not think of him.

Do not go near him.

Do not touch him.

Do not want him.

He is *forbidden*.

I nod to myself and pour some wine.

The next morning is productive. Our head of design hands me an ICOML when I walk into the office, and there are cupcakes to celebrate one of our designers' birthday. It's a Friday, and everyone is in a good mood. Camila smacks me on the butt and says, "Welcome home!" when she passes me in the hallway, not looking the least bit like someone who's biding their time before they make a grand exit.

Part of me wonders if I dreamed what she said. If I fell asleep, then manifested a nightmare so convincing I've continued to believe it.

It's seven minutes past the hour when I'm jogging back to my office. I swing around the corner and Will is waiting there, already seated across from my desk.

"Sorry!" I shout. He twists to look at me, eyes tired. I wonder how early his flight was this morning.

His hair is combed back from his face today, the curls from last weekend a bit straighter, his throat hidden behind a starched blue collar. Not Pantone Royal Blue, summer-sky blue. He stands up when he hears me (I will never be over it). There are maybe eight feet between us, but I can still see the expression in Will's eyes. Curious, patient, cautious.

"No problem." His voice is too warm.

I shut the door to my office to give us some privacy (that whole wall is glass, but anyway). I glance at his arms. Briefly think of the way they hugged my waist against his in that crowded bar less than a week ago.

No-fly zone.

"We should clear the air," I blurt.

His dimple appears. It gives him away even when he's trying not to smile or show his amusement. "Okay."

"I mean, shouldn't we?" I ask. Or have I invented the entire undertone to the way his hands lingered on my face and neck outside Andalo?

"You're right," he says, voice rough. "We should clear the air."

I nod once. "I don't want us to be a distraction for each other."

Will slips his hands into the pockets of his slacks. He laughs briefly, bites his lip, and asks, "Do you plan to stop existing?"

I was wanting you.

My heart shouldn't be singing. "If it makes you more comfortable, we could move most of our meetings to be virtual."

He stares at me, his lips slightly parted. "Do I make *you* uncomfortable?" The question sounds genuine, like he really wants to know.

"No," I jump to say. "It's not—it's not *my* problem. I just don't want *you* to feel like you've gotten yourself into a situation you'd rather not—"

"Being around you doesn't make me uncomfortable either," he says, cutting me off. "You're . . ." Will presses his lips together. "Warm. You're a very warm, caring, hardworking person. Being around you makes me feel pretty good about myself, actually."

His words inflate me until I'm lightheaded. Nobody has ever phrased something that way about me before. The idea that being in my presence could make another person feel better about themselves. That my presence has that kind of positive impact.

"I don't want to go virtual," he says, taking a measured step toward me. "Frankly, that would look bad to my boss, and I just don't think it's necessary. I'm a professional, and I'll act like one. No distractions, business only."

He watches me, waiting for my input.

"What about standing when I enter or exit a room? Can you stop doing that?"

His head cocks. "Why, specifically?"

I panic and change my mind. "No reason."

"Then no," he says, biting on a smirk. "That I can't stop, or my mother might kill me."

"So, we're negotiating," I say.

"Mm." The dimple again.

"No more personal favors."

He nods. "Agreed."

"We should avoid talking about our personal lives."

"Okay. What else?"

I consider. "I think that covers it."

Will's eyes cut from mine, and he twists back. "In that case." He reseats himself in one of the chairs, and I walk around to my side of the desk, taking a seat. There's an entire panel of wood between us, but somehow, it still doesn't feel like enough distance.

"I have two things for you." Will leans forward and slides two folders across the desk. "The first is an action plan for B Corp Certification. The second is research on how to open your physical stores in alignment with your B Corp strategy."

I whip open the first folder and parse Will's research. It's meticulously organized, typed, graphed, printed.

"How long will it take?" I ask.

"Typically six to eight months. But I swore I'd work harder for you than I've ever worked on anything, and I think we could get the assessment filed in three months. After that, B Lab will review your information, and you'd need a score of eighty or higher to pass."

"Eighty or higher," I repeat, my eyes tracking across the paperwork.

After the pop-up fiasco, Revenant *really* needs some good press. This could be the ticket. I don't want to wait any longer than I absolutely must to try for certification.

"So, where are our problem areas?" I ask.

"Suppliers," he says. "Some of them are okay, others you're going to need to replace. The suggestions are all there."

I glance up at Will. His ankle is propped on one knee, and his hands are linked together in his lap. His eyes catch and hold mine.

"This is great, Will. Thank you."

He nods. "I'm happy you're happy."

I push aside the first folder and grab the second one. "And this?"

"Market research on other brands who went from online to omnichannel."

I roll out my neck, eyes trained on the packet, while I try to convince myself that competency shouldn't be this much of a turn-on.

"Thank you," I say, forcing a levelness into my tone. "I'll have a look at all this and follow up with you tomorrow if I have any questions."

Will nods and stands up. He's still got one more folder in his hands. He checks his watch. "I've got a meeting now with Camila. She asked for some research, too."

"She did?" It comes out eager, and Will notices. "I mean, um. That's . . ." I trace my index finger along the edge of a folder. Dusk blue, not Pantone Royal Blue. "Productive," I finish lamely.

Will studies me like he's strategizing the best way to break into a fortress. "Is that . . . okay with you?"

"Of course!" He continues staring, and I finally crack. "I have a favor to ask."

He slants me a look. "You quite literally just told me no favors."

"This is a work favor," I clarify.

"In that case, it's an assignment."

I grab a pen and fiddle with it, then look back up at him. From this angle, the underside of Will's jawline is as defined as a cliff face. "The first night of Camila's bachelorette? She drunkenly told me she's leaving Revenant. But I don't think she remembers saying it."

After a moment, he deduces: "This upsets you."

I shake my head. "I don't want to hold her back. But I just . . ."

"Just . . ." He waits.

"I just want to make sure she's not unhappy. Or that something within my power to change isn't *making* her unhappy."

Will nods. "I can ask if she's happy."

"No! Ugh, boys," I groan softly, dropping the pen to fiddle with the ends of my hair. I curled it today, even added some hair perfume. "Just let me know if she seems . . . disengaged?"

He frowns. "Okay. So, I'm just supposed to take her temperature?"

"Basically."

"I'm not known for my stealth," he says.

"What *are* you known for?"

"I'd tell you if it wouldn't be breaking one of your rules," he reminds me.

"Right. You can text me," I say. "About Camila. Don't put it in an email."

He nods and heads for the door. I watch him walk away, trying very hard *not* to stare at the shape of his legs straining against the fabric of his pants.

He pauses. "Even if she leaves, Josie, it doesn't mean she'll stop being your best friend."

"I want to believe that," I respond, my voice full of a vulnerability I wish was better disguised. "But given my shoddy history with friendships, it's hard not to worry."

Will gives me one last thoughtful look before he disappears, closing the door behind him.

CHAPTER FIFTEEN

Will: She seems fine

    Josie: Fine how?

Will: Fine like I wouldn't have questioned a thing if you hadn't said something

    Josie: what are you guys talking about

Will: the price of tea in china

    Josie: haha no but for real

Will: instead of micromanaging how about you read my research? I worked very hard on that packet for you, Josephine

    Josie: well, you did promise to work harder for me than you've ever worked on anything before

    Josie: sorry, that sounded flirty

    Josie: or maybe I made that up in my head and now I've just embarrassed myself

Will: read the research

That afternoon, the three of us head over to South Congress to check out Revenant's first storefront. We're still searching for a replacement for Margaret (whom Cami ended up letting go after the pop-up, with a generous severance package), but once that person is hired, they'll be in charge of this place.

I didn't invite Will, which means Cami had to have done so. We grab lunch at Torchy's Tacos beforehand.

"Where do you live?" Cami asks Will.

"A loft in Tribeca," he answers, sipping on his soda between bites. "It's not far from the Ellis office. I've lived there for almost five years. I love that apartment."

"What's your favorite thing about Manhattan?" she asks next.

"The food," Will answers quickly. "Trying new restaurants. But the food scene in Austin is great, too."

"You and David really would get along splendidly," Cami says.

Will's eyes flash to mine. I've been watching him nonstop this entire meal, but I finally glance away.

The harmony of his presence here is so easy, so natural, it's borderline alarming. Possibly because the Will Grant I used to know didn't talk easily with anyone, not even his sister or his dad, and definitely not me. But *this* Will has the flow of a river current as he eases himself into our day.

The building we're renting for the store is in the middle stretch of the South Congress shopping district. Out front, the Revenant sign has already been hung up along with decals on the window that read *Coming Soon!*

"I *love* it," Cami says, hands over her heart. We're standing on the opposite sidewalk, admiring the sign before a walk-through. She turns to me, her eyes wide. "Can you believe it, J? I know this store is small potatoes compared to the online business, but it just feels really—"

"Special," I finish. Over her shoulder, I can see Will watching me. "I know what you mean. Five years ago, I'd just accepted that I couldn't keep up with orders anymore and hired my first manufacturer."

"*Six* years ago," she says, "I quit my first big-girl job at Whole Foods to become your marketing director."

"A position you made up," I clarify.

"A *company you* made up!" she rebuts. Cami laughs, bolting across the street. I tense as I check for cars. "Take my picture!"

Dutifully, I pull out my phone and snap a photo of her posing in front of the sign. She does a jumping jack, blows a kiss.

Will shifts beside me as Cami heads for the front door, keys in hand.

"You know what?" he says. "Camila seems pretty damn happy."

My reply is a noncommittal noise that stays lodged in the back of my throat.

Inside the store, the fixtures have already been placed, the racks drilled into the walls. I wander toward the back room where the inventory is boxed up. I grab a steamer and start humming Lizzy McAlpine, de-wrinkling clothes just to busy my hands, listening to Will's low tones and Cami's excited drawl as they talk out front.

I feel more than *see* him meet me in the back five minutes later—the sound of his gait, the weight of his breath, the crackle of air making room for him.

"You ever work in a retail store?" Will asks.

"That's a personal question," I say.

I turn to him, my head tilting up. Neither of us bothered to turn on the lights, and shadows are folding across his face. "Sorry," he says, sounding anything but.

"The summer before I went to college," I answer anyway, since Will spent most of lunch talking about his own personal life and I devoured his answers while Cami asked endless questions about New York. What tourist attractions are actually worth it, does he go to comedy shows, if he ever gets claustrophobic (more so these days, he answered). "I steamed every item before it went on sale that summer."

"So steaming is what *you're* known for."

I snort. "Steaming is therapeutic." I put the steamer down and move the dress to a rack.

Will's shoulders curve as he moves to face me. "In all the press I've read about you, you always credit your oma with inspiring your love of fashion."

I toss him a look. "All the press you've read about me? It wasn't just the one profile?"

He shrugs. "Had to figure out what you were known for."

"As you said, steaming."

"I'll be sure to tell the journalists."

His mention of Oma conjures the smell of licorice tea, the feel of diving my hands into a giant tin of loose buttons.

I cross to the other wall and lean against it, my hands behind my back.

Do you want to tell me about her? Will had asked me that night on the beach.

"Oma was amazing. When I was growing up, my parents would drop me off at her house and we'd spend the day going to the fabric store, picking out a pattern, and then designing something and sewing it ourselves. A purse, a pair of pajamas, a pillowcase, even doll clothes. My American Girl doll had a better closet than I did."

His smile is soft. "Why didn't your family have a funeral service for her?"

"She was wholly against it," I answer, chuckling. "She said nothing would make her roll over in her grave faster than gathering a bunch of people who felt obligated to grieve her in her least favorite color. We did a small family thing instead. But how did you know that?"

"Zoe and I looked it up to see if we could go." Will says this offhandedly, like it's not vital information.

"You guys would have gone?" I ask.

Will nods, scratching underneath his jaw. "Zoe felt pretty guilty about yelling at us after I told her about your oma and my breakup. She was embarrassed. Still a little angry and hurt, too, but yeah. She was planning to go to the funeral. So was I."

I blink rapidly, tears smarting in my eyes. I never considered Zoe was afraid she'd hurt *my* feelings. That day she'd come by my desk and muttered *I'm really sorry about your oma* under her breath—had that been her white flag?

But why hadn't she mentioned the letter? Why hadn't she waited for me to say anything back before she walked on?

Why were we *so bad* at communicating?

It's almost like we were hormonal teenagers or something.

"That means a lot to me," I say.

I pull out my phone and find a picture of Oma, tilting the phone screen in Will's direction. "This is her in an outfit that in-spired what's now called the Always Blouse for women. It was one of the first things I ever designed under the Revenant brand name."

Will looks at the picture. His smile curves farther up toward his eyes, cheeks lifting. "I see the resemblance."

"Really?"

"Definitely. You're both so elegant."

My cheeks warm. "Oma once told me sweating wasn't acceptable."

Will laughs. It sounds like trouble.

"Do you still do any of the designs?" He nods at the photo.

"I help if they want my opinion. To make sure the new designs are aligned with the brand, and whatnot. But our designers are very good. Better than me, and far more educated on that stuff."

He leans against the opposite wall of the narrow back room, arms crossing over his chest while one of his feet catches on his other ankle. For a while neither of us says a word. We only stand there, parsing each other.

"Will?" I ask.

His eyes glint. "Hmm?"

"What happened to your parents' marriage?"

He smirks. "We're not very good at the rules, are we?"

I've never had a hard time with discipline except when it came to social media. I'd tell myself to stop scrolling and wouldn't listen. I'd tell myself it wasn't real and become convinced it was the *only* real thing.

Now, I realize, there's a second area where I'm undisciplined. Him.

"Just this rule," I say. "We can unwrite it."

Will sighs and pushes his fingers through his hair. Not with annoyance. More like he's bracing himself.

"We didn't move to Nashville when Zoe and I were seniors because my dad got a better job. I mean, that's what he told us, but it wasn't the full story."

"What's the full story?" I ask quietly.

"He had a mistress in Nashville," Will explains. His voice drops impossibly low. "It had been going on for five years by the time Dad moved our whole family to be near her." He shakes his head and laughs dully. "He thought he could have it all. His wife and mistress in the same city. Kids at one house, a new labradoodle puppy at the other."

"Your dad's mistress had a labradoodle?" I clarify.

"Yeah, and it was *fucking cute*. He would never have let *us* get a labradoodle. Too expensive," Will goes on. "He didn't let us have a dog at all because Zoe and I couldn't keep our guinea pigs from attacking each other when we were six." He rolls his eyes at the ceiling, like after all this time, the sting has gone out of his dad's betrayal and now he can see the humor.

I smile but it's a weak attempt. "When did you all find out?"

Will's expression switches from mildly beleaguered to downright miserable. "Um. Actually, I found out before Zoe and my mom did."

I pause. "You kept his secret."

Will palms at the back of his neck. He glances sideways. "Mm. Yeah."

"How long?" I ask, horrified.

Will's discomfort is coming out of his ears at this point, but he answers quickly. "The whole school year."

Everything, all at once, immediately clicks into place.

Will Grant—Zoe's moody, quiet, discontent twin brother. Who had just moved almost a thousand miles from home, who had been forced to leave his girlfriend and all his friends behind, only to discover it had all been for the sake of his father having a closer proximity to his mistress. No wonder he was sullen back then.

My hand flutters to my mouth. "Oh, Will."

His face is pained now, open and raw. "I caught them together almost immediately. It was at Centennial Park. I was running—training so I could try out for the football team—and my dad and his mistress were there with the puppy . . . kissing and stuff, on a blanket." I can see the memory flash past his eyes. He blinks hard.

"Your dad asked you to keep his secret when you confronted him about it?"

Will's eyes flick to mine. "How do you know I confronted him?"

I shrug. "I just do. You wouldn't have let that go unsaid."

"Lot of good it did me." He shakes his head. "I was just a kid, and I'd always idolized my father. He convinced me . . ." Will blinks again, stretching out his neck. "He convinced me it was normal. Common. It wasn't that big of a deal. He also said if I told my mom, I'd be ruining our family, that nothing would ever be the same again."

A look of disgust crosses his face. He won't meet my eyes now.

"You kept his secret all year?" I ask.

Will nods, his focus elsewhere. "It was like this physical wedge between me and my family. I was withdrawn. Even you could tell that. I knew it wasn't normal, no matter how convincing my father tried to be. He started spoiling me as if my secret keeping was worth a reward. Flights home to Austin so I could see Amber and my friends. Titans tickets that autumn. A new bike for Christmas. But I was drowning, and it only got worse as time went on. I couldn't look my mother in the eye without feeling like I was on the brink of a meltdown. But I couldn't tell her the truth either, too scared of my father's threat that I'd break our family apart. She knew something was wrong with me, but she thought it was the move, the transition. I couldn't talk to Zoe about it, either. She hated me. I didn't get why at the time—I chalked it up to hormones, I remember—" Will laughs softly. "But now I know it was *because* of Amber that Zoe was so distant. I didn't even have the mental capacity to see the damage I'd done to that friendship."

"Amber wasn't a true friend, the way Zoe told it," I say.

He finally looks at me. "Maybe that's why you confused me so much. You and Zoe didn't want me around like Amber had. I first thought it was because you knew you were a bad influence on Zoe, but actually, you two had more fun on your own."

"Wait. You thought I was a bad influence?" I ask.

"Oh, the worst. I had absolutely no basis for that opinion other than you were beautiful and rich. I gave it up pretty quickly."

"You did not."

"I did, Josephine. But by that point, it was *you* who thought *I* was the bad influence. A mood-ruiner, I think you once called me." He arches an eyebrow, and I flinch.

"Well, if I'd known what you were going through—"

Will shrugs. "I shouldn't be pitied for keeping a cheater's secret."

I'm not entirely sure that's true, especially given the emotional manipulation Will's father put him through, but I don't press the point. "So, what happened? Did you tell your family, or did they find out?"

"I told them. Well, I told Zoe first, and together, we told my mom."

"When?"

He rubs a thumb over his lip. "A few days after you and I kissed. Funny enough, that was a catalyst to get me and Zoe talking again."

"Well, at least there's one bright spot," I say.

Will studies me. "I was relieved, I won't deny it. Relieved to have the secret off my chest. Relieved Zoe and I were on the same team again."

And even though I'm genuinely happy our kiss had a roundabout effect of shrinking Zoe and Will's estrangement, this means she didn't have a friend when she got the news that her father had a mistress, that her family was about to get torn apart. And just on the cusp of her going to one college, Will going to another. Their whole family separating, a four-person unit split into singles.

Camila was right.

Zoe needed a friend, and I hadn't fought hard enough. I needed a friend, and she hadn't fought hard enough either. We were both too stubborn and embarrassed and insecure to be there for each other when it mattered most. When each of our families was splintering.

"I changed my mind," I say to Will. "I *do* want you to give Zoe a message."

His lips lift. "Okay. What's the message?"

"Tell her I shouldn't have given up on our friendship so easily." I try to keep my voice firm, but it's threaded with pent-up emotion. "Tell her I'm still sorry about the rest of it. But I'm especially sorry about *that*, too."

CHAPTER SIXTEEN

Derrick Lovell: I submitted you for the Forbes 30 Under 30 list.

    Josephine Davis: I think Camila would be a better submission.

Derrick Lovell: That's what you said last year. Which is why Camila was on the list LAST year.

    Josephine Davis: Well then, they probably won't want me on this year's list. Too derivative.

Derrick Lovell: Regardless, if a reporter reaches out, you should engage. It's good press and Revenant desperately needs some of that right now.

Will goes back to New York armed with new assignments and I miss him every single day we're apart. I think of him constantly, replay our conversations in my head. They bring me a sense of ease, of peace. I lie in bed at night and recall the low rumble of his voice, the upward hitch of his mouth when I amused him. I count the minutes it took us to break the rules I'd outlined. I wonder constantly what Will meant when he said *It's not that I don't want to.*

Then *what?* If he wanted to kiss me, what stopped him? I need something specific I can add to my own list of reasons not to want him. Is he dating someone in Manhattan? Given what Will told me about his father, I think the answer is no—he wouldn't have come that close to me if he was committed to another woman. Maybe our reasons are the same. Distance, time, avoiding the mess of our past.

I lose sleep, wondering. Thinking of him. Wishing for more conversations with him, breaking the rules with him.

Toward the end of June, our interns finish the classroom portion of their program and switch to office work. Today is the transitional breakfast, where all the interns mingle with their department heads for the first time.

Camila and I are watching from the sidelines, having way too much fun dissecting every expression, every lip movement.

"The intern in the khakis, white button-down," she whispers, "is already crushing *so hard* on the intern in the blue dress."

I follow her words with my eyes to confirm, chewing on a cinnamon sugar donut. Sure enough, the khakis intern is gazing with curiosity at a brunette in a blue midi dress. She's talking enthusiastically at Ilya, the lawyer. Ilya looks like he's doing mental gymnastics to keep up with the conversation, which makes me bite on a smile.

"She's the one from Dartmouth," I whisper back. "And I'm pretty sure the boy came from UPenn."

"They are going to have," Camila says, "the most ridiculous summer of their lives."

"Narrate it for me," I say.

"I'm betting on at least three couples by the end of next week. By the end of July, two pairs will have broken up, while the third grows increasingly serious."

"Then what?"

"*Then,* amongst the recently single, there will be hookups with other interns who are 'just looking to have fun.' As their time in Austin runs out, one of the old couples will come back to each other, begging mutual forgiveness for their late-July wild hair. Meanwhile, the couple that stayed faithful all summer? Guess what?"

"What?" I ask.

"One of them has a serious partner back in their college town."

I gasp theatrically.

"It's all going to come out, that final night during the intern farewell party," Cami warns me. "There will be tears, and proclamations of love, and if we're *really* lucky, two interns fighting over the girl of their dreams, now that this is their last shot!"

I snort into my paper coffee cup, drawing a few eyes. Howie, our VP of tech, shoots me a *Help me* look. He's talking with my personal intern, Eugenia, who has a way of making you feel like she might be better at your job than you are. Her box braids are up in a half ponytail, and her sparkly pink eyeshadow is stunning against her dark skin.

I stand and walk over to them, listening while Howie finishes explaining SEO. He excuses himself to refill his coffee.

"Everyone here is brilliant!" Eugenia exclaims, straightening her skirt. "I've already spoken to every officer and vice president."

"Who's your favorite?" I joke.

"Probably Jason Lorcan, the CFO."

"A sleeper hit," I say, nodding. "I can appreciate that."

"It's pretty crazy you were my age when you started Revenant," Eugenia says.

"Just about."

"How did you manage it and take classes at the same time?"

"I didn't have a social life," I admit. "When I was a senior, I entered a competition for young entrepreneurs and won ten thousand dollars. I used the money on social media marketing, and everything spiraled from there."

That's the point I realize Eugenia isn't listening anymore. Her gaze has drifted toward the door. When I twist to see what she's looking at, I understand why.

Will Grant just walked in.

I don't remember him being on the schedule this week? But my heart escalates into a rapid thrum, pleased without my permission.

"Who is *that*?" she asks.

He does look exceptionally good today, I'll give Eugenia that. Between now and the last time he was in my office with his blue folders, he might have gone on vacation, or at the very least spent a handful of sunny days by a pool, because his skin is glowing and bronzed against his crisp white button-down and black pants. His hair is windswept, making me guess he rode his rental bike to work today. He looks perplexed as his focus drifts over the crowd.

Our eyes find each other a few seconds later and an electric spark runs down my spine. I pull two fingers toward myself in invitation. Will crosses the space to me and Eugenia.

"Are you party crashing?" I ask.

"Depends. Did my invitation get lost in the mail?"

"You're not an employee."

"And yet, I work for you," he counters, tone low but amused. Will's eyes track to the half-eaten donut in my hand. "Are those from Voodoo?"

"You bet your bottom dollar."

"I'm party crashing," he decides.

"Since you're here," I say, "this is Eugenia Thomas. She's one of Revenant's summer interns, and for the next ten weeks, she's going to be my executive assistant."

Will's ocean eyes sparkle as he sticks out a hand for Eugenia to shake. "So, *you're* the Eugenia emailing me about Josie's calendar."

"Thanks for your patience," she says. "I'm still getting the hang of it."

"Godspeed." He flashes her a perfect smile. Eugenia looks positively starstruck.

"Will is a consultant," I tell her. "He's going to help Revenant become B Corp Certified."

"That's amazing," she sighs.

"Just doing my job," he replies.

"Why did you make that sound like your job is being a firefighter who just saved a historic landmark from getting scorched?"

He throws me a look, eyes crinkled. "Got to bolster my self-importance somehow."

"What are you doing here?" I ask.

"Camila knew I was in town for another client and asked me to drop by." Will searches the room for her. "She has something to ask me, apparently."

She's busy chatting, so we acquire Will a blueberry cake donut and then listen while the head of HR makes a brief speech about office etiquette. No vaping inside, please, and you can vlog so long as you aren't sharing privileged information. When the speech is over, Will bites the inside of his cheek and shares an expressive glance with me. His body has drawn closer to mine. The unmistakable scent of his aftershave hits me, so distinctly his.

Out of nowhere, my *want* slams into me again, sharper this time than the night outside Andalo.

It's like four years' worth of untapped desire is cumulating in my center. Does he feel it, too? I think he does; Will's eyes give him away. He looks at me so plainly, as though he's finally given himself permission and can't imagine ever tamping the urge again. Will Grant has manifested into something else, something more significant than a dimple I want to feel with the pad of my thumb, than a chest I want to rest against. I once thought of him as a mistake. Now he's been repackaged in my head as a missed opportunity.

Will swallows as conversations around the room pick up.

Neither of us breaks eye contact.

"You can't look at me like that," I get out.

He shakes his head, and when he speaks, his voice is wistful. "But it's been a while since I last got to look."

An emergency flare goes off in my stomach.

"The rules," I say.

"Aren't working," Will says. "What's the point of them, anyway?"

"What was the reason?" I parry back.

"What reason?"

"The reason you didn't, even though you wanted to."

"Didn't kiss you again?" Will clarifies. He leans toward me as if pulled by an invisible string.

"Yes. That reason. What was it?"

Camila walks up then, putting her hands on our shoulders.

"Garlic Fest," she says.

I smile. Will frowns.

"Pardon me?" he asks, wrinkling his nose.

"Garlic Fest. It's tomorrow, and I think you should come."

"Is that what you needed to talk to me about?" he asks.

"Yep."

I throw Cami a look. She's inviting him to Garlic Fest?

Will rubs a temple with his finger. "My flight back to New York is tonight."

"Postpone it," Cami says easily. "Stay for Garlic Fest."

Will opens his mouth, closes it. His eyes pass back and forth across our faces, and he leans against a desk behind him, crossing one foot over the other.

Then he asks, "What the hell is Garlic Fest?"

"Garlic Fest," Camila elaborates, "is my fiancé David's favorite day of the year."

"It's a chef party," I clarify.

"He's grown this huge . . . *garden* over the years," Camila adds, and then she winks at Will, whose neck erupts into red splotches at the innuendo.

"It's really just a garden," I say.

"A *huge* garden," Cami says.

"Back to garlic?"

"Right. The garlic is all harvested by now." Cami takes a sip of her coffee. "So, every year at the end of June, we host Garlic Fest, and it's this giant outdoor party at our house where David and his pretentious chef friends cook the whole menu, and they invite their pretentious wine friends—"

"And their pretentious bread friends," I say.

"And their pretentious salsa friends," Cami adds. "Anyway. It's tomorrow, and I think you should come, since you're interested in the Austin food scene. Your friend Brooks will be there. I can email you the details."

Will is smiling so broadly now that in a sight of true rarity, both of his dimples are showing. Still no teeth, though. Only Eugenia gets that smile, apparently. "I have," he says, "an abundance of questions."

"Tuck them into your back pocket, and if you still have questions after you come and hang out for an hour, I'll answer them," Cami offers. "Doing so now would spoil the charm."

Will looks at me. "You'll be there, I assume?"

"Oh, definitely."

"With her biker gang," Cami adds.

Will rubs his temple again. "So many questions."

Camila gets pulled into a conversation with her department's intern. Will continues to lean against the desk and just . . . *look at me.* His lips are pressed together, his eyes like thinly cracked glacial ice.

"Sticking around?" I ask.

"I *am* tempted to request a meeting in case I can't have you for a while."

I rest my chin on my hand. "You must realize the suggestive way you phrased that is either deliberate or obtuse, right?"

"If it was obtuse," he drawls, "how would I have realized?"

"Stop flirting with me."

"You're the one batting your eyelashes."

"You started it," I say.

He levels me with a flat, scorched look. "That wasn't even *close* to the way I flirt, Josephine, and anyway, I was serious. You've been traveling so much I haven't had time to schedule anything with you recently."

"I could push my ten thirty with Asset Protection."

"It's nice to hear you prefer me over Asset Protection," Will says. "Eugenia and I are going to be thick as thieves, wrangling your schedule."

I snort. "It can't be *that* difficult to schedule time with me."

"You are literally the hardest person to schedule around that I've ever worked with," Will says. "For instance, where were you yesterday?"

"Los Angeles. There was a port issue. Mice ate through some of our clothes."

He makes a nauseated face. "Well, that's unfortunate, but did you do anything fun while you were there?"

"I got a massage at the hotel salon to de-stress over the mice."

"I mean, did you do anything fun in the *city*?"

"I never go into the city on work trips."

Will's face contorts in alarm. "Why not?"

"Because it's a *work* trip?"

He's silent for a few moments. "What fun is being a CEO who's required to travel half the time if you don't get to explore while you're at it?"

"I have plenty of fun on work trips," I say. "I order room service, I do my CEO classes online, I visit the hotel workout room—"

"Okay, well—" Will grimaces. "When you and I go on *our* work trip together, we're *not* eating hotel food and getting our exercise in a workout room."

I drop my hand away from my chin and stand up straight as his words digest. "Sorry?"

"We'll be eating something local," he elaborates, shooting me an exasperated look through his lashes.

"No, what *work trip* are you and I going on together?"

"That's what I wanted to meet about," he says. "We need to book our flights."

"For *what*?"

He holds up his index finger: "Peru." Middle finger: "Spain." Ring finger: "India."

Suddenly, the packet Will handed me the last time he was here crystallizes sharp in my mind. Those are the locations of his supplier recommendations to replace the ones that aren't up to B Corp standards.

"Right," I murmur.

Since then, I've researched each supplier on his list and agreed they're worth pursuing. But with the first store opening so soon, contacting the suppliers got pushed to the end of my to-do list.

Something like panic must be gathering on my face because Will jumps to say, in a placating tone, "It's okay. I already set up the meetings with the help of your VP of supply chain. We're going in two and a half weeks, if that works for you."

When I look at him, his expression is soft.

"Thank you so much for getting a head start on this," I say, my tone genuine.

"Of course."

"But you don't need to come with me."

"Absolutely, I do," he says.

"I can take the VP."

"He's going on paternity leave," Will reminds me. "That was the whole point of me coordinating the visits with him ahead of time."

"I go on work trips by myself all the time," I remind Will.

"Not to three different continents over a two-week period."

We stare at each other, at a standoff. "Is Ellis even willing to let you go for two whole weeks?" I ask.

Will shrugs. "I can work on my other clients' assignments remotely." He settles against the desk again, waiting me out.

The idea of traveling to three different continents with Will shoots stars up my spine, and not in a way that feels healthy or professional. I imagine us across a dinner table from each other. Saying good night from neighboring hotel room doors. Forming inside jokes, sharing once-in-a-lifetime experiences. The whole thing seems like we might be brushing up against a boundary we wouldn't be able to uncross. It blinks *BAD IDEA* like a tacky glowing Vegas sign.

But at the same time, I objectively know it would be good to have Will there. He's studied the B Corp standards back to front, and *that's* what we'll be evaluating.

"What did Zoe say? When you gave her my message?" I ask.

Will's expression warms. "She said she felt the exact same way. But she wanted to tell you herself, in person. She doesn't want me botching it, I guess." He rolls his eyes.

My chest tightens, nervous and hopeful.

I break my gaze from his. "Okay, let's go to my office and book the flights."

Will trails me away from the party. I sit down at my desk and pull up a fresh browser on my computer screen. "We'll be flying Delta, first class."

"Great."

Instead of sitting, he walks to my side of the desk. Then he gives me the dates for each leg of the trip, and I select them on the airline website. We're starting in Peru, then heading to Spain, and ending the trip in India.

We bicker over flight times. Will says he isn't a morning person, but I've flown enough to know the earliest flight of the day has the highest on-time rate. Eventually, we compromise and even manage to agree on seat assignments.

He isn't crowding me, and yet I can *feel* Will's body towering over mine. If I tilted my chin up, I'd see the underside of his. With herculean strength, I keep my eyes forward, clicking through the screens until we've secured two first-class tickets to three continents in July, bought and paid for on my corporate card.

"Done," I say.

Will steps away from me, tamely making his way to the other side of the desk. I notice a tiny smirk on his face.

"What?" I ask.

"Nothing. I just knew you'd be a Delta flyer."

My shoulders shrug. "I like luxury options occasionally."

Will nods. "I figured that out, too. You're funny about it, though."

"How so?"

"You drive a 2014 Ford Escape you don't care about leaving a ding in, but I've seen you wipe an invisible smudge off your high heels." Will nods to my LV bag hanging off a wall rack. "Every single time I've been around you, you're carrying a different purse, but I've seen your house, and it's ramshackle. In an endearing way," he clarifies. "It's just funny, that's all. You're funny to me."

"I'm just . . . me," I say. "And besides, I'm not usually hosting dinner parties, or picking up strangers off the side of the road in my 2014 Ford Escape."

"Better not be," Will warns jokingly.

"Even if they look like a reformed finance bro?"

"Well." He pretends to consider. "Actually, no, not even then."

The air between us grows tight. Again, I notice the way my bio-rhythms change for him.

"So what was the reason?" I ask.

He looks amused by my change in topic. "The reason I didn't kiss you even though I wanted to?"

"Yep."

He watches me. "Neither of us was sober, that was the reason."

I balk. "That's the only reason? If we hadn't been drinking, you'd have kissed me?"

Instead of answering he asks, "Not good enough for you?"

"Not really."

"What are *your* reasons?" he asks.

I rattle them off: "Distance. Lack of free time. The possibility that I could lose my focus when this is a critical time for Revenant's long-term success." I *don't* mention my insecurity over my yearslong lapse of sexual drive.

"Those are all perfectly legitimate," Will acknowledges.

"But if I hadn't told you we can't become a distraction for each other, you would have—what? Tried to kiss me again?"

"Probably." Will's eyes flick to my lips. "Definitely."

I say nothing, overwhelmed by the bareness of his admission, the roughness of his voice.

Dimples. "Care to explain the biker gang?" he asks, throwing me a lifeline.

"It's not a biker gang like that," I clarify. "Cycling girl group is more accurate."

"What's your favorite bike route in Austin?" he asks.

"I like taking the Johnson Creek Greenbelt and then connecting at Barton Creek. You eventually wind up at Zilker Park. It's scenic."

He says, "Maybe I'll give that one a try tonight."

"Enjoy," I say.

"Given your *reasons*," Will says with an indulgent edge, "are you sure it's okay for me to stay for Garlic Fest?"

"Absolutely."

There is no better solution for squashing the attraction between us than spending some quality time together at the notorious Garlic Fest. Last year, I was sweating alliums out of my pores for a week.

"I'm one hundred percent okay with it," I add with a big, wide grin.

CHAPTER SEVENTEEN

That evening, I don my athleisure and start up my Strava app to track mileage before departing my house on a solo bike ride. My laptop and Wi-Fi hot spot are in my backpack with a frosty bottle of San Pellegrino, a few fashion magazines, and a very large, very old monogrammed towel that debuted at my third birthday party.

I catch the Johnson Creek Greenbelt, cross the bridge at Red Bud Isle, then tool back over the river and along the trail that runs beside Barton Creek. The air smells like warm molasses and smoky charcoal. The wind dries my sweat against my brow, stiffening my skin.

I zoom past Will at one of the creek bed outlooks where turtles sunbathe on the rocks. He's standing a few feet behind a family with young children, but when I get close enough, Will's eyes switch from the turtles to me.

He looks unsurprised, even pleased to see me, like he'd been expecting me to come find him somewhere along this route.

Will catches me less than forty seconds later, his pedaling evening out to match my pace. Our gazes lock, our breaths labored.

"Can I ride with you?" he asks with his voice. And with his eyes: *You came to find me. You knew I would be here because you told me to be here.*

"Sure," I say with my voice. And with my eyes: *If I didn't want to be distracted, I wouldn't have come, so I guess I want to be distracted.*

We're quiet after that, focusing on the speed, the pace, the green-belt beneath our tires.

Ten miles later, I rest my bike in the grass, the view of downtown Austin snagging on the skyline beyond the river.

Will loops his leg over his bike and sets it beside mine, pulling his hands above his head. His skin is glistening with sweat. He's in loose training shorts, an old T-shirt from NYU that pulls up to reveal his tanned, muscular stomach when he stretches. He unclips his helmet and tosses it, runs a hand through his damp brown hair. It sticks back like a wave frozen before the crash.

"That pace was no joke."

I pull up my Strava app. "We were only going twenty miles per hour."

"Only," he repeats, smiling. His voice is husky, his breath still rough.

I take off my backpack and spread out the oversized towel, then collapse onto it, staring at the washed-out sky. It's maybe seven o'clock. Only an hour and a half of daylight left.

"Sit down," I offer.

Will sits on a corner of my towel, drawing his knees up to his chest, hooking his fingers around them. I loll my head in his direction, and he looks down at me. We stay like that for ten breaths. In, out, in, out.

I roll onto my belly and pull my magazines and seltzer out of my backpack. Will takes a long drag of water from his aluminum bottle.

We maintain normalcy for another two minutes as our heartbeats drop to resting rates. I glance at him every twenty seconds. His eyes never leave my face. But I go about my business, intent on proceeding with my evening.

"Would you consider this free time?" Will asks cheekily.

"If you weren't here, I'd already be watching CEO classes by now."

"So I'm distracting you," he concludes, "from the important stuff."

I grab a magazine and open it but glance at him over the top. "It was nice of you to stay," I say. "Maybe I don't want you to be alone tonight since Camila asked you to stay in town this weekend. You must be on your own dime for your hotel for the next two nights."

Will glances at the cityscape. "I wanted to stay. I like spending time here."

"I've noticed. You talk like you love New York but need constant breaks from it."

"I *do* love New York," Will agrees. "And I *do* need constant breaks from it. The lifestyles are different, here and there."

"What you mean is, instead of clubbing with hot girls in bodycon dresses while you drink dirty martinis on your Friday nights, you get to look at *turtles,* and then go on sweaty, dorky bike rides with me—a *coworker*—in the least exclusive location possible," I joke.

"I think you've got bodycon covered, so nothing lost there." He nods at my outfit, smirking. Bike shorts, an athletic tank, not much else. My ass is aimed straight up since I'm lying on my stomach. I blush, thinking of adjusting, but that would only draw his attention back to it. "But yes, to the rest of it."

"Wait. Are you *confirming* you drink dirty martinis with hot girls in exclusive clubs when you're in Manhattan?"

Will winces. "Not willingly."

"Yes, what a chore."

"Lately it feels like one."

"So, it still happens with semi-regularity?" I'm intrigued beyond belief.

"There's a lot of networking that goes on with my job," Will explains. "Showboating, salesmanship, taking clients out on the town. I find it demanding and overwhelming and uncomfortable. I feel like I can breathe when I'm in Austin."

"Are you sure that's not a difference in air quality?"

"It's at least fifty percent a difference in air quality," Will allows.

"And the other fifty?"

"Stuff like this." He jerks a thumb at our bikes, tangled up like old friends. "We just rode almost fifteen miles on the same greenway without being forced out onto a city block."

"Amazing how much space there is when you're not on an island," I quip.

"I had," Will goes on, "the best barbecue of my life today. And it was this new place, less than a year old. I've never seen it on any food media list, but it should be there, right at the top."

I smile. "You really like barbecue."

"I really like *good* barbecue. Good anything. Austin has good *everything.*"

"You're making me hungry."

"There's a food truck over there." He points, and I follow his eyes to a taco truck across the field, the line fifteen people deep. "Do you want something? My treat."

No more personal favors, I remind myself. It was the rule we established in my office, to curb *this,* and Will agreed.

"I mean, if you were already going," I say. "But I'll pay you back, of course."

He dips his chin. "What kind of tacos do you like?"

"Get me whatever the most vegetarian thing they have is."

His head cocks. "The *most* vegetarian?"

"Least meat forward?"

"So, you're a vegetarian, but not a purist?"

"I guess so," I say with a shrug.

He shakes his head, laughing beneath his breath as he stands. "Do you remember when you said you're incredibly easy to read? That was untrue then, and it's untrue now."

"Are you saying I'm complicated because I'm semi-vegetarian?"

"Complicated is not the right word," he says.

"Intricate?" I offer. "Convoluted?"

"Layered," Will retorts.

My heart flares as he walks away.

I watch him cross the field for an embarrassing number of seconds, his body firm and sure and strong, before pulling out my laptop and connecting to my Wi-Fi hot spot. I click play on my latest CEO class and flip magazine pages while I listen.

Will returns twenty minutes later with cauliflower tacos for me, barbacoa for him. I pause the online class.

"No, keep watching," he says. "I'm the one crashing your night. I want to listen."

"You want to listen to a lecture on effective project management."

"Dying to." He takes a bite of his taco and honest-to-goodness *winks* at me.

I hit play, and we keep coexisting in silence. Will polishes off his dinner and I do the same. He sticks his feet out, crosses them, and then lies all the way back on the towel. We're head to foot right now, two opposite charges neutralizing each other.

The class ends, and Will sits back up. I take a few notes on the app on my phone, answer some discussion questions online, and then look back at him.

It's dark now, the sky tinted purplish black. The park has started to clear out. It's one of the rare weekends where there's no concert, no event here at all.

"You make sense here," Will says, the blue in his eyes darkening to match the night. "In Austin, I mean. It fits you."

"Thank you," I say, perking up at this compliment. "I think so, too. Nashville was too . . . restrictive, I guess? I didn't want to go back to the mold I'd made for myself during high school, with my family."

"Have you ever been kayaking on the river?" he asks. "I saw a whole slew of people out there a couple weeks back."

"No," I say.

"That's too bad."

"Camila and I have matching paddleboards."

Will grins. "That tracks."

"Is it horrible of me to say I'm not sure you make sense in New York?"

Will shakes his head, his gaze flicking back to the cityscape, lights illuminating every building. "It's not horrible of you to say. I definitely think I used to. When I was eighteen and I'd just started college at NYU, I loved Manhattan. It was the perfect escape from the family drama of the previous year. A totally new experience for me."

I wait in silence, hoping he'll go on. He does.

"Once Zoe moved up after she graduated, New York became our place. We were at that life stage where you're finally in charge of everything and nothing's gotten messed up yet. We'd always been close except for that one bad year, but New York is where Zoe and I became friends as adults. You know when you learn to not just love your sibling, but to *like* them, to respect them as a person you *choose* to be around?"

I shake my head. "I've never been close with my brother. But I love that for you two."

Will's eyes pity me. "I don't know who I would become if I lost touch with my sister again. She's one of the most grounding people I know."

"Maybe you don't want to leave Manhattan even though you might be ready to, because of that reason," I suggest.

"That's probably true," Will says. "But I can also admit the things I want have changed."

I cock my head. "What is it you want now?"

His eyes dart away from mine, and he wets his lips. "I don't know. Not to waste my retirement fund in rent, and maybe to get a kitchen with a gas-top stove?"

"Shoot for the moon, why don't you?"

Will smirks. "You make it look effortless. Having the lifestyle you want, pairing it with a job you love."

"It's not effortless," I inform him. "It in fact requires every drop of my effort, and then some. The only reason I keep my head above water is because I'm basically a nun at this point."

I flush red as soon as I say it, but Will looks intrigued. "You don't date?" His voice is low, almost affronted.

"Never."

"Not even casually?"

"Especially not casually. That's the kind of dating that requires the most effort."

Will laughs. Audibly. "That's true."

His leg knocks against my elbow. Neither of us pulls back. Neither of us utters out loud that this is sort of like a date.

"If I wasn't here," Will asks, "would you already be watching another CEO class by now?" He's asking out of pure curiosity, not to chastise me.

"Yes," I admit, hating myself for it. "I'm behind on the coursework."

A moment of silence. "I'll go now."

"No." I reach out and grab his leg, squeezing my eyes shut as my forehead rests on his knee. His breath catches in his throat.

It's been *so long* since I've had this kind of company. Male company, easy company, the kind of company you could waste hours with.

I'm battling a war in my mind—push forward, get the work done so I can enjoy Garlic Fest tomorrow guilt free. Or lie here, talk to Will about nothing productive, nothing that bolsters the bottom line, and start my weekend.

Tentatively, almost shakily, his hand rests on my back, and he starts to rub. I feel the warmth of it everywhere. My muscles unclench, my spine straightens, my skin relaxes. I'm embarrassed and confused, so I keep my head tucked low.

"Play the next video," he murmurs. "I'll stay. We'll watch it together."

The issue, I think to myself, is we can do this for one night. Maybe Will even finds it endearing. But it doesn't solve the problem in the long run. Because I can't ask an actual romantic partner to fill the microscopic holes in my busy life forever.

I can't ask that of Will Grant. I respect him too much to let this happen past tonight.

But I hit play anyway and let him rub my back like a lover would. And promise myself I'll be productive in the morning.

CHAPTER EIGHTEEN

For as long as Camila and I have known David Ortega, he and his chef friends have hosted Garlic Fest.

The first time we attended was five years ago, back when Cami and David were in a simple flirtationship, having just met at Container Bar the night before. We were twenty-two and understandably confuddled anyone would willingly show up to a party where garlic is the star of the show, but *He was the cutest,* Cami had said, *and maybe these chef types know something about garlic we don't?*

Spoiler: chefs know something about garlic we don't.

Five years later, it's one of my favorite traditions, and now that she's David's fiancée, Cami has joined the fray as a partial hostess, though I'm pretty sure the most she accomplished today was a single wildflower arrangement. She's still fiddling with it when I walk into her kitchen, her hair in a messy updo, her white T-shirt smeared with dirt.

"Are these too wilted?" she asks, catching my eye.

"Yes," I say. They're drooping in all directions, the stems hugging the lip of the vase.

Cami huffs and turns around, opening the fridge. "Beer?"

"What about a shot?" Giovanna proposes, passing me by to re-fill her water bottle in the kitchen sink. After fifteen miles, she still hasn't broken a sweat. I swear she's poreless.

"*Ohmygod.*" Leonie pushes her palms against her knees, doubling over. Her blond hair nearly touches the floor as Giovanna rubs her back soothingly. "Can you give us, like, five minutes to recover before proposing *shots* at four o'clock in the afternoon?"

Camila looks between us with revulsion. We're all in athletic gear, our cheeks in various states of blush, our hair matted from helmets. "Not my journey," she mutters to herself, cracking the tab of an Austin Eastciders can.

In the backyard, situated between a handful of ash trees and a few dogs rolling on their backs, ten professional chefs are prepping their mise en place at foldout tables. Chopping fennel, deseeding lemons, spatchcocking chickens. Beyond them are three Big Green Eggs, one coal fire, a gas grill, a smoker, and a stone pizza oven David had installed when Cami moved in.

Giovanna and Leonie shower in the guest room while I help Camila pick sturdier flowers from the garden. The others join us to set the picnic tables, working around towering piles of marinated meats and garlic cloves doused with olive oil, wrapped in foil sachets.

"We can finish this, J," Giovanna says, ripping open the plastic on a stack of paper cups. Her hair is still damp, but there's a slight touch of makeup on her cheeks and she's dressed now in a simple sundress. "Go shower."

"I don't need to shower," I say.

I'm still readjusting Gio's utensil placement (to the societally correct arrangement: fork left, spoon and knife right, blade facing inward) on all the place settings when I glance up and notice my friends staring at me.

"*What* did you just say?" Camila snaps.

I look down at myself in bike shorts, an athletic tank top. A variation of what I wore last night with Will.

"I'll put on the jean shorts and a T-shirt I brought, but I think I smell fine," I say.

Gio rubs at the hair just above my ear, pulled into a low ponytail. "Stiff. From *sweat*."

"It's not that bad," I protest. "Do women *always* have to show up to a function with perfectly clean hair and a face full of makeup?"

"*Women* don't," Camila retorts. "But *Josephine Davis* does. The only way I see you willingly choosing not to take a shower, blow out your hair, and do your makeup is if you're terminally ill, or under duress."

I shrug. "I forgot to bring my makeup bag."

"Between the three of us, we've got you covered."

"Guys!" Leonie cries. "If Josie wants to keep it casual, let her! We're at a backyard cookout, not a black-tie wedding."

Camila ignores this, narrowing her eyes at me. She drops the paper napkins onto the table and stomps over, grabbing me by the wrist.

"Ow!" I whine as she pulls me into the house with her.

"What's wrong with you?" she asks.

"Nothing!"

"In the nine years I've known you, I have *never*, and I mean *never*, seen you show up to a social function—personal, professional, familial, or otherwise—without at *least* fixing your hair into a slicked-back bun with your cute scrunchie and using that three-way makeup thingy for your lips, eyes, and cheeks."

"The Ilia Multi-Stick."

"Beside! The! Point!"

"I'm . . ." With my arms, I gesture in each direction, at nothing. "Mellowing out."

"That's the biggest fucking lie you've ever told me, Josephine. Are we *lying* to each other now?"

My eyes narrow back. I cross my arms over my chest, anger flaring at the memory of her words: *I'm leaving Revenant.*

"I don't know, Cami! *Are* we lying to each other now?"

"What's *that* supposed to mean?"

"What do you *think* it's supposed to mean?"

"Okay," she says, holding up a palm, "now I have to know what *that* is supposed to mean?"

"All of those chefs," I say, pointing out the window, "are going to be sweating their balls off when they light the grills in fifteen minutes!"

Camila groans. "Just tell me what's wrong!"

"Nothing's wrong!"

She leans a hand on the counter, studying me. "Are you mad I invited Will Grant?"

"Mad?" I laugh, sounding unhinged. "I'm *thrilled* he's coming!"

"If you're really so *thrilled* he's coming," she articulates, "why aren't you going to take a fucking shower, babe?"

"Because I need us to stop being attracted to each other!" I scream. Irrevocably.

That's when a throat clears over by the front door, and we turn to see the man of the hour frozen in the living room.

Will is dressed in a white brewery T-shirt and loose jeans. He's holding a bouquet of yellow sunflowers in one hand and a six-pack in the other. His wavy brown hair is loose, disheveled. His mouth parts a fraction as his eyes center on the dead space between Cami's body and mine.

Beside him is Brooks, Will's friend from high school.

There's a toddler and a beagle peeking out from under Brooks's legs.

My face flames in embarrassment as I swear beneath my breath. I dart through the opposite end of the kitchen, sprint down the hall, and shut myself in the guest bedroom.

My friends' soiled athleticwear is stuffed in their lightweight backpacks, lined up along the far wall. I go to the bathroom and look at myself in the mirror.

Exactly how I looked last night—and even then, Will and I had been halfway to a date.

I can't *dress up* knowing I'd be doing it for *him*. Every dab of makeup, every swipe of soap across my skin. It wouldn't be for anyone else at this party. All for him.

Camila is right, though; I almost never let people see me like this.

My skin is splotchy, red stains patchworked across my face, my neck, my chest. A third from blushing, a third from the bike ride, a third from digging around in the garden. I lift my nails; they're caked with dirt. When I glance back at my reflection, I can see the oily shine of my hair near my temple. I smell like sweat and soil. A few strands of hair are stuck to my neck.

And even though this was my exact intention, now that I know Will Grant has seen me like this, I start to hyperventilate.

It isn't based on a desire to be the prettiest person in the room. Only a desire to be the most put together. I've always had this meticulous, obsessive compulsion to look fixed up, to appear curated. So when people see me—when they form opinions of me—they never think to themselves, *That girl's life must be on fire.*

I push both palms against the countertop, centering my breath before panic sets in. There's a soft rap on the door.

"Come in," I say, expecting Camila.

I glance over as Will enters the guest room, my heart rate jackhammering again.

The flowers and beer are gone now. He closes the door behind him, looking at me with sharp eyes. I fight internally with myself. Wanting him to see me. Wishing he wouldn't look.

After my second online class finished up last night, Will followed me all the way home. *For safety,* he insisted, and even though it was a personal favor, another rule broken, I didn't argue. Because last night I let myself be selfish with Will. Selfish with his time, with mine. But when I got inside my house and watched him bike away, the spell broke, and I felt mortified I'd gone searching for him at all.

Now he's cataloging me. His left hand clenches tightly onto the doorknob and his right forms a fist by his side. His chest expands and contracts with even breaths as his eyes mark a path down my body.

I hold still as a statue under the harsh lights of the bathroom.

After twenty seconds of this, Will sighs and walks toward me. He leans a shoulder against the restroom doorframe. "Let the record show I tried," he rasps.

"You tried?" I repeat.

"I *tried* to accomplish what you want from me. I *tried* not to be attracted to you. It doesn't work. Never has. Not last night, not today. I want you just the same."

"It doesn't work for me either," I say spitefully.

His eyes darken. Sapphire blue.

"I would have you," he says, voice hoarse, "like this, just as quickly as I would if you were in a ball gown. I think I might prefer this, to be honest."

His words sink in, then pulse through me, concentrating in my core. The aloneness of us, in this very private bedroom, is erasing my "reasons." I resist the urge to thrust myself against his body and let him lift me off the ground, like I know he could. *Would.*

We breathe too heavily, lean too close.

"Josie," Will mutters, sounding wounded.

His hand moves toward me, but I grab him by the wrist.

I repeat his words back from Andalo: "It's not that I don't want to."

He repeats mine: "Want to what?"

I release his wrist. "A shower first," I say.

Will wets his lips. "You or us?"

"Me."

"I'll leave."

"No," I say. Last night when Will offered to leave me alone, I couldn't look him in the eye when I asked him not to, but I do now. He looks as lost as I feel.

"I want to talk," I explain. "I just need to be clean first."

He nods. "Take your time."

I close the door to the bathroom and turn on the shower, stepping under the spray. All the while I strategize how to explain myself to Will. He already occupies too many of my thoughts. Everything lately has been recontextualized around him. If I go to New York for work, would he want to see me? Would Zoe? If he likes Austin so much, why doesn't he just . . .

Move here?

Stop. I have to stop this. It isn't fair to him. I'm not being *fair* to him, making these internal assumptions that he could change his life to accommodate mine. That's no way to build a relationship.

I wash my hair, my body, quickly change into the spare clothes I brought, and dab sunscreen on my face. When I open the door and steam from the shower pours into the bedroom, I find Will sitting on the edge of the bed, elbows on his knees. He stands when he sees me.

"Feeling better?" he asks.

"In a sense."

Will scratches at his arm as he studies me. "What was it you wanted to talk about?"

"The price of tea in China."

He smirks, stepping toward me. "You wanted me with you last night, Josie. You told me to stay the weekend, to come to this party today. I was doing my best to respect your boundaries, but now I'm just really confused."

Be fair to him, my brain whispers to my heart.

I sigh wistfully. "I had this whole scheme."

He asks, "What scheme?"

"To be a huge turnoff all night long."

Despite my tone, Will's smile grows. "Josephine, I am on the edge of my seat waiting to hear what you *think* would have turned me off."

I raise a challenging eyebrow, crossing my arms. "I was going to be very patronizing every time I saw you eating meat."

A divot on his forehead. "You didn't mind last night. I would have known you were playacting. And besides, you're not even a purist, you said so yourself."

"Well, for your information, I'm an aspiring vegetarian."

"How does that work?" he asks.

"I'm always aspiring. Never vegetarian," I answer.

He laughs. It sounds like music. "What else?" he asks, prepared for further absurdity.

"Garlic. Lots of garlic on my plate."

"From what I understand about this event," Will says, "that's not specific to *you.*"

"I was going to talk about myself endlessly."

"A counterintuitive tactic, considering I've been desperate to get inside your head."

"And now we're right back to the beginning!" I cry. "Because if you stopped finding me attractive, maybe you'd stop wanting to get inside my head!"

"If that were true, it would make me an asshole," Will points out.

"Well, you *were* a finance bro!"

I'm losing it, and Will Grant can tell. His dimples have entered the room. But at least the sexual tension between us has mostly dissipated, replaced by a comedic warmth I'm not sure is any less dangerous.

"The entire crux of this issue," Will says, rolling the words, "is your rigid belief that we should not be involved in any way, shape, or form. When it comes to the professional aspect of our coworking relationship, I won't argue that point. It's naughty."

Good *fuck,* the way he says *naughty* is—

"But if this is about Zoe—"

"It's not. I believed you when you said she wouldn't care."

He cocks his head. "Then what?"

I inhale deeply and subsequently word vomit: "I can't let anything become more important to me than Revenant. I can't give room to anything else in my life, can't give space to anything else in my head. And if you and I . . . if we were to . . ." I hug myself and Will frowns. "I think you would become very important to me," I whisper, looking at his shoes.

"Which can't happen," Will concludes. "Because I would be distracting you from what's *most* important."

I flinch but don't deny it.

Revenant is just a business, sure. But maybe my entire self-worth is wrapped up in it, and maybe I don't know how to backpedal, seven years later.

When I look back up, Will is nodding to himself, like he's internalizing this, accepting it. He bites his lower lip. "I want to make a deal with you. Are you game?"

"What kind of deal?"

Will drums his fingers on his biceps. "Tonight, we'll be friends. We'll talk. Hang out. I know this party means a lot to you and Camila. I want you to always have fond memories of it. You shouldn't feel tortured by my presence here. You should enjoy yourself."

I offer him a small smile, touched. His thoughtfulness is unbounded.

Will rolls out his neck. "But at the end of the night, I'm going to tell you the five worst things about me."

It's like a gear clicks into place, and I suddenly understand.

Instead of curbing *his* attraction toward *me,* he's going to curb *my* attraction toward *him.*

There's some serious appeal to this, I won't deny it. Getting Will off my mind would free up a hefty amount of mental capacity I could repurpose to focus on work.

The question is: Are the five worst things about Will Grant enough to permanently squash my feelings for him?

"How do I know you're going to give me the true worst?" I ask.

"Here's a teaser," Will says. "I'll give you the first one right now as an advance. When I was a senior in college, I cheated on my corporate finance final."

Cheating. That's pretty bad. It signifies a weak moral compass. Already, the questions are internally swirling as I study him.

It doesn't line up, if I'm honest. Will doesn't scream *cheater* to me. On women. On tests.

I mentally berate myself when I realize I'm already trying to rationalize this "worst thing" away, to diminish its significance on my opinion of him.

Will looks back at me. He's no less attractive than he was one sentence ago, but some of the mystery behind his time in New York has been eliminated.

I stick out my hand. "You've got yourself a deal."

CHAPTER NINETEEN

As more guests arrive in the sun-drenched backyard, the chefs begin serving their appetizers: grilled bread with melted garlic butter, roasted oysters, fiery salsa and handmade tortillas, tiny cups of balled fruit. A bartender from Agricole I know only as Weird Stanley sets up a booth in one corner of the yard, pouring bags of frosty ice into giant metal tubs. He produces a piece of card stock, which he folds in half and displays on his card-table-turned-bar: *Drink Specials.* All of which are vampire themed.

In the other direction, Camila and David are whispering to each other by the fence line. I can't see her face, but David looks like he's absorbing her stress, hands running up and down her arms. He pulls her against his chest, settling the crown of her head there.

A bright splash of envy hits me, seeing them like that.

I've been *fine* on my own since my last breakup. I haven't even *wanted* to date. Why am I suddenly wishing I had somebody to hold me upright like that? Somebody to whisper with in the corner at a party?

Giovanna materializes beside me. "You fixed yourself up," she notes.

After Will left the guest bedroom, I did some light makeup and braided my hair.

Plus, deodorant.

And some perfume.

And a pair of Cami's earrings.

I turn to Gio. "Do you think Camila's been acting weird lately?"

She gives me a cynical look. "I think *you've* been acting weird lately."

I ignore this. "She hasn't said anything to you?"

"About *what*?" Gio asks, crossing her arms over her chest.

"Nothing," I grumble.

"Are you guys in a work fight?"

"Not that I know of."

Though now my memories are retooling themselves into something more sinister. Is my frame of reference too narrow? Maybe it isn't a recent problem driving Camila to leave Revenant. What if it's something that's been building inside her for years?

"Do you want me to ask her if something's up?" Gio offers.

"Please do not."

She groans, rubbing a hand over her forehead. Giovanna has always been a no-nonsense, cut-to-the-chase type of person, just like Camila. Neither of them hides the way they're feeling, and neither keeps secrets. I wish I could say they've rubbed off on me, but I'm just as meek and insecure with my friendships as I've always been.

Gio has just opened her mouth—no doubt to urge me to just *talk to Cami about it*—when two of Cami's sisters grab us by our shoulders and pull us into a group hug, squealing.

"Reunion!" Patricia shouts before sprinting away to find Camila.

"Garlic forever!" Jane chimes in, thrusting a handle of Patrón in the air.

She pours some of the liquor into the plastic shot glass hanging from her necklace. "For you, our fearless leader."

"Can I start with a beer?" I ask, backing away.

"No."

"There are *children* present," I protest.

"It's not *cocaine,* J!" Jane argues. She detaches the shot glass from the necklace and hands it to me, her face pleading.

I give in, grabbing the glass and pouring tequila over my tongue in one smooth motion. My eyes squeeze shut as I swallow.

When they open, Will Grant is standing before me, offering a lime wedge. No clue where he got it, or how he did it so quickly. I accept it wordlessly, biting into the acidic pulp as my reflexes calm down.

"*Hellooooo* there," Jane says, grinning ear to ear. She fiddles with her bangs.

"Hi," Will replies, his voice deep and warm.

I examine him with fresh eyes. In the early evening light, his hair reminds me of sun-bleached wood. When he smiles down at Jane—who is almost a foot shorter than him—he's giving her the same smile he gave Eugenia. Almost like Will is imbibing Jane's intention and serving it right back to her, exactly the way she wants it.

"This is Will Grant," I say as I wipe my thumb over my mouth to catch a bit of lime juice. "Will, this is Giovanna, my friend from college, and Jane, Camila's little sister. Will is the one who got us that last-minute reservation at Andalo."

Jane gasps. "That was *you*?"

She's enraptured by him, but when I look at Gio, she shoots me a curious look.

"How do you two know each other?" Gio asks.

"Work," I supply.

Her eyes narrow into slits.

"Would you like a shot, Will Grant?" Jane pinches the plastic glass out of my hands and squints up at him against the blasting Texas sun.

"I'd like a beer, actually, but thank you for the offer."

Jane pouts and loops her arm through Giovanna's. "Let's go bother Cami," she suggests.

Gio shoots me one final look before they waltz off.

The backyard is flooded with bodies now. Already, one of the chefs is pulling wilted spinach off a cast iron griddle, plating it on a serving dish, dressing the greens up with fried garlic chips shaped like half-moons and a dollop of crème fraîche.

Will looks around. "Nothing like this would ever happen in New York. I mean that in the best way I could possibly mean it. And if someone even attempted it, it would be far more pretentious. In the worst way I could mean it."

"Clearly you haven't met David's pretentious salsa friends."

When I turn to Will, he's looking back at me with mischief, flecks of silver in his irises in this lighting. The color is kaleidoscopic. Idly, I wonder what I'd name the color, where it would fit in the shade options of the clothing we sell. Lapis blue. Aegean blue. Arctic blue.

"So you and Brooks are hanging out?" I ask softly.

"Let me introduce you," he replies, just as soft.

"Hang on, I just quickly need to chew on some raw garlic first."

"That's only going to repel the *toddler*, not me or Brooks."

He draws me over to a shady corner of the yard, where the red-haired man and his child are lounging on a towel. Their beagle's leash has been looped around the ash tree. It's panting happily, resting two adorable front paws in a plastic bowl of water.

"This is Brooks," Will says. "Brooks, Josie."

Brooks has brown eyes and freckles all over. His red beard is neatly groomed but objectively wiry, and despite the knowledge that he's the same age as Will, I can see some color fading from his hair, almost blurring out. When our gazes meet, he aims me a lopsided grin.

"Yeah, I've seen you around at the restaurant with Camila. So you're the girl."

"So you're the friend," I say. My cheeks warm when I mentally revisit what Brooks witnessed in the kitchen thirty minutes ago. "Who's this?" I nod at the toddler.

Brooks glances over his shoulder at the little boy in a blue-and-purple-striped T-shirt and very small khaki shorts. He's got his lower lip sucked between his teeth, messing with rainbow blocks on a stacking toy. Already the heat is getting to him; his cheeks are rosy.

"That's Marshall. I know what you're thinking."

My lips quirk. "What am I thinking?"

"A toddler named Marshall?!" Brooks shrugs. "It was my ex-wife's suggestion. I call him Marsh most of the time."

"Sit down, if you want," Will says. "I'll get you a beer. Or—" He hesitates, and as I sit down, my eyes track up to his brows, which are furrowing in my direction. "Do you like beer?"

"I love beer," I say. "What happened to the six-pack you brought?"

"It was collected by someone named Weird Stanley," Will says.

"Rookie mistake," I say.

Will's lips curve. "Be right back."

He vanishes. I turn my attention to Brooks and little Marshall. It's sort of astounding, the fact that he's old enough to have a child, an ex-wife, and a few gray hairs. Then again, I'm old enough to be a CEO. Not according to half of Reddit but, like, legally.

"How long have you and Will been friends?" I ask.

"Since middle school," Brooks says. "But we didn't keep in touch after he went to college and worked on Wall Street."

Brooks refills his beagle's water bowl, which the beagle had, seconds earlier, nosed over.

"What's your dog's name?"

"Ernie."

"Hewwo, Ernie." I give him a scratch between the ears. "I want a dog."

"They're a big responsibility," Brooks warns me, like he knows I don't have the time.

"Yeah," I agree sadly. "Toddlers, too, I bet."

Brooks screws on the lid of his water bottle, tosses it into a diaper bag, and reclines onto both palms. He surveys me one more time, his focus lingering on my T-shirt, which proudly reads *DEVILED EGGS AND KEEP THEM COMING*.

"How come you don't want to be attracted to Will?" he asks. "And vice versa?"

I guess I respect his straightforwardness.

"Because it would just be a lot cleaner if we had a platonic relationship," I answer.

"You should dye your hair brunette. He's always been into blonds."

"Like, in a shallow way?" I ask somewhat hopefully.

Am I so desperate to find Will Grant unappealing I'm willing to reduce him to shallowness—the very same thing I got mad he reduced *me* to when we were seventeen?

"No, in an attracted-to-blonds way," Brooks says. "Why, are you shallow?"

"Depends on your definition of the word."

"No depth," he deadpans.

"I can be a little obsessive about the way I look," I admit. "So yeah, I guess so."

He chews on his lip. "I think it's pretty bullshit we tell women who are obsessed with the way they look that they're shallow, instead of recognizing that it's body dysmorphic disorder and cultivating a society that doesn't uphold unrealistic beauty standards."

My mouth drops open as Will reappears. "Getting to know each other?" He tosses a can to Brooks, who catches it with one hand, then holds it up to me in a *cheers* gesture.

"Oh yeah," Brooks says.

Will collapses onto the spot of free towel beside me. He slips two stacked plastic cups that say *Take Your Cloves Off* between his teeth and cracks open a can of beer. It's something local, with dark-purple branding. Not the same thing he brought, but we're all collectivists for the evening. I watch greedily as he drops the cups hanging from his lips into his free hand, and then as the amber liquid from the can spills into the top cup.

So far, wiping out my attraction to him is going horribly.

I clear my throat and ask, "You guys reconnected after the run-in at Agricole?"

Will hands me my drink. "Basically, yeah."

"Fate," Brooks says. "Should have known you'd come home eventually."

"I'm not home." Will stiffens. "You know I still live in Manhattan."

"We'll see," Brooks says.

Will glances away from both of us, and my mind keeps spinning. I guess I'm not the only person wondering if he's considering a life change.

He finishes pouring the other can of beer into the second cup and stretches his legs out, leans his torso against the tree trunk, and takes his first sip.

"That child's mother," he says, nodding at Marshall, "is my high school sweetheart."

"You really had to go there," Brooks grumbles.

"Your ex-wife?" I ask.

"The very same," Brooks says.

"The infamous Amber," I say.

"Yup," the guys say together.

Will grins. "I wasn't even invited to their wedding."

"You'll be there for my next one," Brooks promises.

"How come it didn't work out?" I ask.

"Amber gave an over-the-pants hand job to another line cook at the restaurant. I found out through LinkedIn."

I blink. "Does the line cook still work with you?"

"Yeah. He's the dessert guy now."

"Is he *here*?" I ask.

Brooks nods. "Yeah, he's the one doing the desserts."

"Are they *together now*?"

"No, she's dating an Apple VP."

"That's rough."

He shrugs. "Not really. Me and Marsh get all our technology for free."

A shadow crosses my vision and I turn left, where Josue—one of David's close friends, also in the wedding party—kneels beside our towel.

"Do me a favor, J, can you taste this garlic dressing for the Caesar salad and tell me if you think it needs more salt?"

I grab the plastic spoon from the blender in his hand and give the dressing a lick. "Needs more garlic."

"It does *not* need more garlic."

"Then it needs more salt."

"Like, an anchovy saltiness, or a salty saltiness?" he asks.

I blanch. "There are *anchovies* in here?"

Josue nods.

I turn to Will. "This is why I'm always aspiring."

"Never vegetarian," he concludes.

"Do you need help with anything?" Brooks asks.

"Yeah, that'd be great, unless you're above peeling and deveining shrimp?"

"I'm above nothing." Brooks downs his beer. "Can you watch my kid, Will?"

Will looks wholly unsure. "Sure," he says.

Five seconds later, they've abandoned Will and me with a help-less child. We exchange equally terrified glances. I'm almost positive neither of us has much experience with childcare.

Marshall seems spatially aware there's more room now to move around on the towel; he crawls over to Will, patting his knee. Will lifts the kid onto his leg, rocking him up and down gently while he somehow still manages to sip at the beer in his free hand.

Under the shade of the tree, in the Austin heat, wearing jeans and a T-shirt with a tear on the sleeve, drinking a beer and bouncing a baby on his knee, this man could not look any further from a sleazy finance type if he tried.

My sexual drive is fully driving. I glance around the yard, looking for a friend-slash-excuse-to-abandon-ship before my want multiplies. But Cami is a no-go after our blowup, and if I search for Gio, she'll only force me to talk to Cami.

And anyway, it would be rude to leave Will alone with a toddler, especially considering I *did* agree to his deal that we'd be amicable for the evening.

I look back and study him over the lip of my cup while I sip. The ambient noise around us dims. It feels like all the light in the yard is pointing this way, offering him a radiant sunglow.

"Why aren't you and your brother close?" Will asks.

I consider my answer to his left-field question before responding.

"Robbie's a very traditional, buttoned-up, straight-and-narrow type. He had a plan for his life he executed flawlessly. Met a nice girl in college, proposed senior year, and then impregnated her with their firstborn seven years before she becomes geriatric by the medical standard. Another kid two years after that, another one three years after that. Which means Robbie and Miranda are scheduled to be intimate again in about eight months."

Will fights a smile. "What does Robbie do?"

"Insurance."

His fight with the smile continues. "So, he's a low risk, low re-ward guy."

"One thousand percent. My mom likes to trade stocks," I say, taking another swallow of beer. I lean my body toward Will, shifting my weight onto a palm. Marshall has settled against Will's chest, his eyes half-closed. "She's a part of the Reddit set and everything. My dad begrudgingly endures it, but Robbie and my mom fight about it every chance they get."

"Let me guess," Will says. "*Robbie* thinks if she's going to invest, it should be in a ten-year bond or a treasury bill."

"You got it."

"Your mom sounds awesome," he murmurs.

I laugh at that. "She is awesome. You know the type of helicop-ter parent who puts all their worth into their children, and then doesn't know what their purpose is once the children stop needing them? That was my mom. She never worked, never had hobbies, really, until after I went to college. She and my dad used to be more traditional than they are now, but I love the people they've become."

Will nods, rocking his head against the tree.

"Do you think that's why you started your own company?" His voice is soft and almost careful, but his eyes are piercing. "Because you didn't want to ever wonder about your purpose?"

"Definitely." I remember what I told him at Eberly: *I want my existence to be meaningful.*

"Is it fulfilling?" Will asks.

I startle. "What?"

"Your job."

"Yes" is my automatic response.

Will sees right through me. "Give me the real answer, Josephine."

I tug my bottom lip between my teeth. "I suppose the real an-swer is my job gives me more anxiety than fulfillment these days."

What I don't admit is sometimes, I wish I could give it all up. Trade my lifestyle for a different one. And yet, every day, I wake up and decide *not* to sell Revenant. I decide *not* to give up the CEO position. Even though I could at any given point.

And maybe that's because—just like my mother—I don't want something I created to stop needing me.

The way he's watching me is new. Most of the time, Will has furrowed brows, his eyes hungry as they rove my face, the position of his body arched toward mine. But now, Will's body is relaxed, his eyes calm. His features have arranged into a smooth understanding, like he's temporarily stopped trying to work me out because I gave him the answer myself.

Beyond us, smoke is lifting off the grills, the smell of charcoal fragrant. The side of my face is catching the brunt of the sun as it falls into the tree line. The colors of the light are changing, painting Will's hair an almost red sheen.

"Do you ever wish you were doing some other job?" he asks.

"Never," I admit, just above a whisper, like it's a confession. "But sometimes I wish I was doing nothing at all."

Little Marshall is now fully asleep against Will's chest, his round cheeks rosy. I envy him. I envy his ability to fall asleep on another human with nothing on his mind beyond his own immediate comfort.

"What would you do, if you had nothing *to* do?" Will asks.

"I think I'd get a puppy," I admit. "Some type of doodle that doesn't shed and costs more money than a month's rent, and sure, you can add the fact that I would want a designer dog to the list of the worst things about me, I don't care."

Will cracks a smile. "I'm allergic to dog hair, so that's fine with me."

"I would start designing again," I say. "Nothing I'd manufacture, not this time around. They'd all be one-of-a-kind dresses or formal wear. And maybe I'd auction them off and give the proceeds to philanthropies if there was enough interest."

"An animal shelter, to make up for your designer dog," Will advises.

"And I would start dating again, too." I say it on an exhale, then pause and glance at Will after the words leave me. His expression doesn't alter, not even a fraction.

"*Who* would you date?" he asks shakily.

"Somebody different from my ex-boyfriend," I pronounce. I don't even wait for Will to inquire; I just tell him. "He loved to play sports, watch sports, talk about sports. And he loved to plan our weekends and vacations around sports—which was fine sometimes, but there wasn't room for anything else, for anything I wanted to do or see or visit. And I didn't ever tell him I felt that way, so it was partially my fault. Clay was thoughtful in all the usual ways. I got flowers on Valentine's Day and jewelry on my birthday, but he never once gave me a personal gift, something that screamed, *I thought of you when I purchased this.* He would tell me when he thought I looked especially pretty and ask me about my day. He was by and large a good guy."

"But he wasn't good for *you.*"

I tip my cup back, send the rest of my beer down my throat. "We weren't good for each other. Our relationship was too passive. It ended the exact same way it began, and I get the feeling relationships aren't supposed to be like that. Shouldn't they change, adapt to the growth of each individual, and also to the couple as a unit?"

Will nods his agreement. "Should be dynamic. A healthy relationship, anyway."

"Exactly. When he got the opportunity to move, I told him to go. And I told him I needed to stay because I was building Revenant in Austin, and I didn't even want to consider relocating. And we just . . . dissipated, like fog when the sun rises."

Will watches me. "You're saying if you had the time, you would date someone you don't feel passive about."

"I would date someone I'm obsessed with," I clarify, heart in my throat.

"Someone you'd change your plans for."

"Someone who makes every other worldly thing pale in comparison. Someone who matters to me more than the rest of it. Someone who storms into my life and turns everything upside down. Someone I can't keep myself from."

The sunlight halos him. Will's eyes get bluer. I think of the rules we keep breaking. The excuses we keep making. Even this "deal" tonight is just a way to keep talking guilt-free.

Brooks reappears then with an armful of fresh beers. He sits and cracks them open for us. Will and I pass over our empty cups so he can top us off.

"Made those shrimp my bitch," he says. "Thanks for babysitting."

"Marshall is perfect," I say.

"Do you want kids?" Brooks asks me. But his eyes track to Will.

"I don't know," I say honestly. "I haven't given it much thought."

I've given more thought to Will as a father in the last ten minutes than to myself as a mother over the course of my whole life.

"Want to know a secret?" Brooks grins wickedly. "Right this second, Grant is imagining getting you pregnant."

"If your spawn wasn't asleep on me, I would end you."

CHAPTER TWENTY

After the sun fades and Camila plugs in the twinkle lights that span the backyard, Brooks packs himself a to-go container of food and bids us farewell to put his son to bed. Leonie slips an icy glass of white sangria into my palm. I fish out a piece of apple and suck on it. Will and I have migrated to the line of people waiting for the buffet of garlic-inspired dishes. The music has been turned up in direct accordance with the rowdier, alcohol-bolstered voices. The coolness of the evening sends tiny shivers up my skin, and I can feel tightness from sun exposure in my cheeks every time I smile.

"Will you be eating meat this evening?" Will asks as we pick up paper plates and diverge to opposite sides of the long serving table.

"Not intentionally. Though that steak with chimichurri does look amazing."

"Brooks's shrimp." Will picks up a pair of tongs and grabs a few, adding them to his plate.

"No poopy veins in sight," I say.

"I'll be the judge of that, aspiring vegetarian."

"What if, for tonight, I was an aspiring *pescatarian*?"

"That's between you and your god."

I shrug, grabbing a single shrimp. "Lack of self-control around meat. Add it to the list of the worst things about me."

We move forward in the line, and Will says, "Just because I'm giving you my list doesn't mean you have to give me yours."

"It's only fair."

He sighs, exasperated. "Not everything has to be fair, Josie. Most things aren't."

"Spoken like a true Jordan Belfort apologist."

Will glares, which makes me laugh. I grab a blueberry muffin I'm *really* hoping doesn't contain garlic and top my plate with it.

Aside from Camila and David, who are at the chef table up front, the rest of my friends are seated already. I lead Will toward their table and introduce him to Leonie. She and Gio inspect him with friendly suspicion.

As soon as I sit down, Leonie says, "So, J, I hear you bought a two-thousand-dollar vacuum cleaner from a door-to-door salesperson last week."

I glare at Gio. "I told you that in embarrassed confidence."

Gio shrugs, smirking as she dips her chicken taco into a pool of salsa. "It was too funny not to share."

I grip my halfway depleted sangria. The liquid is sloshing around in my belly. "She had eleven brothers and sisters, left home at seventeen and emancipated herself so she wouldn't follow in her parents' footsteps of addiction, and was saving up to buy a car so she didn't have to take the bus. She was interested in getting a cosmetology education and—look, it was a *really impressive* vacuum cleaner."

When my eyes cut to Will beside me, he looks delighted by this information. "Elaborate," he says simply.

"It has one million functions. There's an entire bag of attachments.

It *mops*. It shampoos the carpet! She had these little cotton pads, where you could see the dirt getting sucked up. Did you know—" I pause, remembering the saleswoman's pitch. "Did you know there are dust mites on our mattresses?! This vacuum has an attachment for mattresses!"

Gio and Leonie burst into a cackle of laughter. I don't think they're taking the issue of dust mites seriously enough, but at least Will isn't laughing at me. He's resting both of his elbows on the table, shoulders leaning in my direction. I feel the barest graze of hair on his forearm brushing against mine.

"Dust mites on mattresses are a *legitimate* concern," I say. "I googled it."

"I believe you," he says.

"It's worth the money, in my opinion," I add.

"You led with the seventeen-year-old who needed a car," Will says. "Which means you were always going to buy that two-thousand-dollar vacuum cleaner, even if it only vacuumed."

After a lot of cajoling, I promise to send a picture of the vacuum with all its attachments to everyone once I get home. Leonie tops off my sangria. I eat my plate of food, including the single shrimp, and am duly informed by Josue when he swings by our table that there *is* actually chicken schmaltz in the rice, sorry about that. Will and I split the blueberry muffin (no traceable garlic). We drink a little more, talk about everything, about nothing.

"I need to get going," Will says eventually. "One of my other clients found out I stayed in town and wants to go on an early bike ride tomorrow."

"Where are you riding?" Gio asks.

"Decker Lake."

"Great spot," Leonie says, nodding her approval.

"I still owe you four more worst things about me," Will whispers, right into my ear. Goose bumps form in that spot and expand everywhere.

"I'll walk you out," I whisper back.

A heaviness falls over me as Will says his goodbyes, making a point to hug Camila and shake David's hand. Though he isn't necessarily a "charmer," I'd still call him charming.

Charming on request, maybe.

By the time he meets me at the gate that leads to the front of the house, something in my gut has shifted.

"Did you have fun?" he asks.

"I did. Thank you for . . . making it fun," I say.

I unlatch the gate. Will and I pass through. The *click* of the latch securing back in place pulls me into the moment. The scent of grass cooling in the night air. The hum of music blending with voices, the dull noise of crickets.

I'm expecting Will to head toward the street, but instead he keeps to the edge of the tall fence line until he makes it past the next corner. I follow him.

When I turn, he's leaning one shoulder against the wood slats. I step toward him and lean my shoulder against the fence, too. A mere six inches separates our chests, which are breathing in and out, in and out. Coming close, then retracting in a steady pattern.

For a minute, neither of us says a word. We just stand there, letting our bodies hum in the dark quiet of each other's presence. It feels like every molecule in my body is reaching toward him. Begging to touch him.

"Number two," Will says. His voice unfurls along my neck, somehow massaging the muscles there I'd tensed. "I hate leftovers."

This pulls me out of my trance. "I'm sorry. *What?*"

"I hate leftovers," he repeats. "I don't like taking food home from restaurants, and if I'm cooking, I always try to make exactly the right amount of food for the number of people consuming it. Which is usually one."

"You—" I pause, processing. "*Why* do you hate leftovers?"

"They aren't appealing to me," he explains. "I hate thinking about food being cooked, cooled down, and then reheated." Will shivers. "It just doesn't seem *hygienic,* and on top of that, I was forced to eat a lot of leftovers as a kid because my mom cooked everything in bulk—don't even get me started on freezer meals— and I just *hate* them. I would rather eat a banana and a piece of toasted bread with peanut butter for dinner than leftovers I took home from a gourmet restaurant the night before. Also, cooking is sacred to me—a very calming ritual—and reheating leftovers in the microwave has the exact opposite effect."

I stare. "You realize some restaurants serve food that has been previously frozen?"

"Yes," Will says, blanching. "I can almost always tell."

"What about, like, *preserved* things?" I ask. "Like kimchi?"

"That's fine," Will says. "Though I'm pretty rigid about expiration dates."

"Wow." I rub a hand over my forehead. "Hating leftovers really *is* one of the . . . maybe not the worst, but certainly one of the most idiosyncratic things about you."

He nods. "I've been told."

"I *survive* off the Trader Joe's frozen section."

He smirks. "Well, there you have it. Our first sign of incompatibility."

It's a weak holdout, but better than nothing.

After a minute of processing I say, "I'm ready for number three."

Will's face grows solemn. "I snore. Terribly."

I burst into laughter, which, had there not been a cicada or two nearby, might have been overheard by the party guests.

"I have allergies—dog hair being one of them, but also pollen and ragweed—and my snoring is worst in the spring and fall, but frankly, it's tragic all year round. Plus, I've got a deviated septum." Will presses a finger to one side of his nose, and I notice the tiniest curve there. "I've had multiple women leave, or ask *me* to leave, a one-night stand at three a.m. because they could not sleep over the sound of my snoring."

My laughter simmers but doesn't subside. "You woke up after sex with a stranger and were told to leave because of your *snoring*?"

Will nods. "More than once."

"When was the last time you had a girlfriend?"

"I dated someone when I was at NYU for about a year. She said she didn't end it because of the snoring, but she complained about it often enough that I'm not totally sure I believe her."

"What was the provided reason she dumped you?"

Dimples. "I didn't *drink enough.*"

"*What?*"

"She was a bit of a partier. I couldn't keep up."

"You were cramping her style."

"Evidently."

"I watched you drink tonight at a very normal rate."

"Thank you," Will says. "Back at you."

"Okay. What's the fourth worst thing about you?"

Will holds up a palm. "Hang on. These aren't power rankings. They're just the five worst, in no particular order. If you want to rank them later, that's your call."

"Deal."

"Number four is: I love sports."

He holds a serious face for about three seconds before the corner of his mouth kicks up, and I start laughing again.

"No!" I cry.

"Yes," he responds, the word defiant. "I put that in the list of worst things the minute you mentioned it earlier. But the truth is, Josephine, I *love* Texas football, and I also root for the Nashville Preds. The NFL, I couldn't care less about. But I'm really into college football and professional hockey."

Part of me thinks that's adorable—and anyway, who am I to

judge his interests when I don't want to be judged for mine?—but the whole point of this exercise is for me *not* to find anything Will tells me endearing. I expel a sigh, curling in on myself.

"Aside from the cheating thing you mentioned in the guest room, I'd argue these are more quirks than bad traits," I say.

"Well, I saved the best for last."

"You mean the *worst* for last."

Will scratches at his arm. Despite the warm smile on his face, barely visible even from this close, I sense the shift in his composure. Up until now we've been mostly joking, but whatever Will is about to tell me has more weight. His smile drops a fraction at a time—until it's gone, washed away by night. Somehow, it makes the stark color of his eyes intensify as they hold mine.

"Right before I left my previous job," he whispers, "I was responsible for ending a marriage. So, on top of my parents' marriage, which I also ended—" He winces. "That's two now. My responsibility, both of them. And I didn't do it gently or kindly the second time. I was thoughtless about it. Selfish. I broke someone's heart."

He pauses, gulps. "The point is, I have a habit of ruining things. Marriages. Friendships. Even business partnerships. I'm the common denominator. The person that causes your relationship to break. I try to do the right thing. I've always, *always* tried. I've never set out to hurt people. But I do anyway, every time. And I'm terrified, Josie, that somehow, some way, I will break something that matters to you *again*."

This, I realize, is Will Grant's most shame-filled self-realization.

His lowest opinion of himself.

He broke Amber's relationship with Zoe.

Zoe's friendship with me.

Zoe's opinion of her father.

Their father's marriage with their mother.

And this other marriage, too—whoever that couple once

was—which Will claims to have ruined in a way that inflicted obvious pain.

I could tell him other people's relationships ending isn't Will's fault—but that's not really his issue, anyway. It's *how* things end. The role Will plays in it. His regret, his remorse, his self-loathing over his involvement. If he hadn't kissed me on the beach, would Zoe and I have stayed close? If he hadn't kept his father's secret all year, would his mother have suffered less heartache? If he hadn't dated Amber, would Zoe have never put distance between them?

More than anything, I want to pull Will into my arms, promise him he isn't a villain.

In the very next blink, I do exactly what I want.

"You are not a bad person for telling your mother the truth," I whisper against his neck. Will's arms circle my waist, and he pulls me closer. "You are also not a bad person for keeping it from her because your father asked that of you. It's not your fault Zoe and I stopped talking. She and I shoulder that blame in equal measure. And I don't need context on what happened with that other marriage to know you feel remorse for your hand in how it ended."

Will's lips ghost along the crown of my head. One of his hands tangles in my hair. His other squeezes my hip, and I feel moldable.

"What if I was okay with being your collateral damage?" he whispers.

My breath hitches. "What?"

"What if you took from me what you wanted and left the rest? I can take it." His voice is deep in his throat, breath warm on my skin. "Use me. Please. It would be an honor. I can exist for you only in moments like this one. I can be scarce when you need me not to exist."

I don't miss the way he changed the conversation away from his insecurities, but my brain is too foggy to switch back. "That's not going to work," I say, my spine arching.

"Why not?" He sounds frustrated.

"Because I don't do anything halfway."

Will rumbles out a laugh and presses one kiss to my temple before his arm loosens and he steps back. I inhale ragged breaths as we look at each other.

"No," he agrees. "You don't."

He looks past me, steadying his own breath.

"I'm sorry," I say, the words wholly insufficient.

"Don't be, Josephine. You owe me nothing."

"I owe it to you not to cross my own boundaries. Which I keep doing."

He looks back at me. "I don't exactly mind when you cross them."

Silence swallows our want.

"Thank you for agreeing to my deal," Will says, his voice husky and low. He shoots me one last loaded gaze and vanishes into the dark.

CHAPTER TWENTY-ONE

I've always put my anxiety into work. I scrape the bad feelings off my skin, gather them into manageable pieces, and bury them around the office—between file folders, underneath desks.

It's always been like this.

When I was a teenager, I'd get anxious my mother wanted to live my life for me. Make decisions for me, pass judgment on my body for me, make social plans for me, care about schoolwork *just enough* for me. (*Don't be too smart, darling, it'll only get you into trouble.*) When it got to the point where I wasn't sure if I was made of straw or blood and bones, I'd disappear to Oma's house and sew something. *That* was a tangible use of my hands. Proof I had meaning, that I was productive. That my existence was tied to the world.

When Oma died—when I was a senior in high school with two months left, friendless and lonely and heartbroken—the only way I knew how to feel close to her was to *make*.

Good grades, clothes, plans.

Decisions.

I *decided* to delete my social media, *decided* to attend the best college to admit me. I worked hard, took on extra credit, and wound up with a better second-semester GPA than I or my parents thought possible. I started working at a boutique, steamed every item we put on sale even though my boss told me it wasn't necessary. At the end of the summer, I went to college and turned over a new leaf.

I wasn't the friendless girl with cute clothes and passable grades. I was the quiet girl with *homemade* clothes and straight A's.

Junior year, when I started dating Clay, and for some reason started to feel like I was made of straw again—a tumbleweed, whose thoughts weren't important, whose decisions didn't *matter,* whose existence wasn't tied to the rest of the world—I founded Revenant.

It's always been like this.

Anxiety equals productivity.

You're panicking? *Do something.*

Don't do something *about* it. Just do *something.*

Even now, as I pull back on sleeping hours and spend later nights in the office, I'm at least partially aware of what I'm doing. You can't coexist with the worst parts of yourself for twenty-seven years and not *sometimes* pull back the curtain.

I go on a few rides with Gio and Leonie, make amends with Camila after our voice-raising in her kitchen, but I avoid talking about what's really eating at me with all three of them. I make excuses about work stress when they broach the subject of my mental state.

All in all, I girl-boss so close to the sun that nine days after Garlic Fest, I almost pass out from exhaustion.

I'm on my way out of my office, having stood up abruptly when I realized I was late for a meeting, when my head begins to pound, inky black spots poking at my vision. I sway, knocking my hip on my intern's desk just outside my door.

I tumble a bit at the obstruction, catching myself with my palms on the surface of her desk and sending my laptop and planner flying.

"Oh!" Eugenia gasps.

My eyes blink closed when I realize the black in front of my eyes is growing. "Sorry," I mumble.

Firm hands grip my wrists, lifting me away from the desk. "Just . . ." Her voice trails off. She pulls me back and pushes on my shoulder. "Sit down for a second."

I obey, lowering myself to the floor and resting my head between bent knees. Eugenia rubs my back while I take a few breaths. My office is at the end of the hallway; I'm desperately hoping nobody comes past and sees me like this. Vulnerable. Overwhelmed.

"This is embarrassing," I grumble.

"You've been putting in a lot of hours lately," Eugenia notes. "Your body caught up."

I can feel a tiny heartbeat behind my eyelids pulsing in agreement with her words. I haven't slept, eaten, *breathed* evenly since Garlic Fest.

I inhale, exhale. Do it again.

Every day I get closer to my two-week trip abroad with Will Grant is another day I've been piling obscene amounts of work onto my desk. Even Derrick asked why I'd been calling so much lately, and he's usually the one sending angry texts when I don't answer the phone.

I've made a point *not* to create a toxic hustle environment. I've made a point to encourage our employees to maintain their work-life balance.

For everyone besides me.

I'm usually better at hiding it than this.

"You're usually better at hiding it than this," Eugenia says.

A garbled laugh trips out of me. I pry my eyes open, focusing on her. She's on the floor, too, seated facing me in her pink jumpsuit, her braided hair draped over one shoulder, her legs crossed, posture straight.

Over the past ten days of Eugenia managing my calendar, I've become a scarily productive version of myself. She's asked me on several occasions if this is too many meetings per day, if I'd like her to block thirty minutes for a lunch break, twenty minutes for an outdoor walk. I lied when I registered the concern on her face, told her that the day I got back from San Francisco last week, I took the afternoon off and spent it lounging in the sunshine. (Actually, I spent that afternoon indoors at home, catching up on my CEO class coursework.)

"I know an overachiever when I see one." Eugenia points at herself.

"You've gotten me at my worst," I admit. "I've been self-medicating with work ethic."

"At first," Eugenia says, "I thought you were just trying to get everything squared away before your trip abroad with Will Grant. But Josephine, you spent thirty minutes on the phone yesterday haggling over a warehouse *toilet paper contract.*"

"What if we fail the B Corp review because our toilet paper isn't made with recycled materials?" I practically shriek.

"Nobody wants to wipe with recycled toilet paper!" Eugenia shrieks back.

"It's not recycled toilet paper, it's toilet paper made with recycled—" She holds up a palm, and I cut myself off, huffing.

"What's going on?" she asks. "Really. You can talk to me. About anything."

I swear, there's something easier about admitting your problems to people you hardly know at all.

"I feel guilt," I blurt. "The guilt is what's pushing me to act like this."

"Guilt," Eugenia repeats.

"I feel this overwhelming, heart-wrenching guilt," I say, all in a rush, confused and unsure and wobbly. "Because I have a crush on him. Will Grant."

"No kidding."

"You aren't surprised?"

"I saw you two interact. No, I'm not surprised."

"Well, we've been on a few accidental dates. But the problem is, he's just—" I push my fingers against my temples, out of breath. "*Fitting* himself into my world. Will comes *here,* to Austin, and works for me. He does favors for me. He fixes personal problems for me. It's not right, it's not *fair.*"

"Maybe fixing things for other people is his love language?" Eugenia prompts. "Maybe it doesn't have to be fair."

He'd said the same thing: *Not everything has to be fair, Josie. Most things aren't.*

"I want it to be fair," I whisper. "And I feel guilt that it isn't."

"Then make it fair," Eugenia proposes. A realist, like Cami or Gio.

"I. Can't."

"Why not?" she asks.

"Because Revenant matters more. It *has* to."

The guilt swallows me from both sides.

I haven't been giving my full attention to Revenant since I ran into Will—hence my overcompensation over the past few weeks. Sure, it's just a business, but we all profit share. These employees are depending on me to *care.* To put in my best effort. *I'm* depending on me to care, to not give up what I started. I love this company. I want it to succeed, to get B Corp Certified, to be meaningful to the customers.

But even amidst being distracted by Will, I *still* couldn't match the care he showed me. Contact solution, a shoulder to cry on, a distraction, a consultant, a quiet companion to keep me company when I had classes to take but felt lonely. I haven't intended to be selfish, but that's what happened. Will Grant has molded himself into my world because I don't have the time or energy to be fair with him.

"I can't have it all," I whisper to Eugenia. "I think, maybe, I've been killing myself with work as a subconscious reminder of that reality."

She considers me, chewing on her lip. "Then I guess I can't either."

I frown. "What do you mean?"

"I want to be like you when I'm older," she says, measured and precise.

I blink twice and immediately backtrack on my admission. "Wait. I'm not saying nobody with my type of job could ever be in a relationship."

"You're just saying I'd have to make sacrifices *you're* not willing to make."

I cock my head. Is this a trap?

"Eugenia, you should date if you want to," I say with extra conviction. "Like I said, I genuinely wasn't interested in a man for a long time until now. I know you have a crush on that other intern. The freckled kid who always comes by your desk. Don't think I haven't noticed you giving him your smiles."

Her face freezes. "I do not give him my smiles."

"Eugenia, you do, too."

We glare at each other in a standoff.

"I can't get romantically involved with another *intern*," Eugenia says. "I have a plan for my future, and no boy, no matter how much I might like his freckles, is getting in the way of it. Didn't *you* break up with your boyfriend after college?"

"How did you—"

"It's on Reddit."

My eyes narrow. "What else about me is on Reddit?"

"You lie about being a vegetarian. You refuse to do press. You and Cami aren't best friends anymore and actually hate each other. You don't have any social media accounts because you got canceled in high school."

I flinch. "So, nothing nice."

"Since when has anybody put something *nice* on Reddit?"

That makes me laugh—for the first time in more than a week. It gathers in my belly, expelling itself alongside the frantic nervousness I've been carrying in my gut since Will left me by that fence line at Cami and David's place.

"For the record, I'm an aspiring vegetarian."

"For the record," Eugenia replies. "You don't need the label of vegetarianism—or a B Corp Certification, for that matter—for me to know what kind of person you are."

It's a nice sentiment. If only I were biologically capable of caring less about perception.

"I'll be better after the supplier trip," I say. "I don't want you to think this is healthy or normal behavior."

"Oh, I'm aware. I know you're, like, a borderline millennial, and I'm ambitious, make no mistake. But at the end of the day, romanticizing the grind is not in my generational makeup."

I smirk at her. "Neither are corporate flings, apparently."

"I can make an exception for the CEO and her very hot consultant."

"We aren't going there," I say.

"Yet," Eugenia says.

My brain spins back to my childhood, recalling my brother, Robbie, repeating, "This is what happens when an unstoppable force meets an immovable object," over and over during his Batman phase. He said it all the time.

Unstoppable force, immovable object.

Will and me.

I can't put into words why I think of us like that, but I do. And I'm worried what it means. Or rather, what it *will* mean, when it's just the two of us.

Alone, together, on the other side of the world.

CHAPTER TWENTY-TWO

To get to the first supplier we're visiting in Peru, I must fly first to Atlanta (where Will and I plan to meet), second to Lima, and finally to the Alfredo Rodríguez Ballón International Airport in Arequipa—a Peruvian city close to the southernmost tip of the country and nestled right below the Andes Mountains.

Will has already arrived from New York by the time I deplane in Atlanta. I meet him at a Panda Express near our gate for the Lima flight. He's dressed in professional clothes—slacks and a button-down—but his honey-brown hair looks messy and tugged-at. He's devouring orange chicken and fried rice when I walk up to him, wheeling my suitcase alongside me.

He stands up that very instant, swallowing.

"You really need to stop standing when you see me," I say.

"It's a sign of respect," he says.

"Respect me less."

Will's eyes heat, one brow rising comically. "Are you—"

"Not like that!"

Will laughs, and the sound is warm enough to liquefy my spine. He scoops his sweatshirt off the seat across from him and I sit, eyeing the book on the table near his food. *Madhouse at the End of the Earth.* The jacket of the book is torn in one spot.

Don't show interest. Don't show interest. Don't—

"What are you reading?" I ask, completely un-fucking-able to help myself.

"It's about explorers on a ship in Antarctica," he says, his voice jumping with . . . boyish excitement? "And it's a true story, but sort of fictionalized."

"You like to read?"

"Yes." He says it very simply. Our eyes move from the book back toward each other.

Something about the (surprisingly aggressive) Panda Express lighting draws out the individual marks on his face in stark relief. A few freckles, a tiny scar on his upper lip. A mole on the rim of his ear.

"What about you?" Will asks.

I blink. "I forgot what we were talking about."

His mouth curves up. "Do you like to read?"

"Oh. I don't really have time for reading anymore." I hold up the fashion magazines I just purchased at a news store. "Even these are more like market research."

Will frowns. "That's too bad."

Don't share personal details. Don't share personal—

"When I was younger," I say, the words spilling out of me in a gush, "I devoured books at Sea Island, where my family went during my school breaks."

"I remember," Will says, his eyes warm as he stretches back in his chair. "You took Zoe with you over fall break."

"Right," I say. "We both spent that whole break reading by the pool. Zoe kept her nose buried in some dystopian sci-fi or dragon fantasy with wars and kingdoms. I went for summery beach reads about teenagers and love and family and first jobs at shrimp shacks."

"That tracks," Will says.

"I could read one per day during the summer months, too," I go on. "Wouldn't even leave the beach unless it was to get in the ocean or run up to our house for some lunch. Up until I turned eighteen, I would read until the sun set and my sunburn formed goose bumps."

Will's lips part just slightly, in awe at my oversharing about my teenage reading habits. "What changed when you turned eighteen?"

I shrug, my shoulders concaving. I roll up the magazines in a tight wad. "I guess I stopped thinking of that girl in all those summer books and me as the same kind of girl."

He's quiet for a minute. I keep my focus on my lap. "Are you going to Sea Island this summer?" he asks.

I shake my head. "I haven't been in years, actually."

"No time for vacations?"

My eyes draw back up to his, hazel against blue. "What do you think?"

"I think *I'm* going to spend some time on this trip enjoying myself," he says, voice almost scolding. "You're welcome to join me. But I'm not going to force you to treat this trip like a partial vacation if you aren't up to it."

We're not *eating hotel food and getting our exercise in a workout room,* he'd said.

"Will, it really isn't supposed to be like—"

"Did you think I don't know when your birthday is?"

I freeze. "Cami told you."

His head tilts just a fraction, eyes roaming my face. "Actually," he says, voice dropping low, "Zoe did."

Zoe?

Did Will *tell* her we'd be going on this two-week trip together?

Has he told her . . . other things?

"Your brain is working so damn hard right now," Will says, dryly amused. "You know you can just *ask* me anything you want to know about Zoe, right?"

I cock my head, thinking, and tap my phone screen to check the time. First class is boarding in less than ten minutes.

I use the bathroom and buy a Diet Coke, and then we board our next flight. Will finishes his book while I catch up on some emails.

There's one from Nora Lindberg, the *Forbes* journalist who keeps trying to get in touch about the 30 Under 30 list. She's been after me for years, reaching out once every six months to ask for an interview. But unlike the editor who wrote the profile on me that Will read twice, *this* woman gives me bad vibes. I've read some of her other stuff; she makes a lot of inferences. And via email, she's pushy and manipulative, telling me she's going to write about me eventually, so I might as well control the narrative. Which is alarming and problematic.

I huff at her latest message. Will glances over just as I'm deleting the email. His shoulder brushing mine makes our little row of seats feel more intimate than it should. "Wait a minute. I *know* her."

"Nora Lindberg?"

"Yeah. I know her from New York. She works for *Forbes*, right?"

"Yeah . . ."

Will glances over at me. "She wants you for the Thirty Under Thirty list."

"See?" I hold out my hand. "It's just so *obvious*."

"A lot of people would kill for a shot at that list, Josie."

"Not me."

"It's good press."

"There's no such thing."

Will scoffs. "That's what people say about *bad* press."

I snort in retaliation to his scoff. "There is *definitely* such a thing as bad press."

"Are you really planning to leave *Nora Lindberg* on read?"

"Why did you say her name like that?" I ask.

"Because she's *Nora Lindberg*. When she wants a story, she chases it until she's got it in her grasp. Her profiles are kind of legendary."

"Have you hooked up with her?" The red that creeps into his neck tells me all I need to know. Will glances sideways. Unsuccessfully, I try to push down the jealous knot welling in my stomach. "How many *times* have you hooked up with her?"

"Once," Will rumbles. "And it was three years ago. Last I heard, she was engaged to some music producer."

"Oh, to be a stereotypical New York City power couple."

Will bites the inside of his cheek. "Do you care to elaborate on *why* you hate press, even *business press,* so much?"

"Not really."

"Josephine." Will closes his book and leans an elbow on his armrest, twisting his upper body to face me. "We've got two more plane rides of this, and that's all before we reach Europe."

"Should we order some wine?"

"Your avoidance tactics are extraordinary."

I lean forward. "You know what nobody ever asked Mark Zuckerberg? A single question about his skin-care routine."

"Nora Lindberg isn't that kind of journalist."

"Maybe so, but it doesn't change the fact that most female founders are infantilized and branded the second they hit the spotlight. Or the fact that society turns on us more often and with more ferocity than seems to *ever* be aimed at our male counterparts. I don't want people to think of me when they think of Revenant. It's the surest way I could gut my own company."

Will shakes his head, looking sideways. "Your opinion of yourself is abysmal."

"Better that than an inflated one. Trust me. I've seen how it goes when you step into the spotlight. I've watched other female CEOs get dragged for the same things men get excused for. And anyway, I know myself well enough to be sure I will transform an innocent piece of press into something toxic about my self-worth. How many shares will the article get? How many clicks? How many online sales dollars will it drive?" My voice is almost desperate as I try to explain. I gulp, pushing back the emotion in my throat. "How many hate comments? How many rolled eyes? How many people thinking bad thoughts about me when they could instead not be thinking of me at all? If you don't put yourself on display, nobody wants to hate you. I learned that after I got anonymously slut-shamed on my fucking Formspring account for making out with you in public."

Now Will leans forward, a frown etched into his face. I can easily make out the grain of his blue irises. "I didn't know that happened to you." My face goes red, and his voice breaks. "Right after your oma died. I'm so sorry, Josie."

Against my will, tears well in my eyes. I look away from him, frustrated and embarrassed. A flash of my old resentment comes back—because of course Will, a *boy*, didn't have the same consequences to face for the exact same actions—but it's followed by immediate guilt. What did I want from him? That he suffer equally? That he get privately, anonymously bullied just like me through a now-defunct social media platform that was specifically designed to hurt people's feelings? I wanted our classmates to move on for *both* our sakes, but that's not how teenagers work.

"Thank you for saying that," I say eventually, looking back at him.

Will's expression buckles under a gentle emotion that draws me in, makes me feel understood. Listened to.

"Fuck Nora Lindberg," he says. "She can find another CEO to bother."

"*Exactly,*" I say, grinning.

He rolls his head on the seat back, curving his body toward mine.

"Will?" I ask.

"Hmm?"

"How did Zoe react when you told her about your dad's affair?"

His lips twitch. "She literally beat me up."

I smile and laugh. "Really?"

"Left bruises and everything," he reveals. "It was our biggest fight ever, but I think both of us were relieved we were finally *talking*. About Amber, about you." He swallows. "And then, eventually, about Dad. We worked through all our shit in one night. Then discussed if we should tell Mom, *what* we should tell Mom."

"And?"

"And," Will says, "we told her the very next morning. Mom cycled through about thirty emotions in the span of an hour, grabbed my face, and said, *I'm so sorry he asked this of you*—which is sort of insane, considering I hadn't even admitted that part to her yet—and then she got herself a lawyer."

"She never considered moving home to Austin?" I ask.

Will shakes his head. "She'd found a job she loved teaching pottery at this art studio. I think she would have moved back if she hadn't met Doug, but he came along about six months later, and that was that."

"Do you and Zoe like Doug?" I ask.

"Doug," Will says, "is the best. He makes Nutella pancakes and beer can grilled chicken, and he loves hockey."

"So do you," I say.

"I love hockey because Doug loves hockey," Will says.

"Can we circle back to your stepfather's cooking repertoire ranging from Nutella pancakes to beer can chicken?"

Will laughs softly. "He can make nothing else."

"What else could you possibly need?"

"Something green?"

"True," I concur. "Maybe we could ask Doug to learn a salad or two."

I immediately stiffen when I realize I said *we*.

Will blessedly ignores me and moves on. "Over the next four years, Zoe and I went to colleges in different states. We tried to keep up with each other, but college is busy. She loved visiting me in New York, though, and got a job offer up there after graduation. The problem was, she also had *another* offer in San Diego with higher pay. I told her to do what felt right and promised her that if she went to San Diego, I'd visit all the time."

I smile. "She chose the New York job."

Will nods. "She did. That same year, Doug and my mom got married in Nashville, in the gardens at Cheekwood. It was a really good year."

There's a buoyancy to Will's voice as he recounts this phase of his past. It's easy for him, sharing the good stuff.

I yawn involuntarily.

"Am I boring you?" Will whispers.

"I'm riveted. Promise."

"True or not, you look like you can hardly keep your eyes open."

I rest my head against the seat back, mirroring Will's position. We watch each other through half-closed lids, my chin tilted up, his tilted down.

He says quietly, "Why don't you sleep?"

I do.

CHAPTER TWENTY-THREE

I make it to Arequipa in a dream state. Because even though I technically *wake up* when our plane touches down in Lima, I'm so groggy Will has to all but carry me (and my backpack) through the terminal and onto our third and final flight. I feel like a doted-upon child. I promptly fall asleep again and remain that way until we land.

Consciousness finds me as gentle fingers tap the bones of my hand. My head must have been lying on his shoulder. I tilt it up, catch Will looking down at me with the barest of smiles on his face. Probably amused at some dried drool on my chin or something.

It's eight thirty in the morning. We're in the same time zone as Austin, but my body feels jet-lagged. Thankfully, we don't meet with any suppliers until tomorrow.

As soon as we retrieve our luggage from baggage claim and step into the aridity of the Peruvian terrain, I take deep breaths, sucking the warmth onto my tongue, down into my lungs. It's July, and it *feels* like it even though we're in the Southern Hemisphere.

Eugenia and Will coordinated a private ride for us from the airport into the city, where our hotel is located. I follow him toward a rideshare corner of the arrivals deck.

"How are you feeling?" he asks.

"Disoriented. Did you sleep on the plane?"

"Uh." Will squints, putting a hand over his eyes to look for the makeshift sign with our names in the swarm of waiting drivers. "A bit."

"Why does that feel like a *no*?"

"There's our guy." Will grabs both his suitcase and mine by the handles and starts wheeling them toward a small man in khakis. I greet him in Spanish while he and Will load our luggage into the SUV.

"You speak Spanish?" Will asks me.

"Sort of. I get by. Camila," I add by way of explanation.

He almost-smiles at me, turning for the car.

"I didn't wake up to your infamous snoring," I say once I'm strapped in and Will is beside me in the backseat. "You didn't sleep, did you?"

He slants a look at me. "I once got scolded by a flight attendant who was passing along the complaint from another passenger," he grumbles.

"Oh my God. When I finally hear this snore, I'm expecting to be traumatized."

"*When* and *why* do you think you'll hear it?" Will arches an eyebrow in my direction.

"We've got adjoining rooms, don't we? With a thin door?"

"*Two* doors, actually."

"Is that soundproof enough?"

"Depends on the sound, I suppose." He glances out the window in the other direction.

I'm riffling through a selection of nonsexual verbal returns when my eyes catch on something beyond his window.

"What's that?" I whisper.

"El Misti," our driver says. "The volcano of Arequipa."

It lifts out of the horizon in an almost perfect triangle, with two juts at the tip and folds of green and brown earth cascading down its sides like the pleats of a skirt. The base of the volcano must be miles from here, but something about the way it presents itself to us—to all of Arequipa—gives me the sense that I could reach out and touch it.

I scoot closer to Will, who leans back against his seat so I can get a better view. Between the volcano and our car is an entire city. Tall bushes of flowers with pink and orange petals shoot past as we drive, lining the road and creeping up the man-made structures. The sky is an azure color, starker somehow compared to Austin's constant haze of dust and pollen.

"Have you ever done this before?" Will asks. When I tear my eyes off the window, I catch him gazing down at me.

"Fled the country with a man?"

"Visited a supplier."

"Yes. I've done on-site visits in New Mexico, California, and New York."

"So, you've never traveled abroad for work?"

I shake my head. "When I initially selected Revenant's foreign suppliers, it was all facilitated remotely. By the time we grew enough to add more suppliers, I had the supply chain team, who took care of abroad visits."

"But this time you asked to go yourself," Will notes.

"Yeah, well. Stuey's on paternity leave, and with the B Corp review coming up, I wanted to be sure all our new suppliers are exactly the perfect fit."

Will nods, concealing a private amusement behind his eyes.

Beyond the driver's front window, the downtown area of the city comes into view.

"Hungry?" Will asks.

"If I say yes, are you going to block me from eating something at the hotel?"

He sighs. "Josie, you cannot eat *hotel food* as your first meal in Peru."

"They always have a vegetarian option," I say defensively.

"I'll get you some vegetables, don't you worry," Will grumbles, "if you trust me enough to come into the city with me."

Our driver pulls onto the main thoroughfare, where our hotel sits proudly. The streets are crowded with locals heading to work, and even this early, there are shops and restaurants open in droves, soft music coming from a café with an outdoor patio, tables and chairs spilling onto the sidewalk. When we climb out of the car I'm hit once more with a rush of warm desert air.

Will smoothly tips our driver with soles (I'm not even sure when he acquired them, but it was probably when I was half-asleep waiting to board in Lima). He grabs both of our suitcases and wheels them toward the hotel lobby. When I try to protest, Will shoots me a glare.

"Ten minutes," he says.

"Ten minutes of *what*?"

"Freshening up. That's how long it's going to take me. After that, I'm leaving the hotel. And I think you should come with me."

We pause the conversation while we check in and immediately pick it back up as we head for the elevators.

"I should probably get some work done," I say.

"Suit yourself," Will says. "I'm not going to force it."

He knows what he's doing. He's making me admit I want to spend the day with him. Not because he pressured me but because he merely *invited* me.

"What do I wear?" I ask. If I don't have the right outfit, I'm not going.

"Something you'd want to explore in."

"Explore in?"

Will nods at my Revenant outfit—dusty-blue trousers and a wrinkled white blouse—before his focus travels to my loafers. "Tell me you brought some tennis shoes."

"How else would I take the hotel's six thirty HIIT class tomorrow morning?"

Will groans. "This. *This* is the worst thing about you."

"Is it a turnoff?"

"Not nearly enough of one," he growls.

We pile into an elevator. It's a quick ride. He stares at me with a surly expression from one wall. I stare back at him from the other, considering my outfit choices. On our floor, I drag my feet one in front of the other until we come to our hotel room doors.

"Can I have my suitcase now?"

Will wheels it toward me, pushing down the handle snugly.

"Thank you."

"Welcome. So, are you coming?"

I hesitate. "Yes," I declare before I can overthink it.

Will smiles. "We're going to have fun today."

"Why does that sound like a threat?"

"Because to *you,* it is one."

"You think I feel threatened by the prospect of having fun?"

"I think," he says, voice going deeper, "you feel threatened by the prospect of having fun with *me.*"

"That's not true."

Will's hand comes up to the wall, and his face drops closer to mine. That's when I know he's trapped me. Just before he says, with temptation in his voice, "Prove it."

CHAPTER TWENTY-FOUR

I change into a black tennis skirt and matching tank top, slip my feet into a pair of New Balance tennis shoes, and toss my hair up in a high ponytail. As promised, Will is waiting for me in the hallway, now in a bright yellow Predators T-shirt and a navy baseball cap.

"We could not look more American," I say.

"We *are* American."

"The locals are going to hate us."

"Josephine Davis." Will grabs me by the shoulders and points me in the direction of the elevators. I hate how natural it feels to go where he wants, to settle under his grip. "For once in your life, stop worrying what strangers think of you."

I manage it almost the entire time. When we waltz across the Plaza de Armas, past fountains and manicured trees. When we gaze up at the white stone of the Basilica Cathedral, El Misti visible in the background.

"It's made of volcanic rock," Will muses, rubbing a hand thoughtfully over one archway of the old colonial building.

"How do you know that?" I ask.

"I like architecture." His head tilts up, toward one of the two towers that guard the church. "I was looking forward to seeing this place."

We meander next through the Monasterio de Santa Catalina. Also made of volcanic rock, according to Will, though these structures are pink instead of white—which prompts a whole explanation on the composition of stone I only halfway pay attention to. I'm more focused on the way Will's face lights up when he talks about it. What something is made of. When it was built. Who designed it. Why it matters.

Will doesn't just *like* architecture. He's a dork for it.

In an open-air market, I devour arroz con leche and a potato and sweet corn tamale. Will finds some ceviche, and we eat while we stand, marveling at the fabrics and spices and pottery and artwork for sale. I buy seven garments, unable to stop raving about the craftsmanship, and every time I catch Will's eye, he's smirking.

We explore more churches. Eat again when we get hungry. This time, it's spicy stuffed peppers at a restaurant with a bright yellow ceiling and open windows. Our waiter brings out two complimentary rounds of pisco for each of us—the Peruvian national liquor. We drink it all eagerly before practically skipping to an archaeological museum.

Followed by a café for an afternoon espresso to sober us up.

Then we stumble upon a row of stores I get lost in for an hour. Will disappears about halfway through my shopping expedition. I emerge several hundred dollars lighter to find him waiting patiently for me on a street corner. He's leaning against a brick wall, scrolling on his phone with his baseball cap drawn low over his eyes. The late afternoon sun is painting his skin bronze.

"How long was I out?" I joke.

He glances up at me and smiles, but something about it seems strained. His dimple doesn't even appear. "I was about ten minutes from sending a search party."

"Is everything okay?"

Will pockets his phone. "All good. I think the sun might be getting to me. Are you ready to head back to the hotel?"

My lips pinch. "Sure."

We walk side by side along the warm streets. Will—who's been pointing little things out to me as we pass them all day long— keeps his head down, his eyes focused on the pavement or the crosswalk.

"We haven't had much water today," I note. "Hydrating when we get back will probably make you feel better."

Will nods and offers a gruff noise of agreement. He stays monotone all the way back to our floor, and when we reach our set of doors, he doesn't linger by mine like he did this morning before passing it for his own.

"See you tomorrow," he says, offering me one more pinched smile.

I haven't even said the words back to him before he disappears.

That night, I dream I'm back on the beach getting the phone call from my mother—*Oma passed away. She had a bad fall. Oh, darling, have you been drinking? At least you're coming home tomorrow. I need you, darling, I need you by my side.* There's a fifth of Smirnoff in my left hand. Zoe's talking to her crush, Forrest, the firelight decorating each of their faces. Out of the corner of my eye, I spot Will Grant down the beach.

I tumble through space and time until I'm alone with Oma

in her house. I'm fourteen years old. My first boyfriend, a senior, dumped me last month because I didn't want to have sex with him. My fingers hold down the sides of a garment as the machine hums out a line of stitches. *Golden Girls* is playing in the background, and I laugh a real laugh for the first time in weeks. Oma seems relieved at the sound of it.

The stitches are skipping, I tell her.

She reaches down and pulls the fabric out of the machine and spends thirty minutes removing every stitch. She replaces the needle, replaces the thread. Then she hands the garment back to me and says, *Start over, darling. Try again.*

CHAPTER TWENTY-FIVE

In the morning, I get ready for the day, turning to glare every thirty seconds at the silent adjoining door that bars me from Will. Just when I'm finished getting dressed, starting to panic that I haven't heard a peep from him since his frosty exit yesterday, there's a knock.

When I open the door that connects our rooms, I'm greeted by a clammy, pale face and brown hair that looks almost matted. Dark-purple rings beneath his glassy eyes. Will is dressed in gray sweatpants and the same T-shirt from yesterday. He leans a hand against the side of the doorframe.

"I believe," he croaks, his voice working its way out of him with what sounds like quite a bit of effort, "that I have food poisoning."

"Has this been happening all night?" I ask. "Why didn't you wake me up?"

He huffs out a single, charged laugh. "The last thing I wanted was you witnessing *that*."

"Oh, Will." I move to hug him, but he steps backward, eyes flashing with fear. "I haven't showered yet, Josie. I just knocked to tell you I can't make it to today's site visit, but our driver is already waiting for you downstairs. Will you be able to handle it alone?"

I nod slowly. "Of course."

"I should be better by tomorrow, for the next supplier," he says.

"It doesn't matter. What do you need?"

"Probably some more ceviche." Will's dimple flashes.

"How about crackers and ginger ale, if I can find it? I can look around for a grocery store on my way back."

"That would be great. If it's not too much trouble."

"Not at all." I bite on my lower lip, absorbing the state of him. He doesn't look like he got an ounce of sleep, and that makes for two nights in a row. All I want is to go into that hotel room and start fussing over him, but Will is right. I need to handle this site visit first.

"I'll be back soon," I whisper.

"I'll be here," he whispers back.

Down at the hotel restaurant, the chef lets me know he can send up crackers and ginger ale to Will's room. With that taken care of, I turn my focus to work.

I make it to the supplier and tour the property in a fugue state, though I'm present enough to ascertain it's a viable option for Revenant. No glaring red flags, nice employee facilities, safe conditions, quality product. I *can* do this on my own, but for the first time in a long time, I realize maybe I don't *want* to.

I wish Will was here with me. I wish I could consult with my consultant.

On this. On everything.

About halfway through a sit-down with the supplier to discuss samples and invoicing terms, my stomach twists.

It feels like someone is driving a dull screw into the lining of my insides. As the minutes pass, it only gets worse, and worse, and worse. By the time I leave the place at three in the afternoon, I'm forced to hunch over as I walk back to my ride in an effort to manage the pain.

I don't think it's food poisoning, I text him.

Shit. Are you feeling sick? Will replies right away. I'm already mostly better.

24-hour stomach virus? I guess.

Maybe. Are you on your way back?

I don't reply. Will had the right idea.

When I get back to my hotel room, the last thing I want is him witnessing the fallout.

"Josephine Davis, open this door right fucking now."

"Go away," I moan.

"I will not."

With herculean effort, I crawl from the bathroom across the carpeted floor of my hotel room, making my way toward the bed. My stomach is depleted at this point, nothing left in me to expel, but the virus isn't done with me yet. It's like a million tiny cactus pricks are combing my tummy. More horrid is the knowledge that there's nothing I can do to ease the pain but wait it out. I've had the norovirus before, when I was a teenager on a cruise ship; I know how it works. You hate your life for twenty-four hours, and then you're totally fine.

I can feel a fever setting in.

Will pounds on the door between our rooms again. "I can hear you moaning over there like a dying animal. Let me in!"

"You didn't let *me* in!" I shout back. The effort makes my skull explode.

"Because I thought it was food poisoning!"

"How does that make a difference?"

"You didn't *ask* to come in! *I'm* asking!"

"And I'm refusing!"

Will groans. The door shakes as his body probably slumps against it. "Please?" he tries, voice softening. "I've got mouthwash."

"So do I. It came with the room."

His voice slips under the door and into my bones. "I'm begging you to let me help you, Josephine. I can't take this."

Like a baby fawn that doesn't have full control over their limbs, I pull myself onto my bed before collapsing into the fetal position. It's the only way I'm able to lessen the pain in my stomach. "What help can you be?" I ask, unsure whether it's loud enough for him to hear. "I'm better off on my own."

It's silent for a minute. Maybe Will is realizing I'm right.

There's nothing for him in this room.

"I can get you water when you ask for it," he says, finally. "Or mouthwash if you need it. I can share my crackers and ginger ale. I can find the best thing on TV while you rest your eyes, set it to the right volume. I can warm up the shower to the perfect temperature before you're ready to stand up in it for five whole minutes."

Sounds nice, I have to admit.

"And I can hold you," he goes on.

I think I hear a gulp on his side of the door. On mine, my heart stutters.

"I know your fever's about to hit. I can wrap you up in my arms. Get under the covers with you. Keep you warm. Make you feel not alone. I can let your head rest against my chest and that way, you'll feel another person's heartbeat, in sync with yours. That's what kind of help I can be. Even though I can't take away your . . . physical pain, I can make you feel good in a different way."

It's honestly a good thing my body has been waylaid by this virus. If I was healthy, and I'd just heard *that* speech, I think I might've had an on-cue orgasm.

Still, Will's words settle, then rub against my skin like a promise. All of a sudden, I'm looking at that door between us not as a barrier, but as an obstacle that needs overcoming.

"It doesn't have to mean anything," he says, like a taunt. "If you let me in, I won't turn it into anything more than exactly what you need it to be."

I can take it. Use me. Please.

Part of me knows letting him into this room while I'm at my physical weakest would mean more than either of us is saying out loud. But yesterday might have been one of the best days of my entire life, and despite my best efforts, Will Grant has become one of my favorite people.

Earlier, at the supplier's facility, I'd wanted him with me.

I want him with me now.

I just . . . *want him with me,* and I'm sick, and I'm tired. And I'm sick and fucking tired of trying to be such a perfect businesswoman with no life all the time because perfect I. Am. *Not.*

"I'm . . . really dizzy," I say hoarsely. "I don't know if I can make it to the door."

"You make it to this door, sweetheart, and I will carry you back to bed."

I take a deep breath, wincing as I shift, and slip off the edge of the mattress I just dragged myself onto. I try straightening, but that hurts too much, so I hobble to the door, almost tipping over once from dizziness. When I cross the full five feet of distance and spring the lock free, the knob immediately turns from the other side. Slowly, Will pushes the door in my direction while I back up enough for him to open it fully.

His hair is still damp from a shower, the locks thicker and darker than usual. He's changed into fresh clothes, too.

"You look better," I croak.

His face is nonnegotiable—if that's a face a person can make. "You look as good as always."

Without further ado, Will slips one of his arms along my side and the other behind the crook of my legs. Gravity deserts me as I'm hauled into his grip. I fall snugly against his chest.

It feels like the beginning and the end of something, like the turning point, the final give-up.

As he carries me back to bed, one step as sure as the next, I accept this inevitability: all it would take to make me forever beholden to Will Grant is him requesting it of me.

Carefully, he deposits me near the foot of the bed and whispers, "One minute," before grabbing a glass off the coffee bar and bending to open the minifridge beneath. He unscrews a water bottle and pours, then places the glass on the bedside table. He closes my curtains, turns off the lights, and grabs the TV remote before coming back toward the king-sized bed.

I feel the mattress compress as he lands on it somewhere near the pillows above me. "Do you want the TV on? Food channel, maybe?" I can *hear* his smirk.

"Don't make me regret this."

"How about the nature channel?"

"How about the noise machine app on my phone?"

Will reaches over to grab it from my purse, which I flung to the ground near the bed as soon as I entered the hotel room. "What's your passcode?"

"Three two eight three."

After a pause, he says, "That's Zoe's passcode."

I smile against the covers. "We made them matching back then. I guess neither of us ever changed it."

Now that the room is dark, my eyelids fall heavy. Will locates the sound machine app, and fabricated noises from the rainforest flood my ears. Owls hooting, rain falling, trees rustling.

I'm folded against myself, horizontal on my right side and facing away from Will, but I can hear his every shift as the bedspread rustles. He rises to his knees, bending over me, and sets one hand in front of my face to steady himself. Hair flops down across his ocean eyes.

"Do you want to stay down here?" he asks.

"No. I'm cold."

"Do you want to stay curled up in a little ball?" There's a note of humor carrying through his tone, even as it's mostly swallowed with concern.

"Yes. This is how it hurts the least."

Will's hands settle against my body, almost tentatively searching for the right spots to grip. Every touch is a soothing balm. It spreads from that one spot until I feel him everywhere. Eventually, he hauls me up the bed, somehow without disentangling me from my curled position.

It usually isn't blatant how much bigger he is—it usually doesn't *matter* to me, one way or the other—but I notice now, as Will cradles me against him and my head fits right into the crook where his arm meets his firm side.

He pulls the covers over both of us, letting his legs go long against the mattress, slumping down the headboard to create the perfect angle with his body for me to rest against. I'm practically perpendicular to him, but we fit together seamlessly.

"Are you comfortable?" he asks.

I nod up and down, unintentionally grazing the muscles of his upper arm. "If I had even a fraction more of my faculties right now," I mumble, barely able to form words the way they're supposed to sound, "I would be mortified by how helpless and desperate I appear."

"Everyone needs help sometimes."

My fever hits in full force. I'm desperately thankful for his warm body around mine while my skin erupts into shivers.

I doze in and out of sleep after that, no clue how many minutes or hours are passing. A slip of light is splayed against the far wall of the hotel room, and every time my eyes crack open, I watch the light shrink in direct correlation to the temperature of my body. The ache in my stomach eases as the fever peaks.

I dream of nothing. And then I wake up again to Will's snoring.

My brain is still foggy. I come into consciousness slowly, then all at once, when the sound of his snoring *wrecks* my eardrums. It's a consistent, greedy breath, in and out, in and out, and even though I don't quite have enough oxygen to make it happen, my body attempts a laugh.

I've slipped down further. My head is in his lap. His hands are fisted in my hair. When I try sitting up, his deadweight grip keeps me down.

Carefully, I extricate his fingers from my hair and sit up, testing out the state of my head. The dizziness is gone, and so is most of my tummy ache, but I'm still oscillating between freezing and sweating.

I turn to look at Will, unobserved.

We're *in bed* together.

Sure, we're fully dressed, but the *nakedness* of this situation can't be ignored. He's snoring louder than a freight train, his lips parted, head resting against the headboard, hair dry now but impossibly messy. His eyelashes are brushing against his cheekbones. Kissing them.

I feel the full momentum of my affection for him approaching me in a tidal wave. In mere moments, it's going to knock me out.

The wave arrives, and my affection crashes all around us both.

After an amount of time I don't care to analyze in which all I do is watch him sleep upright, he snore-snorts himself awake on an inhale, eyes blinking rapidly.

"J? You okay?" His voice is almost nothing.

"Does that happen often?" I whisper.

Will's focus readjusts. He licks his dry lips. "What?"

"You snoring yourself awake?"

"Oh." He swallows. "Yeah, pretty often."

I laugh softly, and Will cracks a sleepy smile. Instinctively, his hands lift up my sides, and I lean closer into the touch, my body humming even as it's recovering.

"How's your stomach?" he asks.

"Better."

"Fever?"

"Been better."

He grabs some medicine and water off the bedside table and offers it to me. I gulp it down. He puts the glass back and shifts against the pillows, his arms going back around me with the ease and familiarity of a lover.

"Do you want to . . ."

"Want to what?" I ask.

His face twists with adorable embarrassment. "Um, recline?" He taps his chest twice.

I'm still swimming in my tidal wave of affection for him, so I nod.

Without lifting his shoulders off the headboard, Will pulls me between his legs so my back is pressed against his chest, my head tucked beneath his chin. His heartbeat thudding against the back of my head starts rhythmic but eventually quickens.

After so long of wanting him to touch me—of wanting to touch him—giving in to our bodies' magnetism is the best physical thing I've felt in years. Better than lying in the sun on a pool float. Better than the wind against my face on a ride. Better than cotton sheets, better than a strong buzz. *This* feeling—it's the best one.

I sink fully against him until we create negative space. Nothing else matters beyond this room right now. Not our history, not our jobs. We're just two people who want to be as close as possible in the dark, more than three thousand miles from home.

When I don't hear his snoring restart, I assume Will isn't falling asleep either. I wonder if his brain is emitting fireworks like mine.

"Why did you cheat on your final?" I whisper.

One of his arms circles my front loosely, and his fingers play with the cuffs of my silk blouse. His knuckles scrape the insides of my wrists, soft and soft and soft.

"Because I'd already interviewed for and accepted my first job out of college by that point," he answers, voice hazy. "Failing wasn't an option. I had too much school debt *not* to graduate on time. The culture around that career path—which I was fully aware of before I'd even entered into it—is that you're supposed to do *whatever it takes* to come out on top."

I chew on my bottom lip. "You had a bad grade in the class?"

Will's head nods, rocking mine along with it. His arm moves from my shirt cuff to my opposite shoulder, and he pulls me flush. Flusher than flush. We find more space between us to shrink. A shift here. An exhale there.

"I'd had perfect grades all through high school and college. But I let that one class get away from me, and it was a required pass to graduate. I was taking an . . . elective . . . that semester, just for fun, so I could stay a full-time student." His voice slips into my ear, his breath warming me through, dissipating my body's chill. "I focused more on *that* class than the class for my major requirements, and it wasn't until it was time for the final that I realized I needed a near perfect grade to pass the class."

"What was the elective?" I ask.

A long pause. "What?"

"The elective you were enjoying that distracted you from your major," I say, even though I know he understood me. "What was it?"

After a longer pause, he admits, "Nutrition."

"Like, learning about food science?"

Another *very* long pause. "Yeah."

My smile teases out into the dark. "How did you cheat?"

Will shifts. He's obviously uncomfortable talking about this, but I appreciate that he didn't hesitate getting into it when I first asked. "The professor was known for never re-creating a test, and there was a test bank at one of the fraternities. I knew someone in it, and I paid him to give me a copy."

"I'm not asking about this because I'm judging you," I hurry to explain. "Obviously, cheating is wrong. I know that, and I know *you* know that. I just . . . want to understand more about your five worst things."

He hums. "I think I expected to come out on the other side of that test feeling the same way everyone around me felt at having the upper hand all the time. My classmates, the people at the company I interviewed with. Even some of the professors. Most of them had this sense of confidence, like every move they made was the right one, no matter how morally sideways it put them. And I just never got that feeling."

"What happened next?" I ask. "Tell me about your life."

Will clears his throat. "I was a fish out of water in my first job in investment banking. Cheating hadn't numbed me to the point that I was comfortable taking advantage of the system. If anything, I regressed into more of a stickler for the rules than I'd been before. I couldn't last that way in that industry. The way it's built to operate. I got a new job at the Carlisle Group, which was better for a while. And Zoe was in the city, so we had each other as a support system."

"I saw Zoe's a book critic for *The New York Times*," I say. "That suits her."

"It does suit her," Will agrees. "So does New York. I think she might never leave."

I hesitate to ask the natural next question: "Do you think *you'll* leave?"

Will breathes deeply, his chest expanding and collapsing beneath me. "I never used to think I would. I fucking love New York. I think I always will. But the piece of that city I belonged to warped into something I wasn't proud of."

"What do you mean?"

It's quiet for a moment aside from the rainforest noises. I find it comical we're holding a conversation between croaking frogs and rustling leaves.

"You remember Kyle, the lead consultant you were going to hire before me?"

I nod, thinking back to the sleazy Manhattanite I'd cut loose the day Will asked me to.

"He was my boss for one year. Socializing after work was a requirement to get ahead with Kyle. He'd make us all go out together—two, sometimes three nights a week. It was only a couple of months into the formation of our new team that he started cheating on his wife openly, right in front of the rest of us. At clubs, in Ubers. Work trips were the worst, but he'd even do it in the same neighborhood where he and his wife lived."

It's not exactly surprising behavior to hear told from a perspective like Will's. Though I still hate it when people live all the way down to their reputations.

"I had an especially negative reaction to Kyle's behavior because of my father," Will explains. "I couldn't believe I was in that situation again—of needing to keep a cheater's secret—especially with my actual career on the line. One day, I was out at dinner with Zoe, who read me like a book, all my misery right there, bare for her to see. She basically ordered me to find a new job, and I promised her I would."

His voice is even-keeled and smooth. There's no hesitancy. He *wants* to tell me all of this. The story is tumbling out of him.

"Kyle's was the other marriage you ended?" I ask gently.

"Yes," Will answers, voice low. "At a holiday party in mid-December, a few days before I was supposed to leave the company.

I wanted to end my time there on good terms, but Kyle had other ideas."

"Of course Kyle had other ideas," I mumble, and Will laughs.

I am addicted to making him laugh.

"As usual, Kyle'd had too much to drink by the time the party was nearing its end. He came after me when I tried to leave and started shouting accusations about how I had no loyalty. His wife followed us out to the street. She was standing behind him, looking bewildered, and I couldn't stop thinking of my mom, of how much I regretted all those months I spent *not telling her the truth*. I snapped," Will says, his voice going gruff and nearly pained. "I pointed to her and said, *Talk to your wife about loyalty, she could use some from you.* It was clear from the expression on her face she knew exactly what I was talking about." After a few seconds of quiet, Will adds, "I've never hated myself more, for doing that to her. The way I did it."

I try to put myself in the wife's shoes. In Will's. It would have been embarrassing. But maybe she'd needed someone to just come *out with it* to give herself the courage to walk away.

"She left him?" I ask.

"They were divorced two months later."

More silence.

"Kyle is the one who destroyed that marriage, Will. Not you. You know that, right?"

"Maybe," Will agrees, voice tortured. "I still wish I hadn't hurt her."

"Because even though you keep finding yourself in lose-lose situations, you are a good man, at your core, who knows right from wrong."

"Yeah, well, so are you," he replies, in a tone that suggests we're trading insults instead of compliments. "You're not just good. You're . . . very good."

I snort, and Will exhales a breathy laugh.

"I'm serious, Josie. I think you might be the most hardworking person I've ever met. You also care more about employee happiness than raising venture capital. You care more about B Corp Certification than your profit margins. And somehow, you've managed to get Derrick Lovell to buy in. Do you even know how inspiring a person has to be to have achieved *all that*?"

His praise is awakening a long-dormant part of me that hungers for this kind of approval.

"And you're emotional, too," Will goes on. "Not just some corporate robot. You feel remorse, and guilt, and you feel them deeply. You're scared Camila might be leaving Revenant, and worried what it will mean for your friendship. You have empathy for the girl who sold you that overpriced vacuum. Everybody, including me, knows how good of a person you are."

"Thank you," I say, voice shaking.

His hold on me loosens, but only so he can push himself upright again and pull me back against him. I try and fail not to overthink our positioning. If my abdomen wasn't sore from retching, I think every press of him against me would bolt straight to my core.

"You never answered my question," I say.

"What question?"

"Do you think you'll leave New York?"

He's silent for eight seconds. I count them.

"I really like Austin."

Dangerous, but I smile anyway, playing with a strand of hair hanging by my shoulder.

"You're so fucking gorgeous when you smile like that."

My head shoots up, and that's when I notice our reflection in the blank TV screen. A slip of moonlight peeking through the window is illuminating us just right.

I look like a person who belongs to him, curled up between his legs, with his head above mine and his arms hooked around me underneath the supple bedspread. His lips hover by my ear, and I can see them, and I can *feel* them, too. The careful puffs of his breath warming the side of my face.

But his eyes are on mine in our reflection. His expression is hungry, like the sight of us woven together this way is an image Will is interested in expanding upon.

"Sorry," he says immediately, voice breaking. "I'm sorry. I promised you this didn't have to mean anything. And it won't."

"Will. It would be impossible for this night not to mean *everything*."

"To me, or to you?" he asks tenderly.

"To both of us." I sigh, conflicted. "Maybe it's time for me to give you *my* five worst things."

He smirks. I watch him on the screen as he says, "If you want."

I consider, then begin. "Number one. I'm vain about my appearance. I'm grumpy if my roots are showing, and insecure if someone meets me for the first time and I'm not wearing makeup. If I'm not put together."

"As long as you're doing it for yourself and no one else," he says.

I nod, even though I'm not sure how true that is.

"Two. I come from a well-off family."

After a beat, Will laughs lowly. "The horror."

"I just mean I'm not self-made or anything. I started Revenant mostly with my own savings, which came from my father, and only a little bit from the boutique where I steamed everything."

When I look at our reflection, he's still smiling at me. "Okay. Don't forget I already knew this about you, Josephine."

"Number three, I'm a workaholic. I have terrible work-life balance. I'm obsessive about my company. It isn't conducive to a relationship."

"As you've explained previously," Will says.

"I thought you might need reminding, considering my job is one of the reasons—possibly the main reason—my last relationship ended. Which brings me to the aptly titled number four. It's been that many years since I've had sex. Since I've even *wanted* to have sex."

I say it quick and dirty, blushing blushing *blushing,* and then snap my lips together.

His smile vanishes, and even though I'm looking at a murky reflection of him, something flickers in his eyes.

"Four years," he repeats, tone husky, hoarse.

"Four years."

It must be the fever that got me to admit that.

"And now?" he asks.

"Things are different now."

I very quickly realize I miscalculated, adding this tidbit to my list of five worst things.

I thought it would stall Will. I thought my lack of sexual activity, sexual drive, sexual exploration might freak him out the same way it freaked *me* out. But given the storm on his face, I think it succeeded only in turning him on.

His arms retract from my body, and he shifts away from me.

"Fuck, Josie," he all but growls. "Fuck. Did you seriously just tell me I'm the first person you've felt sexual about in four years?"

"Um, sorry, I didn't think that one through."

Silence. A deep breath.

"Just remind me why I'm here," he says, looking at the ceiling. "The real reason, not the one in my head right now."

I go for lighthearted, breezy. "What? You barging into my hotel room to keep me company because of the guilt you feel for forcing me to leave the hotel in the first place?"

Will laughs, though it still sounds strained. "I actually feel no guilt whatsoever for forcing you to leave the hotel yesterday. It was a near-perfect day. And more likely, we caught this virus in one of the *four* airports we traveled through the day before, not downtown Arequipa."

"Believe what you want."

"I will."

"We should get some sleep."

"We should."

He slides to one side of the bed, and I crawl to the other. Neither of us suggests Will return to his own room. Under the covers, we take painstaking care not to touch, but his presence soothes me, distracts me from my fever.

I fall back asleep to a harmony of rainforest noises and snoring. And I wake up in the middle of the bed, cradled in his arms.

CHAPTER TWENTY-SIX

Despite Will's protests that he can handle the walk-through alone and I should stay in bed, I make it to the second supplier visit the next morning.

Barely.

I *barely* make it, and I'm in such a questionable state of physical wellness—my skin gray, my cognitive skill diminished—the owner *must* be questioning his choice to do business with Revenant the second we drive away.

"He looked at you like you were a ghost," Will notes wryly on our way back to the airport. His gaze turns back in my direction from where he was gazing out the window at El Misti. "You *look* like a ghost."

I glare at him. "Did you mean that to sound nicer than the way it came out?"

He laughs, the sound warm and buttery off his tongue. One day out from the virus, and he's as good as new. "I told you to stay in bed."

"And I told *you* I'm a workaholic."

"You didn't trust me to report back to you with all the right details."

"That's not it," I argue. "It's already too much that you're here in Peru with me. That you help me with my ideas and my plans without question. I can't ask you to do my work for me. I have to show up myself."

In the rearview mirror, I catch the eyes of our driver, Santiago. He's been with us the whole time and had to witness me retching on the side of the road yesterday. Now he lifts an eyebrow at me, silently asking what's going on between the two passengers in his backseat.

"For the record, I question a lot of your ideas," Will says. "But then I research them, and mostly come to the conclusion that you're right."

"Is that how you felt about B Corp?"

"No. I always thought that was a good idea. But this?" Will gestures out the window. "Visiting every new supplier even though half of them are B Corps themselves? When your VP of supply chain told me you planned to do this, I didn't see the point at first. Until I got to know you a little better."

"And?" I prompt.

He studies me. "That first day, when you vanished, I asked Derrick what your priorities were. You know what he said?"

"A good dry shampoo and constant natural lighting?"

"He said you weren't in it for the money, which"—Will dips his chin at me—"rich family, so, makes sense. Or the fame, which"— his dimple pops out—"tracks, too, given everything. I asked him what you were in it for, in that case, and he said, *I'm pretty sure she just wants to feel productive.*"

I laugh softly at that, imagining exactly the way Derrick Lovell would have said it. Like a concept couldn't be more foreign to him.

"Is it wrong to want to feel that way?" I ask. My voice comes out an octave higher than I mean it to, because it's a question with an answer I'd truly like to know.

Will looks at me for a long time. Long enough that the lines around his mouth soften, and the color of his irises changes back and forth from gray to blue in the snatches of sunlight the car windows catch.

"I think the answer to that question is: What would it do to you, if it all stopped?"

I ponder my response all the way to Barcelona.

What would it do to me if I didn't have Revenant?

What would it do to me if Camila left me behind?

What would it do to me if I failed the B Corp review?

I ponder it as night falls and we check our baggage, as we board our plane back to Lima. Then Lima to Madrid. Madrid to Barcelona. I ponder it for eighteen miserable hours of travel, while an entire day of my existence slips by me. A day that will only ever be acknowledged by Will Grant, and not by a single other soul in memory. But it kind of feels perfect that way, him next to me on the plane as I'm swallowed by this sudden existential feeling I don't know how to put into words just yet.

He lets me sit in it as long as I need to.

Finally, when we reach our hotel, both of us dead-eyed and desperate for sleep, Will walks me to my door and I admit to him, "I think if this all stopped, I would fall apart."

He smiles weakly at me, no explanation needed to pick back up on the conversation we ended with an ellipsis six thousand miles back. Will puts one hand on the door behind me, and I settle against it as his height and weight lean in my direction. My body feels so far past the point of tiredness that I'm a walking live wire, strung out by his nearness.

"What does the word *revenant* mean?" he asks.

Chills run through me from head to toe as I remember. That word coming to me *so clearly* when I was deciding what to name the brand for my very first designs. *Revenant.* At the time it had been a cheeky secret, just for me. Reclaiming social media under a different banner.

"It means rebirth, or something that has returned from a long absence," I say.

He nods. "You've done that once already. My guess is *you're* a revenant, Josephine." His voice is low and emotional. "And if you fall apart again, you'll put yourself back together *again.* Because you're strong. The only difference is from now on, I'll be there, if you want me to, to hold your broken pieces."

That same tidal wave of affection crests inside me.

"Did me telling you my five worst things do the job as intended?" I ask.

"No," Will says, smile stretching. "What about for you, when I told you mine?"

I shake my head. Will and I exchanging our deepest insecurities, our biggest faults, only succeeded in making us understand and want each other more.

"I'm tired," I say. Physically, yes, but just—everything. I'm tired of fighting my feelings. Tired of outworking myself.

Tired of being alone.

"Me, too," Will murmurs, his eyes flicking up and down my person. "Get some sleep. We'll carry on tomorrow."

CHAPTER TWENTY-SEVEN

Robbie: Happy Birthday JoJo!

Camila: HAPPY BIRTHDAY MY SPARKLING LITTLE SUN BOMB I HOPE YOU HAVE THE BEST DAY EVER IN BARCELONA! By the way I may have bribed Inez from IT to lock you out of your email for 24 hours sorry not sorry!

Mom: Happy birthday darling, I've sent you several articles via email on Barcelona crime

Dad: Happy birthday JoJo!

Biker Gang:

Gio: Happy birthday J! Hope you get a bike ride in today <3
Leonie: omg josie happy bday lovebug

True to her word, Camila managed to bar me from my own email account. I'm fixing the Outlook app with a stern look, willing it to let me through, when a knock sounds at my hotel room door.

"Happy birthday!" Will says as soon as I pull it open.

"Camila locked me out of my work email," I complain.

His bright smile melts into a diluted smirk. "Camila's a genius."

"That was never under review, but now her *loyalties* certainly are."

"Josephine," he scolds. "Today is a Saturday."

"Retail's busiest day of the week!" I reason.

Will grabs my phone from my flailing hand and stuffs it into the front pocket of his jeans. He's back in street attire today, though without his baseball cap, which I kind of miss.

"What do you want to do today?" he asks.

I grin. "How pissed would you be if I said a hotel gym workout followed by a room service feast while we watch my CEO classes online?"

He gives me a put-upon look, still not breaching the doorway to my room. "I'd say it's your birthday, and let's do it."

I consider him, crossing my arms over my pajama-clad chest. Part of me wants to see if he'd go through with it. Waste an entire Saturday in this beautiful city in a hotel room with me.

"You'd get stir-crazy."

"Not necessarily." Will shakes his head, very slow. "We could absolutely keep ourselves occupied in this hotel room. All day."

My body flushes, all the exposed parts of my skin heating at his implication. His darkening Blue Ridge Mountain eyes fix on my body, which is covered by only a pair of tiny silk shorts and a thin tank top. He presses his lips together, hands resting on each of his hips as he forces his eyes up to mine.

I don't—fully—

I'm not *exactly* sure how it happens—

There's a time slip, if I had to guess—

Because one minute, Will is looking at me with a dare in his eyes, and the next, I wind up airborne, my legs wrapped around his waist as his arms support my weight, and we're kissing against the doorframe of my room.

Finally, finally, finally.

They aren't frantic, our first kisses. Our mouths have no trouble connecting, and Will doesn't struggle to hold me aloft. He pins me easily, just the way he wants me, his toe wedged between the door and the frame to keep us from being locked out. I loop my hands into his plush hair and pull his face toward mine.

Lightly, Will groans into my mouth as his lips pinch and pull and tug harshly against mine. I feel the vibration of that sound travel *down* into my stomach, then go off there like a bomb. His lips tease, taste, slow and then slower *and then slower,* like he's winding himself down, even as his hips push forward into mine, creating our hinge point.

This is where our bodies join, the hinge point informs me. *Move the rest of your body all you want, just stay connected here.* Even as his teeth pinch my lips but don't *bite* them, even as his groans go softer, smaller, like he's trying to stop making audible noises of pleasure but can't quite manage it, I focus on the place we aren't supposed to separate just as Will inches back.

"Wait," he says, breath labored. "Josephine. Sweetheart. Are you absolutely certain you want this?"

"It's my birthday," I reply, voice wobbling. "Please."

Something dark flashes in his eyes, and his lips come back to mine. Tender and gentle, methodical, unhurried.

This is him holding back, I realize. He's giving me time to re-adjust to the way it's supposed to feel with a partner.

But I've *never* felt like this with a partner, and I don't know how to process that. I've never felt so in tune, so physically matched to someone. His thumbnail scrapes lightly across the

back side of my thigh, and what that really means is he just decided it's where I'll get a tattoo that reads *Will Grant was here.* His
nose brushes back and forth against mine while we take a minute
to catch our breath, hips rocking, and what that really means is
*Here's your permission to breathe, Josephine. From now on, it's mine
to give, mine to take back.*

He takes it back, closing the gap between our mouths once more
while my back arches and our stomachs inhale and exhale against
each other.

The *ding* of the elevator somewhere around a hallway corner is
what finally makes him carry me inside. My ass lands on the desk
and the door latches closed. His hands start roving, up and down
my sides, into my hair, thumbs on my cheeks, my temples. His lips
by my ear, teeth tugging on my earlobe.

Will's left hand pushes just so on my shoulder until my upper
half is horizontally spread across the desk. His body bends over
mine like a magnet. He's standing between my legs, which are
limply spread to fit him, and his hair falls over his eyes as he gazes
down at me with those *blue eyes brown hair, brown hair blue eyes,* and
I am literally about to die.

I'm going to perish.

I'm two seconds from passing away.

"You're so hot," I blurt.

Will laughs hoarsely. He leans on one arm, causing his triceps
to bulge. With his other hand, he cups the side of my face and
traces my lower lip with his thumb, pinching at it, mesmerized by
it. "*You're* so hot. Fucking *look* at you, J. Swollen lips, bright red. I
think it's prettier than any lipstick you've ever worn."

He kisses me again, still laughing softly, deep in his throat. His
hands slide over my stomach, across the bare skin where my pajama
top rode up. "Can I take all your clothes off and touch wherever I
want on your body?"

I'm not even joking about it this time.

I'm not being facetious.

I literally come. And it's coupled with a gasp that sort of very obviously *lets him know what just happened and I am truly going to DIE*—

"Did you just . . ." His hand on my stomach settles there, more heavily, as he watches me try to hold still all the way through it. I blush and say nothing, go rigid as a statue.

When I won't meet his eyes, he gently grabs my chin until our gazes finally lock. "You are the end of everything for me," he says, his voice drawn out and strung up and pummeled and ruinous. "How many times do you think I can get you to do that?"

"But the Spanish architecture!" I gasp.

"Funny thing about buildings." His head drops to the space between my breasts. "They don't go anywhere."

"I want to," I say on a sigh, my eyes fluttering closed as he kisses just above the lacy border of my top.

"Me, too, J. It's actually *all* I want—"

"I want to look at buildings with you."

Will pauses. "I thought you wanted a hotel workout," he mumbles against my skin.

"Hang on." Will's body lifts off mine as he pushes against his palms, and our eyes catch. "I like this," I say. "I want this. But my body isn't used to it. Not just sex, but, like, *kissing*. And being turned on. My body isn't used to being *this* turned on."

"I know. I *love* it," he emphasizes.

"I need . . ."

His lips settle against my forehead. "Tell me exactly what you need, Josie."

I take a deep breath in, filling my lungs with his heady scent. "I need to go look at buildings with you. To give myself time to . . . calm down. It isn't that I don't want this. But I want to be *good* at it when we do it."

"You want to be good?"

"Yes."

"Well, I don't need you to *be* anything—"

"Please, Will. I want to be in it with you."

He tucks his head and breathes. Breathes some more.

"Okay," he whispers after a few seconds. There's nothing resentful in his tone. Just a calmness that almost feels anticipatory. "Let's go look at some buildings."

He takes a step back from the desk, adjusting himself in his pants. I sit up, hands pulling my top down to meet the waistband of my shorts. "I need ten minutes to get ready," I say, finding my footing against the carpeted floor.

Will nods, his eyes a sky-bright color. The evidence of my hands in his hair is blatant, but it works on him.

"I'll wait in the lobby."

He turns to go, but something makes me say, "Wait."

Will twists back, his gaze patient.

"I'm not using you. This isn't just about wanting to have sex."

Will's expression warms. He smiles easily, both of his dimples flashing, his kiss-bruised lips pulled up. "What's it about, in that case?"

It's hard to put into words, but I try. "Maybe I've been thinking about this all wrong. About dating distracting me from work or having a partner causing me to be less productive. Aren't people stronger together? Better versions of themselves around another person? I mean, Camila is a hard worker, and she's productive, and she's also in love," I say. "Not that I'm in love with you!" I jump to add. "And not that I'm assuming you'd ever want to actually be my, like, official *partner,* I'm just explaining why I—"

Will crosses back to me, his lips taking mine again in another long, slow kiss.

"For the record," he grunts, landing two small kisses on my nose.

"I would very much want to be your official partner. The truth is I've been disguising the way I feel about you as best as I can. But I'll stop that now. If you want."

His words launch an avalanche. They create waves. They crack earth.

I cling to him, rubbing my nose against his soft shirt. "I want."

Will tips my chin up and kisses me. Softly, softly. I feel positively lost in him, happier and more carefree than I've felt in a long time. "I am happiest," he says, "when I'm giving you what you want."

I change into jean shorts and a T-shirt, braid my hair, splash cold water on my face. When I get downstairs to the hotel lobby, I spot Will talking to the concierge.

He looks down at my feet when he notices me. "Closed-toe shoes. Perfect."

"For?"

"Cycling." Will grins and nods to the concierge. "I rented us some bikes."

I grin back, feeling giddy.

Outside, we climb onto two cornflower-blue cruisers with wide handlebars and kickstands, our reusable water bottles filled, helmets firmly secured. Our hotel is on the outskirts of the city, close to the supplier we'll be visiting in two days. We find the bike lane on a busy street and ride it into the heart of downtown.

The first place we stop is a small café with a faded red awning and a Tripadvisor sign in the window. Will locks up our bikes and pays for my drink—sadly not an ICOML, which wasn't on the menu, but instead (on his recommendation) a café con leche that's honestly delicious.

While we sip our beverages at an outdoor table, the sun still shy, the air scented with fried dough, his hands find mine. Will's fingers lightly graze back and forth across my knuckles.

It's such an intimate gesture. Possibly the most intimate thing we've done so far. My breath tightens.

"You said your body isn't used to it," Will murmurs, a quick smile flitting across his mouth. "I'm going to remind you, all day long."

My body warms. I feel combustible. "How used to it are *you*?"

"Are you asking for my body count?" He hitches a brow.

I shrug. "You don't have to get specific, but—"

"I dated thoroughly, in Manhattan," Will says.

"Thoroughly," I repeat.

His thumbs continue their pattern across my knuckles. "Yeah. But it's been a while. Five months, maybe. And not that I—" He flushes. Clears his throat. But his tiny caresses never stop. "Not that I'm expecting anything tonight. But in case you were concerned, I've been tested since the last person I've been with."

"Same," I reply, blushing now, too, even though I'm relieved we're having this entirely necessary conversation. "But Will, I just realized. I'm not on birth control anymore."

His eyes darken. "I can buy condoms."

"You didn't bring any?"

He shakes his head. "I thought I knew where you stood."

As if to disprove both our assumptions, I lace our fingers together.

"Did you ever have a girlfriend? Besides the one who dumped you in college for not drinking enough?"

Will's lips curve up. "No. My next-longest relationship lasted about six months, I think."

"Why?"

He cocks his head. "Why what?"

"Why don't you think you ever found another long-term girlfriend?" I clarify. "Considering how thoroughly you dated?"

Will glances behind us at nothing. He palms at his neck, fidgety. "I think it was probably because I was attracting the wrong kind of woman? I mean, they were nice girls. Just not right for me."

"You were attracting New York tens who wanted a FiDi boyfriend who works out at a fancy gym like Equinox and love-bombs his girlfriend with designer presents."

Will's lips part and his eyes dance. "Uncanny."

"I love being right."

"CEOs usually do."

"Did you have an Equinox membership?"

"Everybody was doing it," he says.

"You just wanted to fit in," I say. "Why didn't it work out with the New York tens?"

He shrugs, lifting his coffee back to his lips with his free hand. "Couldn't envision myself introducing them to my mother. To Doug. To Zoe."

My stomach twists. If I hadn't already met his family, would Will have been able to envision introducing *me*?

"What was it you were looking for?" I ask.

Will sips on his drink while I stare him down. "Sorry?"

"If that variety of woman was what you *had* but not what you *wanted,* what was it you *wanted* but didn't *have*?"

He sets down his cup and recites his criteria, deadpan. "Blond, five-nine, three freckles on her left jawline. Quick as a whip, strong interior, soft edges. Chews on her bottom lip when she's lost in thought. Hums Lizzy McAlpine under her breath when she thinks no one is listening."

"Will—"

"So beautiful she'd break the New York scale."

"Oh my God, you did not—"

"Driven, successful, friendly, brilliant—"

"Will!" I shriek softly.

"Like I said, Josie." He picks his cup back up. "All day long."

I smile and blush toward my café con leche, equal parts embarrassed and thrilled.

We tool around the city after that, quiet, content with existing near each other. Will stops at a convenience store and emerges with a nervous wink, but we don't discuss it any further.

Over brunch at a spot not too far from our coffee pit stop (Will got the recommendations from a New York friend, who he may or may not have thoroughly dated), I manage to keep him focused on work through nearly the whole meal. We talk through the six-week timeline between now and Revenant's scheduled meeting with a B Corp representative at the end of August, discussing everything that needs to be done after this trip.

"What will you do after you pass?" he asks as we're walking out of the restaurant, back toward our bikes.

"What do you mean?" I ask.

Will pulls on my waist when I start heading in the wrong direction. "I mean, after you finish your CEO classes, and after you pass the B Corp Assessment review, and after you open Revenant's first brick-and-mortar store—then what?"

I set my sunglasses across the bridge of my nose. "Then Revenant will be a B Corp Certified omnichannel retail company with a CEO who's got a master's degree."

He shoots me a look. "Cute. Not what I was getting at."

"Care to elaborate?"

Will bends down to unlock the bike lock binding our front wheels together. "What's the plan after all that?"

It's an innocent question, but for some reason, my stomach bottoms out when I realize: "There isn't one."

He stands, wrapping the bike lock in a tight loop around his wrist. "I think I already know the answer, but is that unusual for you?"

I nod, in a trance. "I've spent the last seven years growing Revenant based on a very clear path for what came next. There were *steps,*" I say. "Work I couldn't get out from under. One thing and then another thing and the next thing and the next, snowballing into . . ."

I drift off, refocusing on Will. He's watching me with careful attention, the barest sign of a smile behind his eyes. "Into a B Corp Certified omnichannel retail company with a CEO who's got a master's degree," he repeats.

I grab the handlebars of my bike. "And maybe a little more free time?"

"For a boyfriend," Will prompts.

"Why, are you interested in dating me thoroughly?"

"So fucking thoroughly, you don't know the half of it." His eyes float to my mouth, his tongue dipping out to trace his bottom lip. "I want you to be my girlfriend more than I have ever wanted any earthly thing."

I want him the same way. I want him desperately, selfishly.

Because I also want the *me* I am when I'm with him.

The *me* who leaves the hotel room to explore.

The *me* who craves human touch.

The *me* who can't stop laughing, whose mind is in constant savasana.

Will kisses me again—in broad daylight, two hunks of metal separating our lower halves. He braces one hand on top of the bike rack and uses his other to cup the back of my neck. He draws me in, tasting like sunlight. My heart beats fast. I settle my hands on his shoulders, tilting my head so I can kiss him back.

Time disintegrates.

It feels like fate.

Like *fate* made his bike hit my car. Like *fate* gave us jobs that would pull us into each other's orbit again ten years later.

"Is your body getting used to it yet?" he asks, breath heavy when he pulls away.

"No." I take a step back from him, eyes blinking. "My body is reacting more uncontrollably every time."

"Well." He shrugs, halfway grinning. "Makes two of us."

CHAPTER TWENTY-EIGHT

W e piddle around la Sagrada Família, the Cathedral of
Barcelona, and another basilica whose name I instantly
forget before winding up at Parc Güell, surrounded by mosaic-tiled
walls and stunning views of the city below. It's the kind of tourist
attraction that truly warrants a visit—*all* of Barcelona has been that
way, in fact—and with the sun bouncing in fragments across the
thousands of colored slabs around us, ten different languages being
spoken in the vicinity, and a tantalizing smell wafting in our direction from somewhere beyond the park gates, I can't think of a single
other way I'd rather spend my twenty-eighth birthday.

"You were right," I say to Will softly.

"Hmm?" He pushes his sweat-dampened hair off his forehead
and pulls an elbow up onto the park bench behind us.

"I've missed out on a lot, holing up in my hotel rooms all this
time."

He passes over the water bottle. "You had a lot to juggle."

"In my defense, I did once *try* to get out and about in New York City."

Will's head turns in my direction. "Yeah?"

"During a VC pitch visit. The firm invited me out for dinner and drinks."

Will groans, laughing. "Oh no. VC guys are mostly douchebags."

"I wanted their money, so I agreed. But, like, the vibe of that entire night pretty much cemented my hatred for New York."

His body freezes. When Will speaks, his tone comes out like a scolding. "I'm sorry. Did you just say *you hate New York*?"

"I know you've lived there for a while—"

"Nearly ten years." He turns his upper body to face me, a look of desperation etched into his features. "Four years in college, six years after. I've lived there for longer than a while."

"Right, so I know you *like* it—"

"*Like* it?" Will scoffs. "New York is *in* me."

I bristle. I wasn't expecting this reaction since he keeps flirting with the idea of leaving.

"Well, it's not in *me*," I say. "It's crowded and smelly and loud and expensive and everyone's either a VC douchebag or an art bro with a superiority complex."

"That is wholly unfair."

"I just don't like it!" I say. "I've never liked it, not a single time I've gone for work."

Will continues to look at me, a dumbfounded expression on his face. He stands up and starts pacing. Back and forth, right in front of me. I watch him with a half-concerned, half-amused expression.

"No," he says eventually, more to himself than to me.

"What?"

"No." Will kneels, literally *kneels* down before me and says, "One day, I'm going to change your mind."

"About New York?"

"Yes." He looks so earnest I can't help but grin. "This isn't funny, Josephine. I've never been more serious. I'm not asking you to live there. I'm asking you to be excited about the prospect of visiting that city. If I'm there, and you're visiting me, or if I'm not, and we're going on a trip together. I need that to be something you could enjoy."

I laugh, and he cracks a dimpled smile. "New York means that much to you?"

Will nods. Looking so fucking sincere, I want it to be mine. My sincere, mine only. After everything Will has done for me, I will do this for him. I will learn to love New York for him.

After all—just because I don't understand something (yet) doesn't mean I can't respect its importance.

I kiss him. Slipping off the bench, I straddle his propped knee and grab his head and tilt it up and kiss him hard. Our lips taste like salt and sweat, like a full day of looking at buildings. Today is my birthday, and he's so cute I don't know how to handle how much of a crush I have on this gorgeous, supportive, life-changing man.

We've got high school diplomas from the same school, shared mistakes, too, and that's the least important out of all of it. Here, now, between high school and this moment, Will spent ten years in New York growing into himself, learning what kind of person he wanted to be while I was in Texas doing the same thing. And now we're both in Barcelona making out in broad daylight for the second time today because we grew and learned enough on our own to find and maybe even deserve each other.

I want to believe I *get* this. I want to believe I deserve to have a person to call mine. To believe I've earned it, believe I've worked hard enough that I can slow down and savor it.

Today only, I refuse to let a single doubt creep in.

⇜ ✳ ⇝

We eat tapas for dinner, more aspiring than vegetarian, and split a bottle of wine we cork after one glass and take with us, so we aren't too tipsy to cycle back to the hotel. On the ride home, the evening air slips over my skin, fingers its way through my braids. I smell the ocean, taste it, hear it hovering against the edge of the city. Maybe tomorrow we can go to the beach.

"How was your day?" the concierge asks while he collects our bikes and gear.

"It was perfect," I respond, smiling at Will.

In the elevator, we're surrounded by strangers, but Will and I press toward the back of the cab. He looks at me with hot, magnetic eyes until we reach our floor.

We walk around the corner to our set of doors.

"How is your body feeling?" he murmurs, his fingers dancing over mine.

"Like a shower," I say. I was hot before dinner, but now, after the windy bike ride under a setting sun, I'm almost shivering.

His fingers drop away from mine when we reach his door.

I'm operating on pure instinct. With a lightning reflex, I reach out and grab his hand, pulling him farther along to my door.

"Water—conservation," I say thickly.

As I fumble with my key card, practically trembling in anticipation, Will comes up behind me, pressing his lips to the back of my neck.

"I have wanted you for weeks," he mumbles. "Years. A decade."

Together, we stumble through the door.

In the entryway across from the bathroom, I push Will against the wall and kiss him soundly. He palms at my hips, tilting my lower body inward so my stomach is pressed against his, my shoulders arched back. He tastes like wine now, like Barcelona, the city on the tip of his tongue. Will lets me taste it again through him.

"I wanted you weeks ago, too," I gasp. His mouth skates down past my jawline, across my collarbone. "You reminded me what it was like."

"To want?" he mumbles against my skin.

"To feel greedy for something I shouldn't have."

Abruptly, Will lifts me off him. He walks me to the opposite side of the entryway, planting a gentle fist against my stomach until my back molds into the wall. His pupils are dilated so much I can hardly see the ocean in his eyes now.

"You *should* have me. You *do* have me. I think," Will says, pinching my bottom lip between his fingertips, "from now on, forevermore, you will probably always have me."

I smack his hand away from my lips and kiss him again, pushing us back against the other wall. Will groans into my mouth, his hands dropping to massage my butt. I push our hips together—our hinge point—feeling the fullness of his erection against my core.

"Will," I say. "I had sex with three guys in college. I don't even remember if I liked it. Even with my ex-boyfriend, it didn't feel like this. I don't know . . ." My voice stutters as his eyes lock on mine. "I don't know how to be good at this for you."

His hands move from my ass to my hip bones, and he pushes me back against the other wall. One hand pressing below my throat, his other hand tracing up my thigh. "I will *show* you how to be good for me. And J?"

"Hmm?"

His mouth drops to my ear. "I'm glad you brought the other men you've been with into this room. We're going to show them how little they ever did for you."

"How little . . ."

He kisses me sharply. My brain fogs. "Your sex either wasn't good, or it wasn't good enough to *remember*?" His voice is incredulous.

"It was years ago," I murmur.

His hands pull out the elastics at the ends of my braids.

"Sweetheart." Gently, Will tugs my head up to the perfect angle so all I can see is him. Jumbled brown locks, bright blue-gray eyes, quarter-inch lashes, damp lips. "On my honor, you will die remembering this night."

We kiss and touch each other until I'm so turned on, a low moan parks itself in the back of my throat. It doesn't leave, doesn't ebb. Will's hands find mine. He tugs me the few steps into the bathroom and flicks on the low light. I find our bodies in the mirror.

Disheveled would be a nice way to put it.

Will steps up to my back and sits his chin on my shoulder, holding my eyes in the reflection. The same way he did in the television screen in Peru two nights ago.

"Do you want to take your clothes off?" he asks, voice hoarse.

I nod.

"Go ahead."

Slowly, I unzip my jean shorts, peel them down my legs until they drop. Then my T-shirt. Will steps back as I yank it over my shoulders and toss it into a corner. Underneath I'm wearing a lacy periwinkle bra and a plain black thong.

"Can I help you?" he whispers.

I nod again.

His gaze concentrates as he works open the clasp at the back of my bra. It pops apart, and Will traces a single index finger underneath the straps, lifting them off my shoulders one at a time. The bra falls on top of my shorts at my feet. Will's eyes lift back to the mirror. First to my eyes, and then down to my chest.

"You're perfect." His head drops to kiss my shoulder. Then his lips trail down my back, and he kneels. "Perfect for me."

Will's hands squeeze my ass softly, just before he hooks his fingers into my underwear and pulls them down past my hips.

"Do you remember when we were reunited, and I was already on my knees for you?"

"Will." I can barely manage his name.

"Turn around."

I do as he says. Will's fingers trail up my calf as he kisses each of my knees. His lips mark a path up my thighs, then hover by my naked core. Not for long, though. Like, *really* not for long. I start gasping again, his telltale sign that he's undone me, and his lips jump to my stomach as he laughs and mumbles, "I hope neither of us ever gets used to that."

"I'm sorry," I say, my insides still fluttering. My hands clutch at his shoulders.

"Take that back," he mumbles into my skin.

"It's embarrassing," I manage. "That never happened with the others."

"It's on the very top," he says, kissing my belly button, "of the list of the best things about you." Slowly, Will stands, his hands moving from my waist to thumb at my breasts. "Go start the shower."

In a daze, I pull open the glass door and turn the handle. Through the slowly fogging window, I watch as Will rids himself of his clothes. Then as he grabs a foil package from his pants pocket, rips it open, slides the condom on. He locks eyes with me and walks toward the shower door, stepping through, closing it behind him.

Heavy, wet air hangs between us, blurring the lines of his body. I want to look down, to see all of him, but I can't take my eyes off Will's as he catches my waist and walks us both underneath the warm spray.

For a minute we just stand there, almost hugging—if a hug included the slide of someone's naked body against yours in a way that feels addictive. We listen to the sound of each other's breathing even out.

Will's lips trace the rim of my ear. "Is your body ready now?"

Already, I'm geared up again. I try to say yes but don't quite manage it. Instead, a series of noises that absolutely do not form a grammatically correct English sentence leave my mouth.

I've never had shower sex before, though I've listened with tears of laughter in my eyes as Cami talked me through the logistical nightmare of her and David trying it in a space that was admittedly much smaller than this one. But Will doesn't look concerned with logistics as his fingers play between my legs, as my body wilts against him.

"Waiting on a confirmation," he says.

I manage a shaky "Yes."

His hands move to my hips. Deftly, he hauls me off the ground and pushes my back against the tile. On instinct, both of my hands reach up to wrap around the showerhead.

I don't know how he manages it—if I was more lucid, maybe I would have paid better attention—but *somehow*, he enters my body in a single, perfect movement without ever readjusting his hold on my ass.

"*ThankyouEquinox,*" I say on a garbled exhale.

Will laughs, his eyes twinkling at me. He presses closer, officially hinging my body to his. "Tell me, Josie. Do you think you'll forget this?"

I shake my head, unable to form words at the feel of him inside me.

He kisses me languorously, the rest of his body frozen still. "This is only going to work the way I want it to," he says, nose dropping between my breasts, "if we go very slow."

"Mkay," I sigh out.

"You be still."

"Not going anywhere," I joke with a smile.

His lips tilt up, and at the same time, he starts to move his hips. Slowly.

Slowly.

Slowly.

Something about the angle Will is employing is working against my body so thoroughly I see stars. My back arches when he groans and bites softly at my shoulder. The space between our bodies is negatively charged, like electricity about to give off a static *crack*. I'm lightheaded.

"How does it feel for you?" he asks, voice muffled against my skin.

Transcendent.

Impossible.

"It feels good," I say. Though the way I say it—breathy and broken and vulnerable—tells him what I mean but can't articulate. That it feels a lot better than *good*.

"You are so good," he says, picking up his pace by only a fraction. It's a tempo designed to drive me crazy. "The *best*. Because it's you, and your body might have been *made* for me. Look how perfect we fit, Josephine. Look what our bodies can do."

"I know," I say. "This is insane."

Our foreheads rock against each other. "So good," he says again. "You are so—so—"

I break apart around him. Not for the first time since we started this, not for the last time before we finish it. My hands drop from the showerhead to his neck. Will's movements never cease, drawing it all out.

"Good," he finishes.

CHAPTER TWENTY-NINE

I f you put me under threat, I couldn't tell you a single other thing about our time in Barcelona.

It's lost on me.

I think the visit at the Spanish supplier goes well.

In Bangalore, all I'm able to commit to memory is the shape of Will's dimples when I ask if he wants to cancel his hotel room. The way our wrinkled sheets look against the morning light. The particular graininess of his voice when he whispers, against my ear and chest and stomach. The pleasure he yanks from my body. Again. Again. The delicious aroma of Indian takeout we have delivered because this time, *neither* of us wants to leave the room.

My body never really calms down for him. It's like a test he's prepared to fail every day, a test he's flabbergasted he gets better at every time.

"I don't understand," he mumbles against my shoulder one day in Bangalore, just as I orgasm the very second he enters my body. "And I never want to."

We visit a dye house, a garment factory, two more suppliers. All in great shape, all of whom pass my litmus test.

Will asked me to remember what it's like to be with him—

Which means everything else is forgettable.

CHAPTER THIRTY

With the trip over and a pile of unread emails to sift through thanks to a) Camila locking me out of my account and b) my recent sexual reawakening, I *shouldn't* have time to overthink the realities of what happened between Will and me.

I *shouldn't* have lain awake the first night missing his warmth.

I *shouldn't* have checked my phone for signs of him like a teenage girl.

The minute he left my presence at the Atlanta airport, headed back to New York, with a caress against the back of my neck and a half-growled *See you soon* against my ear, I should've recalibrated to focus solely on work.

That's the agreement I made with myself: *You can have him in doses if he doesn't distract you the rest of the time.*

But it's been two days, and it's obvious that's just not fucking happening.

The weather outside is too nice. Sales are going too well. The interns are laughing at one another's desks. My body feels more unwound than it has in years.

Right now, everything is good.

I try to tell myself that doesn't mean a shoe is about to drop.

Camila appears at my door with a wolfish grin. "You look fucked!" she says.

"*Camila Sanchez!*" I hiss.

She cackles, shutting the door to my office. Like a little gremlin, she tiptoes closer. "Holy cow, look at that glow on your face. Was it good?"

"How did you know—"

She slaps both of her palms on my desk, her grin growing. "I know you canceled one of the hotel rooms in Bangalore."

"How?!"

"I bribed Reese from Accounting to keep me apprised of your corporate credit card charges." She wiggles her eyebrows.

"Bribed how?"

"Don't you worry about it, CEO mine."

"Was it the same *bribe* you used on the IT girl to lock me out of my email?"

"I've got this place dialed," Camila says, examining her nails.

"Where have you been?" I ask. "I've been back for two days and haven't seen you in the office."

She shakes her head and flings her hand at the air. "David and I took a trip. Don't change the subject."

"From your dubious professional behavior?"

She bends down and leans her elbows on the table so we're eye to eye. "From your good and proper *fucking*."

"Stop saying that!" I whisper-shriek, looking at the glass door.

"Oh, relax, half the office picked up on your good mood over the past two days. They told me to come in here and get to the bottom of it."

"Am I usually in a bad mood?" I ask.

"Not *bad*." Camila shrugs. "Busy, distracted, stiff."

I frown. "I'll work on that."

"How 'bout you let Will Grant keep working on that?"

I groan, sinking dramatically from my chair all the way underneath my desk. Camila drops down and crawls beside me, giggling.

I grab her hands in mine. "I have the biggest crush on him."

She squeals softly. "I *knew* it, J. From the moment you told me he got us a new reservation at Andalo, I *knew* you two were going to become something. But I didn't want to jinx it because of how long it's been since Clay, and I didn't want to freak you out, or say the wrong thing, and frankly, I was worried you were going to talk yourself out of giving him a chance if I spoke it into existence—"

"It's okay," I whisper, dropping her hands. "You probably would have been right about that. I've been wrestling with it. The idea of . . . a boyfriend."

A boyfriend! she mouths.

I laugh, thinking back to the last time we acted this way because of a man. It was the day after the first Garlic Fest we'd ever attended. Camila had spent the night with David for the very first time. She came home to our house, the biggest, dorkiest grin on her face, and we sat down on the couch and shared a bottle of champagne and orange juice while she told me every little detail—all the reasons she liked him, all the things David had said about why he liked her.

Camila Sanchez has a rocky relationship history. In college, she let boys treat her like shit. Some would cheat, some would ghost, some would gaslight her, and she'd find reasons to forgive them all. Twenty was when we finally got to the good part. She was happily single, and for some reason, that made me able to look at men again with a semblance of attraction. Clay came into the picture—a nice guy whom I will always wish the best for, despite our relationship failing to last. He came and went, and Camila stayed.

Her college boys came and went, and I stayed.

When she and David got engaged, I was crouched behind a shrub waiting to pop a gold confetti bomb.

After I chose to end my four-year celibacy, she's under my office desk with me, giggling.

"Want to get some margaritas and talk?" she asks.

It's four o'clock—so *technically* not too early to leave for the day—but still, I say, "I feel like I haven't put in enough face time at the office lately."

"And you know what? Everybody managed," she replies. "We've done a good job with this place, Josie." There's something wistful to her tone that sets my heart on edge.

If she wants to talk, I can't deny her.

"We *have* done a good job," I say, smiling. "Let's drink."

At Suerte, I tell Camila about the trip start to finish as we drink tequila and munch on chips and guacamole. She laughs her ass off when I describe the way I politely asked Santiago to pull over so I could hurl on the side of a Peruvian highway. Camila swoons when I tell her about Will begging to just *hold* me that night. She laughs *again* when I describe his snoring, which I've already grown so accustomed to after three nights in Bangalore that it's hardly noticeable anymore when I'm drowsy.

"And Zoe?" Camila asks. "Have you talked to her yet?"

I shake my head, heart thrumming. "I want to. Will told me Zoe wants to reconnect with me, too, but we haven't had a chance to see each other in person yet."

I'm giddy just thinking about it, but nervous, too. What a strange twist of fate that the very thing that drove Zoe and me apart is what could bring us back together.

We order another round, sip it down to the ice as we talk about the wedding six weeks from now and the Revenant store opening in one month. A couple of guys send us shots from the bar. We promptly swallow them, send a round back to them as thanks, then ask for our checks and giggle as we bail out of the patio exit before the men have a chance to come over and flirt.

Outside, the weather is screaming *Keep drinking.* We Uber to Rainey Street.

"I haven't been here in years," I say as a bus full of girls drives past.

"Slushies," Camila says, pulling me into a bar. We grab our juice boxes and people-watch from the upstairs patio. The sunlight dims, crowds flooding the street below us.

"Do you remember," she says, sometime after the sun has vanished, "that time in college when I peed on the floor?"

"Which time," I deadpan.

"The other time was just water!"

"It was *not* water," I say.

"It was!"

"It. Was. Not," I say. "I don't understand why you can admit to peeing on the floor one time but not twice."

Cami laughs, throwing back her head. "Okay, fine, it was pee both times."

"I fucking *knew* it!" I scream at her, slapping down my empty slushie.

She disappears and comes back with two more. "Do you remember that time when I dated that guy who jizzed on my padfolio?"

"Who leaves a padfolio on their bedside table during sex?" I shriek.

"We met at the job fair!" she shrieks back. "Who has *that* bad of aim?"

"Joe does!" I'm screaming for effect, but also because the nighttime music has come on, doubly amplified. "Remember when me and Gio faked a literal death to get you out of that one date with a man named Basil?"

"Oh yes, *Bahh-sil,*" Camila says fondly. "I hope he's doing well."

I laugh a lot harder than the situation calls for. I haven't had this much to drink in a *minute,* and it shows.

"Remember when I forced you to start an Instagram page for your designs?" Cami says.

"I remember you used threats of violence," I say.

"I don't regret a thing. I don't—"

She cuts herself off, and I can feel it. She's getting close to some kind of admission. There are tears she's pushing back, that she's trying to blink away.

"You're my best friend, Josephine. You're my best fucking friend and I'm never going to forget the way you were there for me, in college, when I was knee-deep in family problems and could barely keep up with my schoolwork and I let men dictate my happiness. I'm never going to forget the rock you were for me, through all that."

She brushes her thumbs under her eyes. I don't know whether to say something or let her get this out. I can feel my eyes welling, just watching her try.

"And working with you at Revenant, it's been a dream come true. I have loved it. I love what we did together. I'm so thankful to myself for quitting my Whole Foods job and doing this with you," she says, now audibly crying through her words. "I'm so thankful to you, for trusting your best friend with your business. And now we can both leave for days at a time, and it all keeps running smoothly. We gave it legs to walk on," she says.

"Only took six years of teamwork," I manage.

She laughs messily. "We don't give ourselves nearly enough credit for what we built. At our age? It's amazing."

I nod, wiping a tear from my cheek.

"But now," she says, "I have to do something else."

She crumbles then, face in her hands. I pet her hair as she sobs, nodding and smiling at a dude who walks past us giving me an *Is she okay?* look of worry.

After a few minutes, Camila looks up and mumbles something about wanting to go to business school. Something about David getting funding to start his own restaurant in New York City. They have a real estate agent; the house will be sold soon, and they're moving after their wedding, just in time for Cami to start school in Manhattan this fall. She's already found her replacement—an internal hire. She's also found the person who will replace *that* person. I don't have to stress about anything. It will be a seamless transition, she promises.

I absorb every word, my lips trained into a smile as she rambles on without hardly breathing. But the *why* of it all doesn't really matter.

Because the point is: Camila is leaving—Revenant and Austin—and that's what's best for *her.*

And the point is also: she's still my best friend, and I'm still hers, and this isn't going to make me fall apart. Because it isn't bad news. It's good.

I rub at Cami's shoulder as her sobbing ebbs.

"In college," I say, "you wouldn't have dreamed of leaving the city where your family lives. Not because you needed them, because they needed you. They needed too much of you. I guess what I'm trying to say is I'm just really fucking proud of you for putting yourself and your marriage first."

She breaks down again, and I do, too. She pulls me into a tight hug. Over her shoulder I notice the same guy from before. He comes up to us this time, asking what's wrong.

"Everything is fine!" I say, attempting a laugh and a smile.

He grimaces. "You sure?"

Camila turns around to face him. "You're ruining the moment!" she barks.

He shakes his head and walks away when I start laughing. My face feels swollen. Camila's makeup is a mess.

"You don't seem shocked," she says.

I wink at her. "This is the second time you've told me."

CHAPTER THIRTY-ONE

I show up on the doorstep of Will's East Austin Airbnb with one bottle of Tylenol and one bottle of red wine. He rented the fifth town house of a ten-unit complex that can't have been built more than a few years ago. It's not far from an outdoor wine bar I visit with my biker gang sometimes.

He swings open the front door, then points to the Tylenol. "You feeling okay?"

"It's this weird tradition my friends and I formed back in college," I explain. "People always bring alcohol to stock your bar, but never pills to stock your medicine cabinet."

"That is weird," he says.

"Yeah." I grin.

He accepts the Tylenol. "You know this place is a rental, right?"

"A two-week rental!" I say excitedly.

He got permission to work remote for a while and focus on his three Austin clients. I'm over-the-moon thrilled to see him—to have him here for days on end—but my guilt is still clawing at me, bruising my insides, scraping at my peace of mind.

Here we are again. Will bending for me, me letting him. It isn't fair, and sooner rather than later, something has got to give.

When I step inside, I'm not sure what I'm expecting. Maybe slate-gray walls and steel furniture? A desk with three monitors, a bare-bones kitchen?

Instead, when I look right, I'm greeted by the largest, deepest beige couch I've ever seen, in a sunny living room. There's an olive tree in one corner and surround sound music playing softly. The scent coming off the kitchen is delectable.

I've barely deposited the wine on the entryway table when Will hooks his arms around me, his hand cupping the back of my head. He crushes our lips together like it's the only natural greeting. *Hello. I missed you. I want you. I'm happy to see you.* I move my mouth against his, repeating the unspoken words right back.

He pulls away, eyes dancing, and twirls a lock of my hair around his finger.

"Did you cook?" I ask, nodding toward the kitchen. I can just make out a grater from here on the visible part of the countertop. "When you suggested dinner in, I assumed we were ordering take-out."

Will's dimple flashes. His eyes move from my face to my outfit, an oversized T-shirt dress and old white sneakers. "I cooked." He shrugs. "I cook."

"So *that's* what sets you apart from the other Equinox men in the West Village."

"I live in Tribeca."

"Close enough. Did you cook for the women you thoroughly dated?"

"Not a single one," he says, grabbing the wine and turning toward the kitchen. "I don't have the setup for it in my tiny apartment."

It's a hilariously juxtaposed comment as I follow him to *this* kitchen, which might be the most stunning thing I've ever laid eyes on. The cabinetry is a forest-green color, the countertops a beautifully marbled off-white. He's even got a range hood for his stovetop and an overhead cookware holder hanging above the kitchen island.

"This place is for sale," Will comments innocently.

I raise my eyebrows as his implication lands. "That so?"

Will sets the wine beside a cutting board piled with soft, springy herbs. He stares at me, expression calculating. "Want to know a secret?"

I nod.

Will steps away from the counter and pulls open a drawer. I circle around the island until I'm beside him, eyeing a thick piece of paper he places on the counter.

"Is that a . . . *culinary school diploma?*"

"Mm," he says.

"With your name on it?"

"Looks that way."

Gaping, I turn my face up to his. "Explain!"

Instead, he hauls me into another kiss.

I melt against Will's body as I remember the feel of him. It's been a week since we returned from Bangalore, and with all the catching up we both had to do at work, neither of us has caught a break until tonight. Every atom in my body heats up to a boiling point at the physical contact. I want to fuse myself to his body, recycle his air through my lungs.

"I'm so confused," I whisper when I pull away.

"You're the only person from my personal life besides my family I've ever told," he whispers against my lips.

"That you went to *culinary school?*" I ask through the haze of digesting what else he said: *the only person from my personal life.*

I am planted in Will Grant's personal life.

Will pulls away, looking back at the diploma. "A couple years ago. I took night classes. It was around the time things at work started to get bad. I was miserable, and wondering if I was going to feel that way for the rest of my life," he says. "I applied on a whim. But when I got accepted and started learning . . ." He looks back at me, his eyes feverishly bright. "I *loved* it. I used most of my consulting salary to pay off the tuition, so I'm debt free. I completed my credentials by working as a late-night line cook for a while, and even that was exhilarating."

"I—" I glance around the kitchen. There are finished entrées warming on the stovetop, something baking in the oven. "Just for fun? Or do you want this as a career?"

"I didn't know the answer to that when I signed up for culinary school," Will says. "Part of me convinced myself I was only doing it for fun, as a hobby. But the point is, now I have the option to just . . ." His words fade off.

"Drop everything," I whisper. "And change your mind."

Will's expression clears.

"You didn't say a word," I say. "I never would have known."

But the way he picked restaurants abroad. The fact that he hates leftovers, that he can *usually tell* the quality of a dish's freshness. His obsession over meeting David Ortega, a lauded local chef. *This* explains why Will almost failed a class in his major so he could focus on his nutrition elective, why he stayed at his day job even when he was miserable—so he could pay for culinary school.

All the signs were there.

"I chose the career I chose," Will explains, his gaze intense, "because there were a few years after my parents got divorced when our financial situation was precarious. We'd never been well off, but after, it got worse. My mom didn't make much money, between her pottery job and my dad's alimony payments. Zoe and I assumed all our own debt with our college educations. A high-paying job in investment banking was the safe bet, and when that didn't work out, consulting was a natural transition. It's not even that I hate my career anymore. But I've been disappointed by a lot of the people in my industry, and I hate the way it's made me feel about myself. The things I've done being a part of it."

His words wash over me like a dense, calming fog.

"I'm telling you all this," Will whispers, one hand snaking around my waist while the other pushes hair out of my eyes, "because I don't want you to freak out when I say what I'm about to say."

"You're moving to Austin," I guess. Wish. Hope. Pray.

He nods, a tiny smile breaking through his solemn expression. "Already put in an offer on this place. I hope you like it."

I try to inhale, but it feels like sucking cotton down my windpipe. My muscles are locking up.

"I am freaking out a little bit," I admit.

Will pulls me against his chest. His hands skate up and down my back. "Talk me through it," he murmurs.

"I'm, like, *really* happy about this," I say. "It feels like the biggest present in the world, a present I don't deserve and haven't earned yet."

"Josie. You are certainly part of the equation, but I didn't make this decision just for you. I want this for myself. I've wanted it for a while now, even before we found each other." Will's fingers leave my hair, dance along my knuckles. He likes to absently touch me, I've noticed. "Zoe and my mom both think it's a good idea. I have enough savings at this point to buy this place and even take some time off, figure out what I want to do next."

Time off. What a beautiful, terrifying concept.

"Won't Zoe miss having you around?" I ask.

I recall what he said at Zilker Park: *New York became our place.* Will Zoe hate me for taking Will away from their place?

"She's got the New York dream job, a tight friend group, and a boyfriend who worships at her altar. I can't fault him," Will says with a wry laugh. "And not for lack of trying. They've been together for two years now, and I think they'll be together forever. My mom is happy and healthy with Doug in Nashville. And you—" His hand tightens on mine. "You don't need me either."

"That's not true," I protest.

Will shakes his head. "I mean that in a *good* way, Josie. All the women I thoroughly dated in New York were people I thought I could take care of, and I basically encouraged them to play into it. Hell, I even thought of *you* that way, in the beginning. I thought if you hired me, I could take care of all your problems for you." His voice lowers, his mouth at my hair. "But I was never meant to be your hero. I honestly think you were meant to be mine."

I swallow a lump in my throat. "I don't always ask for help when I need it. I could be stronger in that way."

"I know," Will says, his smile catching near his cheeks. "I *was* there in Peru when I had to convince you to open the door."

I laugh through a swollen throat. "*You* didn't even *tell* me you were sick."

He shakes his head. "We're going to argue about that forever, aren't we?"

"Forever," I agree, and it feels like a dangerous promise. "The truth is, Will, I want to be with you all the time. Every day, every hour. So I *do* need you, just so we're clear."

"It's mutual. Even if I tried to explain it to you," Will whispers, his hands on my face now, "I don't think you could ever know how badly I ache for you. The way you feel to me is like an inevitable rightness. Like I'm finally trusting my fucking instincts."

His words unfurl along the back of my neck and spread across my skin underneath my clothes, dissipating every feverish shiver.

"I think about the day we reconnected—how I ran into the

back of your car, but it felt more like you crashing your way into the rest of my life—and I work myself into a panic, imagining all the other scenarios of that morning where it didn't happen. Where we never saw each other. It's *not real*, because we *did* see each other, but somehow, I give myself a small heart attack at least once a day picturing a possibility where we might not have.

"Everything I think about is in reference to you. Would you wear this? Have you seen this movie? How many of those vacuum cleaner attachments have you tried so far?"

"Nine," I whisper.

"I want to be there while you test each one and pick your favorites. I want to carry you around in my arms and then put you down and let you stand on your own two feet while you build something out loud that used to live inside your head. I want to stand on the sidelines and clap for you and then take you somewhere private and fuck you. But mostly, Josie, I want to be a good person with you. Because you make me feel better about myself, just by being you."

All I manage for a very long time is one single, shaky breath.

His hands drop from my hands to my waist, and in a quick movement, he lifts me onto the kitchen counter and steps between my legs. "Back to the culinary school diploma," he rumbles. "Do you think I'd be crazy to do that? Give up the past six years of my career to pursue something completely different?"

"Would you leave Revenant in the lurch?" I joke.

"You know me better than that."

"I do," I agree, my palms on his chest.

Will pushes a lock of hair behind my ear. "I would wait until your B Corp Certification came through and then set you up with the second-best consultant you'll ever have."

I smile and say, "I don't think it's crazy. I think it's miraculous. I sometimes wonder how much of myself I let corporate America take. How much I could take back if I stopped participating."

"I know what you mean," Will murmurs.

"You always know what I mean."

It's quiet for a moment. A string of Grace Jones lyrics floods the empty space. The longer whatever is in the oven bakes, the more sugared and perfect the kitchen smells. Will noses along my jawline, kissing lightly.

"Have you ever seen those soft living videos on TikTok?" I ask.

Will's eyes narrow as he pulls back. "Wait a minute. Do you have *burner accounts*?"

"No, but sometimes the social team lets the password slip, and I scroll!"

He blinks. "No shot. Admit you have burner accounts."

"I *swear* I don't," I say. "If I did, I'd never get anything done. You can check my phone."

Will eyes me suspiciously. "Well, regardless, I don't know about the soft living videos."

"It's these people who live in quaint houses overlooking the ocean or the middle of a mountain range and they just . . ." I gesticulate with my hands. "Pick lavender and bake sourdough and write a novel on a typewriter and bird-watch! Or crack open coconuts they drink on the beach while watching the sunset. Or build furniture with their bare hands!"

"Baking sourdough," Will says, wincing, "is really fucking hard. The rest of it sounds all right. Are you interested in soft living?"

"I think about it sometimes," I admit. "When I'm stressed out. Or second-guessing myself, or wondering if this is all worth how much it drains me."

Will rubs a thumb along my jawline, his eyes absorbing the planes of my face. "How often does that happen?"

"Not very."

"And now?"

I smile, meeting his eyes. "Camila finally told me she's leaving."

His face morphs from curious to concerned. "She did?"

I nod. "She's moving to New York so David can open a restaurant he gets full creative control over, and she can go to graduate school."

Will's hands drop to my bare thighs, where he rubs soothingly. "Looks like we aren't the only ones with these kinds of thoughts."

"Burnout avoidance," I suggest.

After a moment of consideration Will says, in a gruff voice, "I already burned out, Josie. That happened a couple years back."

"I think I did, too," I whisper. "But I only just noticed."

He presses his lips against my forehead. "I want to make you a deal," he whispers.

"What deal?"

"If you wake up one morning and decide you want to try out soft living," he says, breath dancing along the wisps at my hairline, "we do it together. Even if it's only for a little while. If you want to drop everything, then I will, too."

It's an idea that stuffs me with anxiety just as much as it thrills me. Revenant is my proudest accomplishment. I don't want to abandon it, not now that things are just starting to calm down. Reminiscing with Camila about how far we've come only reminded me of how much passion went into building that company.

But I'm not the same girl I was when I was twenty-one.

I'm tired.

I've got two years left of my twenties.

And I think I'm falling in love.

"Deal," I say. "But I hope you won't wait on me if you already know what you want."

"I won't wait," he promises. "I can be your private chef, and you can be my CEO. I will have dinner on the table when you get home, on one condition."

I bite my lip as he tilts my chin up. "What condition?"

"Josephine." He steps in closer, drowning me in the cinnamon scent of him. His hands weave back into my hair. His face hovers centimeters above mine. "Will you please, *please* be my girlfriend?"

My heart stutters, leaping out of rhythm. I let our lips graze. "Can I taste dinner first?"

A noise of displeasure lodges in his throat. He crushes our mouths together. Kisses me harshly, teeth nipping at my lips. "Sorry. Did you think it was for *you*?"

"What other . . . aspiring vegetarians do you know?" I gasp between kisses.

"This meal is for real vegetarians."

"I could be one of those."

"You can be anything you want."

Will pushes me to lie flat against the countertop and leans on his elbows, bracketing my upper body. His hair falls over his eyes, which are shining with that flinty, concentrated azure color.

"I'll be your girlfriend, Will Grant," I say.

He has wiped away all my holdouts. He showed up, and showed up, and showed up. I cannot go back to the Josie I was before he found me, even if I wanted to.

"Thank you," Will says. "I did wrong by you then. Thank you for giving me the chance to get it right now."

CHAPTER THIRTY-TWO

Will feeds me roasted sweet potatoes served over a homemade lemon garlic aioli, garnished with chile-and-honey-buttered pepitas. He got flour tortillas from Matt's El Rancho, stuffed them full of fried cauliflower and guacamole. There's a salad with three ingredients—leafy greens, lemon juice, olive oil—and it might be the best thing I've ever tasted. For dessert, he pulls chocolate chip cookies out of the oven, slathers homemade strawberry ice cream between two of them, and rolls the whole thing in coconut flakes. It's more delicious than a home-cooked meal has any right to be, and when I say as much to Will, he rubs at his neck.

We eat the cookie sandwiches on his back porch, where the sun gleams into our eyes and melts the ice cream until it's dripping down my hand. He polishes his dessert off and then sucks on my fingers, his hot eyes on mine the whole time.

"What's the verdict?" he asks.

"I will eat all your leftovers."

"Somebody's got to."

"I will buy sound machines and earplugs to block out your snores."

"I'll visit an ENT to see if there's a surgery I can have," he promises.

"I don't mind the snoring," I say. "It's just a reminder I'm not alone."

We sit on that porch even after the sun goes down. Will's hands curl around my body, adjusting me until I can lie across him and fall halfway asleep while he tells me more stories about New York, cooking school, his secret double life as a line cook. All the places he wants to take me when we visit Manhattan together.

"Will we see Zoe?" I ask.

"Definitely," Will says. "She's already talked about having you over to her place on the Upper West Side."

"Does she know you put in an offer on this place?"

Will's lips curve up. "Zoe's the one who sent me the listing."

After a beat I admit, "Our relationship will always be different now. Hers and mine. I want to be her friend again, but I know it won't be like it was before."

He sits with this. One of my favorite things about Will is he never hurries to fill a silence during a loaded conversation. He speaks only when he's sure of what he wants to say.

"Zoe's different now. Just like you're different. Just like I'm different," Will says. "Of course it won't be like before. It *can't* be. But that doesn't mean you two can't have a friendship that's new and special."

I nod against his shoulder, silently agreeing.

My relationship with Camila will change, too, now that she's leaving Austin. Maybe this is all just totally natural—important people weaving in and out of your life but never making a permanent exit.

I can hold on to my memories of me and Zoe—reading books side by side at the Sea Island beach, giggling in the back of a classroom, screaming in the bleachers during a football game, whispering our self-doubts to each other from a shared bed—and I can greet her as an adult with our mutual hurt long overturned and buried.

I'll tell her I'm in love with her twin brother. But *she* meant the world to me, too, and that happened first. They are two independent facts.

I will tell Camila I'm going to miss her so much—that it will feel like a part of my soul has been sliced off to be carried with her—but I know it's time for her and David to go.

I don't realize I'm crying until Will wipes at my cheeks wordlessly, then carries me upstairs to his bedroom and holds me. Neither of us speaks a single word. We hardly even make a sound, as if the silence could be cracked into sharp pieces if it breaks.

When I start to kiss him, he pours his care into the way he kisses me back. With every shiver of my body, every movement of his hands exploring my skin, it's like he's sharing my big emotions, giving them another place to live for a while.

"You are my girlfriend," Will whispers to me as the sun rises the next morning. Light spills through his gigantic windows, cloaking us in a hazy warmth.

"I promise not to have a baby with your best friend," I whisper back. My index finger pushes in against his dimple, memorizing the shape of it. "And I promise not to dump you because you don't drink enough."

"I promise not to move to Canada to play hockey," Will whispers.

"I think Clay lives in California now."

"I've always hated California."

"You are my boyfriend," I whisper to him. And whether Will knows it or not, those four words are actually code for I'm-head-over-heels-in-love-with-you.

We say it back and forth over the next couple of weeks as Will puts in his notice, transitions his clients to their new leads, and packs up his apartment to move to Austin. Every day, it means a little more. Because it usually comes at the beginning or end of a very real conversation about our grandmothers, our most embarrassing moments, our thoughts on Austin's mayor, the pros and cons of living in Zilker versus East. My casual mention that I got on birth control. The embarrassment of our high school mascot in Nashville, Humboldt the Honeybear.

One day, the director of social media approaches me at work and says, "Does Will Grant still work for us?"

"Yes," I say nervously. "Why?"

She holds out her phone. "He's been DM'ing the Revenant account with, like, dog videos and food porn and something called the soft life aesthetic? Like, the type of stuff you'd send to your best friend or your significant other."

I scroll through the messages, resisting a smile. "What's the password?"

Marianne groans. "You can't use the business account as your personal Instagram, Jo! Are you *dating* him?"

"That wouldn't be advisable."

"I'm not giving you the password," Marianne threatens, grabbing her phone back.

"Why not?"

"Because the last time you logged on to the account you accidentally reposted a meme about hot delivery men."

I blush, remembering that meme, then burst out laughing.

"Make a personal Instagram, dammit!" Marianne shouts at me
as she walks away.

> **Josie:** Marianne won't give me the insta
> password. Can we look at all your DMs together
> the next time I see you?
>
> **Will:** That is going to take at least forty-five
> minutes.
>
> **Josie:** You sent forty-five minutes' worth of
> posts to a business account? Fetish much?
>
> **Will:** BRO MAKE A PERSONAL ACCOUNT. I
> WOULD FUCKING LOVE AN EXCUSE TO STARE
> AT PICTURES OF YOU

Later that night I download the app and create an account under the username @picturesofjosie. I take one selfie—my hair in
a high bun, a hole in the collar of my T-shirt, smile wide, and a
big thumbs-up—then post it. I easily find and follow Will, whose
Instagram is about as stale as the accounts of most men in their
late twenties. But I scroll through his photos anyway. Pictures from
college, from sports games, with family members. There's one photo
of him and Zoe in Washington Square Park.

She's beautiful. Always was, but she's grown into herself now. In
the photo, she's wearing a red power lip she positively rocks.

I get the notification that he followed me back and bite on a
smile.

> **willGrant27:** More.
>
> **picturesofjosie:** 1 per day.
>
> **willGrant27:** fine. can you at least make the
> account private? I don't want anyone seeing these
> but me.

> **picturesofjosie:** why, because they're so
> scandalous?
>
>   **willGrant27:** because I don't want to share presents
>   from my girlfriend

Will moves to Austin toward the end of August, with one more week left at Ellis, totally remote, and one client project pending (mine). I wish I could road-trip with him from New York to Texas, but I can't manage the time off from work. Still, I show up to help him unpack with a box full of wine and a plastic bag of medicine from Walgreens. Brooks stops by with little Marshall, a six-pack of beer, and a big, fat smile on his face. So does one of Will's old clients—the guy Will cycles with, whom he considers a friend now.

He gets to know David better when we go on a double date with him and Camila. Now that their move is out in the open, it's the bulk of what we talk about. The wedding coming up and then a brand-new chapter of their lives, as a married couple.

Later at my house when we're lying in bed, I ask him if he'd ever want to pursue a career like David's.

"Working in a kitchen is just as stressful as working on Wall Street," he muses. "I'm glad I got that experience, and hats off to David for making a career out of it, but I don't know if it's what I'd want to do."

"What, then?" I ask.

"I have an idea percolating with Brooks," he says. "Can I tell you when it's ready?"

"Sure. Whatever you want."

Will pulls me against him and I rest my head on his chest, listening to his heartbeat. "I should have known," he says to the ceiling, absently.

I tilt my chin up. "Known what?"

"That finding you would be the thing to finally set me right again."

My rib cage isn't big enough anymore.

I sit up, and Will pulls himself upright, too.

"I want to tell you something about me," I whisper. "I just don't know if I'm going to say it as eloquently as you."

Will lifts me so I'm straddling him. "I'll parse it," he promises.

I breathe deeply. "I have felt like an imposter my whole life. I never believed about myself what other people made of me. My high school classmates thought I was aspirational, but really, I was an insecure wreck who found validation in the wrong places. Likes, follows, shopping expeditions, smiles from senior boys. Then I was this inventive college kid with a viral side hustle, but nobody knew how hard I had to work to scrape out the same grades it took other people zero effort to achieve. Nobody knew I was just lucky with my brand, that it isn't a unique concept, that I was simply single-minded, hyper-fixated, and that's how I managed it. And now, I'm a CEO, which is just, like, this hilarious fucking *joke*. Who the hell would sign up to work for *me*? It boggles my mind every day. If I showed up to work tomorrow and the whole office had quit, I think I'd say to myself *About time.*"

Will says nothing, only rubs a hand up and down my back.

"Then you," I go on, pushing through my hesitation. "If anyone could have spotted the fraud in me, it would have been you. I was worried that's exactly what had happened when you told me you'd declined working with me. I was so bitter during that presentation, so adamant about B Corp, because I didn't want you to think I was an imposter. If you had, I would have believed it, too."

"It was never about that," Will whispers. "I was only scared of hurting you more."

"I know that now," I say quickly. "And ultimately, you showed me that very first day how much you believed in me."

"Of course I believed in you," he says, tucking my hair behind my ear. "It's impossible not to."

"The point is, Will. If you don't think I'm a fraud," I say, gripping his arms, "then maybe I'm not one. You were the first man to see every messy part of who I am and believe in me anyway."

Will pulls back just enough to show me his irises, burning firelight blue with understanding. "I want your messy parts."

"I want yours, too. I want your list of worst things and I want your biggest regrets. I want your bad days. You're not just a good person, you're a good-for-me person. And you make—" I break my stride for a deep breath. "You make me feel like I'm worth something more valuable than my actual net worth."

"Josie," Will murmurs, his hands on my neck, in my hair, lips on my collarbone. "I love you. I am head over heels in love with you."

"I love you, too," I say back, just before he kisses me. We're helpless.

It came out so simply. His call, my response. *I love you.*

In this bed—in this city—we found and claimed each other. My heart feels like it's transforming into something different—bigger and more vulnerable, easily punctured, but better for Will to hold.

He kisses me deeply. Our chests thud in a silent rhythm.

Will's thumb passes back and forth over my breast. His mouth catches mine on a tiny gasp while my body arches toward him. Quickly, he divests me of my T-shirt, kisses and sucks along my cleavage. It's just as electrifying as the first time. A month ago, now.

A month of this. A lifetime, if we can earn it.

I tug at his waistband and feel his erection beneath my hand. He groans into my mouth and pushes me back against the mattress, crawling up my body with the stealth of a jungle cat. Using all the familiarity of two people in love, he pulls down my underwear and pushes into my body, quick and seamless and intimate. We both sigh at the feeling, too exquisite to name. Somehow, it gets better every time.

His elbows land on either side of my face. Will's body starts to move—gentle but firm thrusts I meet as best as I can—and he continues to murmur, "I love you, I love you." It's almost inaudible, incredibly disjointed. But the words send me to the edge. I come before him, as always, and he huffs an incredulous laugh, as always, and adds a *fucking* in the middle of his next *I love you.* Twice.

I fucking love you, he says. And then, after a few more seconds while his speed picks up: *I love fucking you.*

I struggle to keep my eyes open, so enveloped by the feel of his body pushing mine to the brink *again,* but he's watching my face like it's the most fascinating thing he's ever seen, his eyelashes framing his beautiful blue eyes. I try to keep hold of them.

My hands pull against the planes of his chest as my body starts to lose control. It's in Will's hands now. Part of my control has been in *his* hands since that first day. We rock against each other, his hips working hard now, broken *I love yous* on each of our tongues, and just before my body contracts around him, I think to myself, *This is the happiest I've ever been.*

That's the exact moment I should have remembered: something still needed to give.

CHAPTER THIRTY-THREE

Here's what's funny about crises at work: they never wait their turn. When one comes, the rest follow, like eager little chicks trailing after the mother hen.

The article comes out on Friday, around ten o'clock in the morning: *The Truth About Josephine Davis, Revenant's Reclusive Founder and CEO.*

Written by Nora Lindberg for *Forbes.*

I don't see the piece right away; there's a lot going on. Derrick is coming into town next week ahead of the B Corp review, so I'm scrambling to get my odds and ends taken care of. Not to mention Camila's wedding is in two weeks, and our South Congress store is scheduled to open in one hour.

One. Hour.

Cami is already there, making sure every box is checked with the social media and sales teams, ready to go as soon as the doors open at eleven. I'm wrapping up a meeting when I spot Eugenia through the glass wall. She's aiming me a shifty look.

She's had some trouble with that freckled intern lately. Read: she fell in love with him, and frankly, I'm not that alarmed by her expression considering *he* is in the meeting *with* me. When we finish up and Eugenia hands over my belongings so I can make a quick exit from the building, she says, "Is everything . . . okay?"

"Uh, yeah?" I say. "Why wouldn't it be?"

"N-Never mind," she stutters, falling into pace with me as I head for the door.

"Do you want to come with me?" I ask. "It's going to be great. Cami texted me there's a line already, which shouldn't be a problem because I was *so paranoid* about not having the right inventory selection this time I told our new director to seriously overcorrect—"

"I can't, we have an intern thing," Eugenia interrupts.

"Okay, well, enjoy!" I turn back and shoot her a cheery smile—failing to interpret the dead silence of every single one of my employees staring at me from their desks—as I disappear into the elevator.

In my car, I put on Ryn Weaver and turn up the volume, humming along as I make my way to South Congress. It's a beautiful late-summer day, not a cloud in the sky, the air dry, scorching hot. I park in the retail section of an apartment complex and make my way up to street level, a giddiness running through me as I spot the customer line.

My phone rings. I fish it out of my purse and see Will's name.

"Guess where I am?" I keep my voice low.

"Josephine."

"I'm in line! It's, like, fifty people deep!" I shriek-whisper.

"Josie, you should get somewhere private."

"I'm not planning to *stay* here," I say. "I'm about to head to the back entrance. But I wanted to see. Most of the time, our customers are behind a screen, but these people are real. And they're *here*," I go on, enchanted.

"That's great, J," Will says. There's an edge to his tone I haven't heard in a long time. "I'm happy for you. But seriously, Nora Lindberg from *Forbes* just released a piece on you, and it doesn't sound to me like you've read it yet, so maybe you should step away from—"

"Josephine Davis?"

I pull the phone down from my ear. The girl ahead of me has turned.

"Hi!" I say, extroverting my hardest. I was prepared for this today. People perceiving me. I practiced my warmest smile in the mirror this morning. "Thank you so much for being here."

The girl frowns. She holds up her phone screen to me, and that's when I see the article title for the first time: *The Truth About Josephine Davis*.

"Is this true?"

If there's one thing we've come to expect from female founders, it's that they know the power of their personal brand. Customers fall in love with the often young, always smart, unreachably aspirational founder just as much as whatever product or service she's peddling.

And nine times out of ten, it *works*. So why, I asked myself, is Josephine Davis hesitant to let her customers get to know her?

I talked to former Revenant employee Margaret Dwyer, who was the director of retail experience before she was fired after the Revenant pop-up a few months back. She told me her opinion: Josephine Davis is not very nice.

The employees all hate their CEO, according to Dwyer. Davis is rude, demanding, authoritative, and quick to pass blame. Even worse, Dwyer claims that Davis's own CBO and college friend, Camila Sanchez, has fallen out with her former best friend to the point that Sanchez is planning to leave the company for good.

Kyle Waterhouse, a consultant at the Carlisle Group who had a handshake agreement with Revenant, further substantiated Dwyer's opinion, saying, "Davis fired us, too. That seems to be her calling card when a person makes one single mistake."

I myself have reached out to Davis in a professional capacity on multiple occasions to request an interview, with no response.

The bottom line is: no one is above the news cycle, especially someone in a position of influence, and just because Davis avoids press doesn't mean there won't be a public reckoning when the truth comes out.

My very worst nightmare, come to life.

I don't want people to think of me when they think of Revenant. It's the surest way I could gut my own company.

I tried my hardest to stay out of the spotlight, and it still didn't fucking work.

I guess Nora Lindberg got tired of waiting for me to reply.

Coming back to myself, I realize I've taken the phone from the girl's hand so I could read the piece. She's looking at me now with a thoughtful, curious expression, her brows pinched, her lips tight.

"Is it true?" she asks me again.

"Parts of it are . . . true," I say. My voice sounds like it belongs to someone else. "But I'm Camila's maid of honor."

"Is she leaving the company?" another girl asks from behind the first.

"Yeah," I say. Still too disoriented to think rationally. "I need to . . ."

I hand the girl back her phone, then turn around, making a

beeline for the edge of the store block. I take a sharp ninety-degree turn. My phone rings again: Will. I don't answer. As much as I'd love to hear his voice, the knowledge that he read that article—written by his former lover, who unknowingly eviscerated his brand-new girlfriend—is *mortifying* to me.

I run to the back entrance of the store. Start knocking on the metal door. I can already feel my breath coming short. My body feels like an overripe grapefruit, the pulp inside of me withered and sour.

Camila answers. She's dressed in Revenant clothing, her makeup perfect, her hair in big, tousled waves. The expression on her face is familiar. Down-turned mouth, jumpy eyes.

It's the same face she made anytime she had to leave campus to take care of a crisis for one of her family members.

She grabs me by the shoulders and pulls me into the back room of the store. "You know it's not true," she says. "And *I* know it's not true. You're my best friend. That has never changed, and it's not going to." Her words are blunt but soft.

"Why would Margaret say we had a falling-out?"

"I don't know." She shakes her head. "I *never* said anything even *close* to what she claimed in that article." Cami shifts, dropping her hands. "I did . . . I *did* tell her I was planning to resign this fall. I regretted it as soon as I made the decision to let her go, but, like, I've never been good at keeping secrets! It *killed* me. I had to tell someone."

"It doesn't matter," I say. "I just need to make sure you aren't . . . I didn't drive you away, did I?"

"*No.*" Cami pulls me into a hug. "Listen to me, Josephine. Leaving Revenant is the most difficult decision I've ever had to make, and all my reasons to *stay* were because of how much I love you. You're the first family member I ever got to choose. I swear to you."

I squeeze her tight, her words skimming over me like warm sunshine. "I believe you."

"And before you go spiraling about the whole office hating you, that's a load of crap."

I pull away, wincing. "Unfortunately, Cami, if someone *did* have a problem with me, I think you might be the last person they'd tell."

She groans. "I want this reporter's fucking receipts."

"Let's just—" I take a deep breath. "Focus on the store opening first."

Footsteps head in our direction. We both turn to see Pam, the new director. She shoots me a look I can't parse. "It's 11:02, and people are bailing on the line."

"Let them in," I say. Music is already playing throughout the front half of the store. The refreshments and macarons we got for opening day are probably staged by now.

Pam nods, turning back around. I make to follow her, but Cami grabs my elbow. "Maybe you shouldn't," she says. "Be here."

I shoot her a confused look. "Won't it look bad if I'm not? We should be together in public right now, shouldn't we?"

"It's just that I *know* the internet," Cami says. "Better than you do these days, and I think everyone's going to find it performative if we act like best friends today. It might be better to just operate like we're above it all, at least for one day. In the meantime, I can work on a statement that specifies what that article got wrong. I mean, I wasn't even asked for a *comment.*" She shakes her head. "That's some shitty journalism."

"The reporter reached out to me five or six times over the last few years," I admit. "I ignored her."

Camila frowns. "Just because you didn't respond to a member of the press doesn't mean you deserved this, Josie."

It's like she can read my mind. She knows me that well, knows I'm already internalizing my responsibility. *If I had just responded to Nora Lindberg. If I hadn't ever engaged with the Carlisle Group to begin with. If I'd worked harder. If I hadn't been so distracted.*

If I had never loved Will Grant.

"Go," I say. "I'll drive back to the office."

Camila pulls me in for one more hug. "Don't let strangers tell you who you are." She walks back toward the storefront. "I'll bring you a macaron."

"Pistachio," I specify, aiming for lighthearted.

"You got it."

As I'm turning back for the exit, my phone lights up again.

Derrick.

CHAPTER THIRTY-FOUR

C aption under a viral TikTok video, posted one hour after the
Forbes article releases:

@revenant CEO Josephine Davis is in hot water after ex-
employee allegations are published in Forbes. What do
you guys think?? Anyone ever met her, have some light
to shed?

Comment section:

Such a good recap ty ty
Omg I forgot about the popup drama from a few months
back, thanks for the reminder!
Y'all, Josie is LITERALLY Camila's MOH. They are BEST
FRIENDS. This Margaret dwyer person is just hunting for
clout

Okay but why haven't either of them denied anything yet?
   Sus
I follow that one intern who does the revenant work vlogs.
   It looks fun and they seem happy? Josie was in one
   of the vlogs eating donuts and laughing with this
   hot man

Transcript of a viral TikTok video posted four hours after the *Forbes* article releases:

I knew Josephine Davis in high school and I can tell you what
   she's really like. She was super popular, the girl had it
   all. And then, on our senior spring break, she hooked up
   with her best friend's twin brother even though he had a
   girlfriend!! She ruined herself after that and not even the
   best friend could forgive her

Caption under a Revenant work vlog posted by a summer intern, which is having its second wind of virality two months later:

Day in the life of a @revenant intern! Office donut party in
   the morning, tour of the warehouse in the afternoon

Comment section:

@ZoeGrant is that your brother?

Caption under a viral TikTok video posted six hours after the *Forbes* article releases:

The plot thickens: Josephine Davis and Will Grant are
   coworkers???

Comment section:

Wait okay so Will Grant is Zoe Grant's twin brother, and
 Zoe Grant is Josephine's ex best friend, and Will is now
 dating and also working with Josie?
Drama like this is my super bowl
I love how today the internet has decided our collective
 mission is getting to the bottom of a decade-long
 feud between a bunch of wildly attractive twenty-
 somethings.
They are flirting in that intern's video. They are FLIRTING

Caption under a viral TikTok video posted nine hours after the
Forbes article releases:

WILL GRANT USED TO SMASH THE REPORTER AND I'VE
 GOT PHOTOS

Comment section:

TikTok, do your thing. Are Will Grant and Josie Davis an
 item?
No way Zoe fucks with that
So Nora Lindberg is like out for revenge, obviously??
 Because he picked Josie Davis over her? I mean that
 man is fucking fine, I'd consider stirring some shit up
 too if I were her
Ya he looks like bby henry cavill
I'm team Josie alllll the way now, Nora Lindberg is BITTER

Viral post from Camila Sanchez on her personal Threads account
twenty hours after the *Forbes* article releases:

The allegations made in the *Forbes* article about me and
    Josie having had a falling-out are completely, one
    hundred percent false. Our friendship is as strong as it's
    ever been. She's one of the best people I know. Touch
    some grass.

Replies to the original post:

Is it true you're leaving though????
Oh my god look at this press release from *Food Baby!* David
    Ortega is her fiancé!!!

Linked *Food Baby* article: *Austin Sous Chef David Ortega to Head
up Día De, a Soon-to-Open Mexican Restaurant in Gramercy Park.*

So Camila IS leaving Revenant!!
There's this thing called remote work? Also long distance?
She's saving face so hard in this post. Obviously something
    happened, and now Camila and Josie hate each other
    but won't admit to it.

Caption under a viral TikTok video posted twenty-four hours
after the *Forbes* article releases:

Where to shop instead of Revenant

CHAPTER THIRTY-FIVE

The @picturesofjosie account is my gateway drug. Because I see myself trending, see users reposting content from TikTok, and I just can't keep myself away from it all. My phone is filled with notifications—calls, texts, emails—but the only thing I can focus on is doomscrolling social media platforms. It's like I'm a teenager all over again.

> I never even liked the clothes
> She's really not that pretty IMO?
> Imagine being Camila, in the shadow of your best friend's success all your adult life. She prob got fed up and that's why she's leaving
> The Revenant board needs to fire that bitch

The discourse is never-ending. It's a pile-on fest, something that has snowballed into far more than one piece of bad press. Our sales have plummeted. Today is on track to be the worst day-over-day sales decline on record. I know, because I'm watching the numbers crawl upward at a glacial pace. I did more sales than this in my *first year.*

"Did you sleep here?" My head jerks from the computer monitor to the front of my office. Camila is in the doorway, concern cutting open her expression.

"No," I say.

"That's the same shit you were wearing yesterday."

"I haven't been home."

"So, you *did* sleep here."

"Didn't sleep," I mutter.

She walks over to my desk and grabs my phone. I swat at her, but she darts away and types in my passcode. "You downloaded the apps?"

"In a moment of weakness—"

Camila glares at me, tapping her thumb against my phone. "No," she says, very simply.

"I *need* to keep up with the rumor mill," I say. "For damage control purposes."

She ignores me, continues tapping on my screen. "I don't mean to put words in your mouth, but I think you might be on the verge of a full-on mental breakdown. So no, you don't get to keep up with the rumor mill for damage control purposes. That's *my* job."

"I need to figure out how to do this without you!" I don't mean to shout it, and I don't, not really, but it comes out octaves higher than it should've.

"Well, put a pin in that, because I'm not leaving as soon as I told you I was." She sets my phone back down on the desk.

"No," I say.

"Yes."

I stand, guilt slicing me in half. The *last* thing I want is Cami staying at Revenant out of obligation. "I can do this," I say. "I can fix it."

"And I can help."

I walk around the desk, facing her. "You're fired."

She laughs. "That's cute."

"Cami! You *have* to go to New York with David! Fresh start! Space from your family! Graduate school!"

"I'll defer one semester."

"I am *not* letting you do that," I say, even as tears prick at my eyes with how much I love her, how special it is to me that I have this loyal of a best friend. I've never deserved her, but if I can convince her to go, maybe I'll start to.

"If I leave now," she says, her voice soft, "it will only make things worse."

"Sometimes," I say, "things have to get worse before they get better."

She's wavering. I can see it in her eyes.

I go for the kill strike.

"All this," I say, gesturing around, "is just a *business,* Cami. It's just money. It's just clothes. It's just a big fat house of cards that can be blown over but can also be rebuilt. You're going to have a brand-new husband." I smile softly at her. "In no universe will I hear of any reality except the one where you go with him to New York City in all your newlywed bliss. It's what you deserve. It's what you've earned."

She sighs out, long and slow.

Seconds pass.

More seconds.

"I hate feeling like I'm abandoning you in a time of need."

I grab her hands. "That's exactly why I can't let you stay. It's the same way you always felt about your little sisters, your cousins, your grandma. Which means you need to get the hell out of Dodge."

She smirks. "Not yet. I've got one week left, and we're course correcting. Everyone I've talked to out there is willing to do whatever it takes to turn the narrative around. I didn't even have to *ask* them if what Margaret Dwyer said was true. They came up to me all on their own and assured me it wasn't."

I smile softly. I haven't left my office except for bathroom breaks. I've been avoiding every single one of my employees like the plague. Hearing Camila say they're supporting me is music to my ears, even though I can't shake the feeling that Margaret can't have completely fabricated what she said.

I'm not perfect. Not even close.

"The news about becoming a B Corp is going to help with course correcting. Our review call with the B Lab analyst is tomorrow."

"Are you sure we're going to pass?" Cami asks.

No. I'm not sure of anything, not anymore. But I need her to believe the answer is yes so she doesn't change her mind again.

"Positive," I say, lying through my teeth. "We triple-checked all our documentation and I know we're well above eighty points. It's in the bag."

Thoughtfully, Cami nods and turns to go. "Don't bother redownloading the social apps. I'm headed straight to Inez's desk so I can ask her to lock you out."

"How is that even possible?" I wonder aloud.

"Honestly, babe, the less you know about how thoroughly your devices are monitored, the better."

CHAPTER THIRTY-SIX

Will: Please talk to me

    Josie: I'm sorry. I didn't mean to ignore you. I just can't figure out what to say.

Will: Can I see you tonight?

    Josie: I can't. Derrick is coming into town this afternoon and he wants to look over the materials for the B Lab review call tomorrow. I'll see you then? It's your very last job as a consultant! We'll celebrate after.

Will: I'll be there.

Derrick swans into town with a zero-bullshit tolerance. We work hours into the night, going over every scrap of material that might be called out during our review call tomorrow. Announcing B Corp approval isn't going to recoup all the lost sales, but it will help, and we can't take any chances.

I get a handful of hours of sleep that night. My shower the next morning is just water hitting skin, and my ICOML is just chemicals reacting in my brain to raise alertness. When I show up at the office, I feel as though I've time slipped.

All our executives trickle into the conference room with one addition: Will. My stomach doubles over when I see him. His face is pale, his eyes dull. He looks impossibly sad.

He sits down next to me, hunching in my direction. "Hi." His voice rasps out like a salty wave against rocks.

"I'm sorry," I say.

"Nothing to be sorry for."

"I've been a bad communicator."

"You've been in crisis," he counters, voice low.

"So have you."

He frowns, eyes jumping over my face. "I don't mind being associated with you on the internet, Josie, unless it's something *you* mind."

"Only in the sense that it's perhaps unethical to date your consultant."

"Well, it's a good thing I'm not your consultant much longer, isn't it?" He finds my hand underneath the table and brushes his against it. His touch calms me, centers me.

Reminds me none of this is as important as I am making it out to be.

At ten o'clock sharp, the review meeting begins. A projected screen on the wall flashes from solid black to a view of our analyst, who smiles tightly at us.

"Good morning, all," he says. "I'm afraid I have some bad news."

There was no way you could have known, he says.

Your Spanish supplier was a B Corp, he says, *until they failed their recertification. We change our standards all the time, and this year, they didn't make the cut.*

Unfortunately, it means the score for Revenant has also dropped below the passing threshold, he says.

You can reapply in the future, he says, and eventually, he ends the call.

My mom always used to say trouble comes in threes.

1. The internet hates you.
2. Your company failed the test of goodness (and the internet still hates you, just, you know, as a cute little reminder).

I'm beginning to fear I already know what number three is.

When I head for the garage, I have every intention of wallowing on the UT Austin campus for the rest of the afternoon. But it's sweltering hot, and come to think of it, I've barely eaten in forty-eight hours, haven't drunk much water, or slept well, or taken enough deep breaths that aren't riddled with stress. My brain starts to fog. My vision spots.

I make it to the edge of my car and slump against it, pushing my forehead against the cool metal exterior in an effort to regain control over my body. I don't know how long I linger there—maybe seconds, maybe minutes—before I feel a hand rest lightly on my back. He rubs back and forth, coaxing life back into me.

"I'll drive," Will murmurs.

He half scoops me, half walks me to the passenger side door. I schlep my body into the seat and rest my head against the window after he closes me inside.

Will drives in complete silence to my house, where he again half scoops me, half walks me to my bed and deposits me in the center of it, under the covers.

I gaze up at him, a single tear fogging into existence in the corner of my left eye. He sits on the edge of the bed and gently kisses my forehead, the tip of my nose, my chin.

"Everybody hates me," I say with a tiny sob, feeling pathetic. Useless. Paltry.

"But I love you," Will says.

"I'm so tired," I say, barely managing the words as my throat chokes closed. "I'm exhausted from trying so hard."

"Sleep."

"I don't think that's going to help."

"You have to start somewhere."

I close my eyes, relish the feeling of his thumb rubbing tiny circles on the edge of my jaw. He never falters until I lose consciousness.

I dream of Barcelona. I dream of the almond shape of Will's perfect blue eyes, the way he'd stand there patiently while I brushed my thumb back and forth across his top lashes as many times as I wanted. I dream of the way he'd smile when he thought I said something funny. Every variation of his one dimple, of both, of what kind of smiles brought them out. I dream of his voice and the way the tendons of his hand flexed when he shook the hand of the business partner we met in Barcelona. I dream of every atom that separated our bodies during that tour. I dream of his hands gripping the underside of my knee when we sat down for lunch, the way I could feel it in at least a dozen other places on my body.

I dream of everything I remember about that day. Except I can't dream of a single detail about that supplier's facility because I didn't pay any fucking attention.

CHAPTER THIRTY-SEVEN

My house smells like sugar and cinnamon when I wake. Bleary-eyed, I stumble out of bed and cross to the window. It's completely dark outside. I've been asleep all day.

I follow my nose to the kitchen. Will is sitting at the island in a chair too small for his frame, the bluish light of his computer screen lighting up his wan face. When he sees me, he glances up, his gaze evaluating.

"Did you bake muffins?" I point to the pan on top of my stove.

"Bought you a muffin pan, too."

I walk from the hall to the stove, reaching for a muffin. Before my hand makes contact, Will yanks me up by my waist and deposits me on the counter.

"You enjoy putting me up here," I comment.

"How are you feeling?"

"Hungry."

Will frowns, reaching behind him to grab a muffin. "They're raspberry."

I accept it and peel back the paper. When I take my first bite, some of the sugar dusting rains onto the floor between us. The corner of Will's lip curls into the ghost of a smile.

"How are they?"

I give him a thumbs-up while I chew. "What time is it?" I ask through a mouthful.

"Nine. You slept for ten hours."

I raise my eyebrows, both alarmed and unsurprised.

"Camila came by, but she didn't want to wake you."

I swallow. "She didn't say anything about extending her employment, did she?"

"No, but she *did* say something about forced PTO. For *you*. She's seriously worried about you." After a second he adds, "I am, too."

"Today was bad," I agree. "I'm not usually that bad."

"Wrong. You're usually better at hiding it."

I laugh brittlely. "This muffin is delicious."

Will glances down at it, then back up to me. "Yeah, well, I knew you liked raspberries."

"How?"

"That's the popsicle flavor you ordered in Barcelona."

His mention of Barcelona reminds me of my dream. My expression must shift; his does, too, like a mirror. "What's on your mind, Josie?"

I sigh. Lick the sugar from my fingertips. Will licks his thumb and uses it to sticker some of the sugar off my thighs before he presses it to his tongue. I temporarily lose concentration before my brain recalibrates.

"I didn't do a thorough evaluation of the Barcelona supplier. Or the ones in Bangalore, for that matter. I was too . . . love drunk."

Will's eyebrows draw together. "There wasn't anything we *saw* on those visits that could have prevented what happened today."

"But that's the point, Will. We didn't *see anything*. Or at least, I didn't."

His lips fold downward. "You act like we walked past a glaring red flag and ignored it."

"I just . . ." I put the muffin down and focus my attention on him. "I was distracted that day, is what I'm saying. I was distracted the entire rest of the trip."

"By me." His eyes search mine, plunging past my walls and hunting around the vulnerable parts of me that aren't saying what I really mean.

"Yes. By you."

For a few more seconds we're quiet.

"I did it again," he whispers, his blue eyes warm but sad.

"Did what?"

He looks sideways. "Ruined another thing for you."

My regret hits me like a boxing punch. I was only explaining my own shortcomings. I didn't want Will to *blame* himself for this.

I tip his chin back until he's facing me again. "You keep envisioning yourself as a catalyst for ruin," I say. "But Will—the truth is you're only a catalyst for change. And maybe it starts messy. But it always ends better."

"How is *this* better?" he asks, looking desperately disappointed. "This is exactly what you were afraid of." Will's hands move up my thighs to my waist, clutching tight. "Before we started this, you told me you were afraid I'd become very important to you, and it would distract you from what's *most* important. Revenant. I tried not to do it—tried to fit into your life in a way that allowed for both—but if you don't think it's worked, I've failed."

My eyes mist as I watch him watch me. My fingers trail over his cheek. "That's just it. You didn't become *very important* to me. *You* became what's most important."

I pull on his neck until my face is buried in his shoulder. "I love you," I whisper. "I don't want to part with you. I wouldn't be able to go on without you. But I don't know what to do now. I don't know how to balance it all. I can't *do* it."

I cry against him as he holds me, his hands rubbing circles on my back. "I love you, too, J. So much. But I can't do it either. If you aren't happy, if you aren't fulfilled, I can't be—I can't help—" He cuts himself off, unable to articulate, and keeps rubbing circles.

My body feels like a wrung-out dishrag, wrinkled, used up. After a few minutes, Will pulls back and puts his hands on my cheeks. His eyes lock on mine.

"You and I are going to have an adult conversation about this," he says. "And at the end of that conversation, we will not have broken up. Agreed?"

I nod. "I couldn't break up with you if the world depended on it, Will Grant."

He smiles tightly, looking conflicted by my admission. "You start. Say whatever you want, and we'll work through it."

I take a deep breath, feeling nervous and safe all at once. "When I picture your perfect partner, I don't picture a workaholic. I don't picture a basket case who can't open a social media app without coming close to a mental breakdown. I still feel like a villain half the time, Will, especially now, with the *Forbes* piece, and I just . . . I want *better* for you than me."

He presses his lips to my forehead—a gesture I've come to realize is meant to soothe *him*, primarily. "You say workaholic, I say driven. You call yourself a basket case, but I'd call you self-aware of your boundaries. And besides, the reason you're my perfect fit is because you're imperfect. I happen to love your imperfections."

"And any other time, I'd be selfish enough to let you," I whisper. "Because I want you that much. But this time, I bit off more than I could chew. I thought I could have it all, but I'm not that kind of girl. People don't root for me; they pray for my downfall. I'm going to be spending the rest of the year working my ass off to make sure Revenant doesn't tank for good. It isn't *fair* to you, to ask you to stand by me through that."

"*Fuck* fair," Will says, his face heating. "*Fuck* fair, Josephine. I don't need fair, I don't *want* fair. I've never even *heard* of a relationship that's entirely fair. Together, we make it whole. *Together,* we add up to one hundred percent. I can meet you more than halfway. I'll meet you at the seventy percent, eighty percent, ninety percent mark on your worst days if I have to, because I know you're giving me everything you can. And besides—you know what isn't fucking *fair?* It's not *fair* that people in Wisconsin and Florida and Oregon are acting like they know a single fucking thing about you."

I shake my head, voice weak. "Even Camila couldn't make it all work. She needed a change, wanted something different for herself, for her marriage, but I don't have that option because I *made* this business. I don't get to walk away from it like everyone else does."

Will comes back to me, puts his hands on me again. "Remember when I asked you what would happen if this all stopped? And you said you'd fall apart?"

I nod.

"You haven't fallen apart. You're in a tough spot, but you're whole."

"For now," I counter.

"So do something about it *now,*" he replies. "Don't keep going one hundred miles per hour when you burned out a long time ago. It won't *work.*"

"But I don't know where else to put my self-worth," I say, very slowly. It's a heartbreaking, vulnerable admission, but Will loves me enough to hear it. "When Revenant succeeds, I feel good about myself. When Revenant fails, I feel like a *failure.*"

His eyes shine. "I know that *you* know how unhealthy that is, sweetheart."

"I know. Believe me, I know," I say with a sob. "But I've always been like this! I've always stacked myself up against standards that are at least partly out of my control. Beauty standards, social media statistics, B Corp scores."

"The only person who has the power to change that," Will says, "is you."

His body slots between my legs. I rest my head on his shoulder, staring at my mint-green sewing machine on top of a stack of books I wish I had time to read.

After half a minute, Will asks, "Have you ever seen a therapist?"

I shake my head. "I've thought about it. Never scheduled anything."

"Do it, for me," he says.

"I will. I promise."

He steps away from me and settles against the opposite counter, hands slipping into the pockets of his trousers. He watches me thoughtfully, head tilted just so.

"I'm going to give you some space to sort this out. I'm not going anywhere," he clarifies when my face floods with alarm. "But even I can admit you need to figure this out on your own. I want to be there for you, Josie, I really do, but I'm not sure you know what you want yet. What your path forward looks like in a world where you stay whole."

"I want you," I say. "I love you."

His eyes darken. "I love you, too."

He comes back to me and kisses me tenderly, coaxing my head up, narrowing my world to only him. Will's lips taste like sugar, mine like salty tears. He slides his mouth against mine, soft but bruising. We kiss for seconds, minutes, years.

He is, without a doubt, the most important thing to me. In only three months, that's what he became. What could Will mean to me after six months, a year? How much paler will the importance of anything else be in comparison to him?

"Do what you have to do, Josephine," Will whispers against my lips. "Be honest with yourself. And rest easy knowing whatever solution you come up with, I'm going to love you through it."

Without another word, Will grabs his computer, his backpack, a raspberry muffin that means a lot more to me than a nine p.m. breakfast—

And he leaves.

He takes my permission to breathe with him when he goes.

CHAPTER THIRTY-EIGHT

Will giving me space doesn't push him further back in my brain. It doesn't transition him from the thing I want most—the person I spend all my spare time thinking of, hoping for, considering—to a memory I can call upon *only* when I want to.

I imagine myself at Will's place the first night I saw it, when he whispered into my neck *Everything I think about is in reference to you.*

Cami wasn't kidding about the forced time off. Derrick calls me the morning after Will leaves my house and says it's nonnegotiable, that he'll be staying in Austin all week to help smooth things over with the employees, the press, the customers.

"You stay home," Derrick tells me over the phone, "or take a vacation or something. Just don't come into work."

I left my computer at the office, so I don't really have another option.

The next day is Saturday. I wake up to the first blush of fall on the breeze, chilly and golden leaf scented. Gio and Leonie ride over to my house. I greet them at the front door in a slip of a nightgown, my hair piled in a bun, my thoughts groggy with sleep.

"Want to fuck around?" Gio asks. She smiles up at me, her face playful beneath her helmet. I smile back and nod, even though riding a bike will only make me think of Will. Of the two of us riding our bikes together past the sunbathing turtles on the Johnson Creek Greenbelt.

Everything I think about is in reference to you.

That's the problem with loving someone. When it happens, that person comes out of their box, and they start to fill every crack and shadow in your life. The memories of them get slippery, ethereal enough to move silently and appear before you at any moment.

Still, I change clothes and pump air into my bike tires, then climb onto it and ride away from my house with my friends.

We find a sparkling, dewy glade and spread out a picnic, sipping on grapefruit sodas and passing around a single spliff. We talk about the studio space Leonie rented for her yoga business, Gio quitting her grocery delivery gig because she's finally earning enough from social media on its own.

They're both working, earning a wage from something they're proud to do, and the difference between them and me is, it's not quietly killing them.

Drop everything, my mind whispers, *and change your mind.*

What had Camila said? *But now I have to do something else.*

I'm high, and feeling existential, and terrified of these thoughts.

"What are you thinking about, J?" Giovanna asks.

I sigh out a deep exhale, staring at the clouds. "I'm thinking about what my life would be like if Revenant had never existed at all."

The ground doesn't crack open. Lightning doesn't smite me.

Gio flips over and stares at me for a long time. "I can't fathom it," she says.

"I would have a softer, more anonymous life," I say.

"Do you wish that would have happened?" Leonie asks.

"No," I admit. "No, I wouldn't change a thing about the past. Only, possibly, the future."

I sleep soundly for a third night in a row, no alarm clock to rouse me in the morning. For hours, I stay in bed, hovering in a state of half consciousness, awake and then not, dreaming and then not. Around eleven I finally get up and make a carafe of coffee, and while I wait for the first mug to cool, I eat two raspberry muffins.

As I taste and chew and swallow, I imagine Will checking on me from the door of my bedroom while I slept that first day. I imagine him grabbing my car keys and heading to H-E-B, coming back with bags full of ingredients and unloading them on my counter. I imagine him pulling out a bowl, making a noise of exasperation when he fails to find a whisk.

Everything I think about—you.

I pull open my refrigerator door to see if I have any unexpired cream for the coffee.

It's completely stocked.

Vegetables, fruits, coffee creamer, black bean burgers, cauliflower korma, a giant bowl of salad he made himself topped with chickpeas and pepitas. Seltzers and wine and bottled iced tea.

I collapse onto the floor in tears, overwhelmed beyond belief I get to be loved this way. We started off rocky, but Will has shown me again and again and *again* how much he cares, how far he'll go.

I want to be this way for him.

I need to figure out how to get myself to that place.

Suddenly, the quiet of my house feels engulfing. Ever since Camila moved out, I have felt a loneliness in this place I can't even comprehend. Now, with her moving away, the feeling punches me in the stomach as one final, devastating blow.

I shut the fridge, search for my phone in a panic to text Will thank you just before a knock comes from the front door. My head snaps up, and I run across the hardwood floors of my house, peering through the tiny window as I stretch onto my tiptoes.

It isn't him. It's a delivery man, with a truck parked at the curb behind him.

I pull open the door. The man smiles at me. "Josephine Davis?" I nod hesitantly. "Sign here." He hands me a tablet.

"I wasn't expecting anything," I say as I sign my name.

"Well, you should clear some space. There are a lot of bolts here that someone wants you to have."

I tilt my head. "Bolts . . . of *fabric*?"

The man nods, turning away to head down the steps.

He brings them in two at a time. I offer to help, but he shakes his head at me firmly and asks me where I'd like them. I clear a space in the living room so he can line them up on the floor. There are cottons, silks, polyesters, chiffons, satins, rayons.

"That's the last of them," he says, hands on his hips.

I fish a twenty out of my wallet and hand it to him. "Who are these from?"

The delivery man shrugs. "It was your name on the invoice."

When he leaves, I crouch down on my carpet and start running my hands over the fabric. Already, my mind is spinning, inventing designs in my head.

Did you send the fabric? I text Will.

You once told me that if you had nothing to do, you'd start designing again, he replies.

I don't have the energy to tell him he shouldn't have. It just means too damn much that he *did*.

> **Josie:** Thank you. I don't know how to repay you
> for this, but I'll think of something.
> **Will:** Is it okay if I swing by tonight to drop off one
> more thing? I won't stay, but this is important.
> **Josie:** Of course. I love you
> **Will:** Love you too

I smile down at my phone screen, my heartbeat rocketing skyward.

All the things that mattered most two days ago seem inconsequential now. I have no craving to go online and read opinions about myself I know are untrue. I have no craving to overwork myself because I found five spare minutes to answer emails. The only thing I crave is to *make*, with my *hands*.

I clear off my kitchen table for the first time in months, pull it into the center of the room, and line up my three sewing machines on it. I check the bobbins, dust off the dials. In the back of the closet in Cami's old room, I still have all the patterns Mom gave me when Oma died. I pull those out, too, pick a few of the fanciest to experiment with.

This time, when my mom's contact lights up my phone screen, I answer.

"I'm sewing," I tell her.

I hear her breath audibly cut off, stopping whatever rant she was about to embark on in its tracks. Because what I meant but didn't say is *I'm healing*.

And Mom remembers from years ago—right after Oma died, right after Zoe and I cut each other off—when I'd been slashed open twice and tried to sew myself back together. She remembers it wasn't until I put my focus into *this* that I started to see the light at the end of the tunnel.

"What are you sewing?" she asks.

"A dress, I think."

"A fancy one?" she asks hopefully.

"Very fancy," I say. "I came into some high-end fabrics."

"If it turns out nicely, you should wear it to Camila's rehearsal dinner," she says.

"Maybe I will."

"Now," Mom says, settling in. "Do you know what you're going to say during your maid of honor speech?"

I'm having a hard time putting into words what Camila means to me. Mom says she can write down the ideas since my hands are occupied. We talk on the phone for two hours. When we're finished, I have half a dress made. The top part, mostly, which is a fitted princess style, in a midnight-blue color that looks almost purple in the window light. I put it onto a mannequin I find in my garage.

"Darling, I have to go. We have dinner tonight with those *frightful* Spanglers."

I smile to myself, holding up a bolt of chiffon fabric against the bottom half of the mannequin. "Okay. Thanks for calling."

After she hangs up, I spend another thirty minutes deciding whether to go for a different fabric with a full, billowing skirt or keep the same material and do something slimmer.

I've just decided to go with the fancier skirt when my doorbell rings.

Will.

My heart feeling lighter than it has in days, I sprint to the front door and fling it open.

Only it isn't him standing on my front porch.

It's Zoe.

CHAPTER THIRTY-NINE

She looks just like the sophisticated woman in Will's photos. No more round cheeks, no more Kool-Aid streak in her hair. I've preserved Zoe Grant in my mind as a seventeen-year-old girl, but she's an adult now. With fully developed frontal lobes, just like the rest of us.

Zoe's always been a few inches shorter than me, but the way she stands is full of a confident presence. Her face is clean, her hair still damp from a shower. She's dressed in sandals and a simple white sundress with small yellow flowers.

"Hi," she says, her voice sending me all the way back to that study hall when I asked if I could read her short story and she said, *Oh my gosh, you're secretly weird, too!*

I gulp. "H-hi," I manage.

In the next breath, we're hugging.

Instantly, I feel like an emotionally charged teenager again, clutching my first best friend close as tears prick at my eyes, dance across my cheeks, and land on her shoulders. She sob-laughs against my collarbone and I choke out a laugh of my own. When I pull back to look at her, she beams a thousand-watt smile at me.

"I missed you," we say at the exact same moment, and then laugh awkwardly.

Her expression is open and clear. She evaluates me warmly as I evaluate her.

Out of the corner of my eye, I see Will's car peel out of my driveway and take a left. I love him, I *love* him. I love the way he knows I can want him all the time, but I *need* to see Zoe in this instant more than anyone else.

I hurry out of the entryway and beckon her inside, blushing furiously at the state of myself. I'm in bike shorts and an oversized T-shirt, my feet bare, my messy hair in a bun on top of my head. I don't think I've showered in a while, honestly.

Zoe's eyes roam over the bolts of fabric, the mannequin, the muffins still on the kitchen counter next to a few of my dirty coffee mugs.

"Can I get you something to drink?" I ask.

"Sure," she says, offering me a tight-lipped smile while she blushes. "Do you have wine? I think we might need it."

My laugh is giddy and euphoric and nervous now that the reality of this meeting has settled in. I make my way to the fridge and grab the bottle of white from the door. "Or do you prefer red?"

"I like white," she says, giving me another half smile.

It's painfully quiet as I grab two dusty glasses out of the cabinet, give them a rinse, and then struggle to uncork the bottle. Zoe walks close to the mannequin, examining my half-built dress.

"What are you making?" she asks.

"It's a formal dress," I say, uncorking the wine bottle with a soft *pop*. "If it looks okay, I might wear it to my best friend's rehearsal dinner next weekend."

"Camila?"

I lift the wine bottle, pouring the first glass. "Yeah. Camila."

She keeps studying the gown. "Looks like something the Princess of Elthior might wear."

When I glance over, Zoe throws me a wink. It softens some of the discomfort.

"Do you still write fiction?"

She shakes her head. "I only write about writers these days."

"*The New York Times Book Review* is very impressive," I say.

She walks over to the kitchen island, scooping up one of the glasses. "I guess we're both just very impressive."

We head out to the back patio, settling into chairs with soft cushions I pull out of a storage bin. The early-fall night is still that Texas brand of warm. The crisp wine sliding down my throat feels like a boost I desperately need.

My heartbeat thumps. Fast. Every one of my biorhythms is in jeopardy. There are so many ways this conversation can go, and I'm terrified of all of them.

Zoe sets her glass down on the table between us, looking equally shy. "I'm sorry it's taken me this long to see you."

I shake my head. "Me, too. I mean, Will mentioned you wanted to talk, but you wanted it to be in person, and I totally understood. I could have come up to New York. I *should* have."

Zoe sighs, breaking into a smile. "I think we were both nervous."

"Yeah."

"I owe you an apology," she says.

"Me first," I say.

"No," Zoe says, though she's still smiling. She grabs her wineglass and takes a deep gulp, then looks out at my yard. "I know I don't have to explain to you what your friendship meant to me that year."

I shake my head. "You don't. Because it was the exact same level of importance for me."

"You know how people joke about an ex teaching you something valuable about yourself you carry forward into your next relationship?" she asks.

"Sure," I say, thinking of Clay, and even of my high school boyfriend. I learned lessons from them both that have made me a better girlfriend for Will.

"I think it applies to girlhood friendships, too," Zoe says thoughtfully. "Every friendship that came after you, I found it easier to navigate the tough spots. I learned how to talk it out. How to reason through the actions of another person. It's helped me in romantic love, too, but it started with you. A best friend."

She looks back at me, her expression faraway. "What I'm getting at, Josie, is I think we had to make a big mistake so we could learn from each other. And even though that's kind of tragic, it's poetic, too."

I swipe a tear from my eye, struck by the beauty of her phrasing. Lessons learned.

The pact I made with Camila comes to mind: *If you ever hurt my feelings, I'll tell you, and we'll have a conversation about it. Same goes for you if I hurt yours. And we do our best not to hurt each other in the first place. Deal?*

I was a *better* friend to Camila because I hadn't been as good at it with Zoe. It *is* tragic, and it *is* poetic, too.

"I spent my entire freshman year of college wishing I could talk to you," Zoe goes on. "I felt so horribly guilty for shutting you out, for never responding to that letter you wrote me. On paper or in person. I read it and panicked. My body locked up and I didn't know what to do. And then Will told me about our dad, and—my priorities were skewing every hour. I *knew* you were hurting, that I'd driven this metaphorical knife into you even deeper. I knew all of this, and instead of fixing it, I just wallowed in it, until I convinced myself that too much time had passed, that you were better off not hearing from me at all."

She turns to me, her eyes wet. "I'm sorry, Josie. I'm sorry I didn't have more faith in you. I'm sorry I didn't say more to you about your oma's passing. I have regretted it every year of my life since, and when Will told me he'd run back into you, that he'd offered to be your consultant, I felt this . . . *relief*. Like a weight off my chest, like it was fate."

"Zoe," I say, my voice pained. "Even back then, when I didn't know what was going on with your parents, I *still* didn't think you owed me anything. *I'm* sorry. I should have known you'd be hurt when Will and I kissed. And I also shouldn't have let you push me away. Your family was hurting, too. We could have been there for each other. I'm sorry about a lot, but I'm mostly sorry you needed a friend during a hard time and didn't have one."

Zoe reaches across the table and squeezes my hand. I squeeze back while a very old hole in my heart patches itself. "I forgive you. And anyway, we were teenagers," she says, rolling her eyes. "It was basically a simulation."

I laugh easily and gulp more of my wine.

"This was meant to happen." Zoe dips her chin, a tiny but confident nod. "You and Will were meant to find each other again, to fall in love. I'm a big believer in fate."

"I remember," I murmur. "That four-letter word is still both of our phone passcodes."

She laughs. "No way."

"Way."

We talk about everything, all night long. Jobs and cities and fashion and books and vacations and *Where Are They Now: Woodmont High Edition*. We drain the bottle, drain another. I consult with Zoe on what type of skirt to sew for the dress. We take blurry selfies to send to our mothers. Zoe doubles down on the greatness of New York City, throws out five different weekends she'd love for me and Will to visit. I don't even bother checking my work schedule before promising to pick one before she leaves town.

Later that night, she squeezes me and slips down the driveway, back into Will's car. He watches me through the windshield and I mouth *Thank you.*

He dips his chin, mouth quirked.

And the Grant twins drive away.

CHAPTER FORTY

The intern send-off party is now doubling as Camila's goodbye gathering. She picks me up from my house at four p.m. and we drive together to Zilker Brewing. In the car, we blast all our favorite songs we listened to on repeat during college.

"You look how I feel!" I shout over the wind, which shoots past in humid gusts outside our open windows.

"Lightweight? Carefree? Unbothered?"

"All of the above!"

Camila slants me a grin. She flips on her blinker. "I'm getting married this weekend."

"You're getting *married* this weekend!"

"I'm moving to New York City!"

"You're going to be a *wife* and a *student* in New York City," I say.

"Will you visit? As soon as you can?" Cami asks. "I'm not talking about a dinner when you're in town for work, I'm talking about a real visit."

"You name the day, Cami. I'll be there."

"I know it isn't your favorite city," she says.

"I want to give it another chance."

She smirks at me. "You really are in a good mood. I take it the conversation with Zoe went well?"

I gape at her. "You *knew* about that?"

She rolls her eyes at me. "You think I just left your house without conspiring with Will on a *plan*? Give me a little credit."

The second we show up to the party, my own career woes are forgotten. What's amazing about college interns is their drama will always knock out your own.

Of course, once the party gets going, I receive curious looks from some of our employees. There are even a few who come up to me and urgently whisper-promise that they never said a *word* to Margaret Dwyer and don't know anyone else who did, either. I thank them and otherwise get very uncomfortable about it, even though their sincerity means so much to me.

It isn't that I've ever expected to be liked by everyone. But it's nice to be liked by, at the very least, quite a few.

And then, the intern drama begins.

It starts with three girls who burst into tears at interspersed twenty-minute intervals, each of them looking forlornly in the direction of freckled-intern Andrew whenever they wipe their eyes. Andrew, in turn, surrounded by the other guys, can't keep his eyes off Eugenia—who has remained by my side from the first instant she spotted me.

"What is going *on*?" I ask her. We're sitting at a picnic table outside the brewery with Camila and a few of the retail staff. The bulk of the interns, Andrew included, are in a huddle a few tables away, gossiping and pointing between Eugenia and the three crying girls (commiserating by the outdoor bar).

"Andrew and I hooked up a few times at the start of the summer," Eugenia explains. "I ended things because it was getting too serious, and then he hooked up with Eva. But Eva's boyfriend back home in New Hampshire found out she hooked up with Andrew, and also, Melanie—who lived with Eva this summer—got pissed because she's apparently had a crush on Andrew the whole time and supposedly Eva *knew* that and boinked him anyway. I don't know why Cassie is crying, that one is lost on me. But look, it's not my problem those girls are in love with him and he's in love with me."

"Are we watching a live reenactment of *A Midsummer Night's Dream*?" Cami asks.

"If so, then you're Puck," Eugenia decides.

"Me?" Cami raises an eyebrow. "Why am I Puck?"

"Don't think I wasn't listening when you predicted this exact scenario at the donut breakfast months ago."

Camila smirks. "I am sort of omniscient, aren't I?"

Eugenia takes another sip of her drink. Her eyes drift over to Andrew's. "I don't *mean* to hurt anyone's feelings," she says, her voice softening into wistful territory. "But I can't have it all, and for the next several years, I need to prioritize my career." She turns to look at me. "Same as you did. Right?"

"I don't think it's true you can't have it all." I nod at Camila, whose eyes soften. "Cami and David have been together since she was twenty-two, and she's one of the most successful businesswomen I know. My college boyfriend and I didn't last not because I couldn't have made it work," I explain, "but because he wasn't the right person for me. When you *find* the right person, your brain moves past wanting to have it all. Instead, you start to think about how you can have as much as possible with each other."

"That's . . ." Camila tilts her head, biting on a smile. "Exactly right."

"I can be wise sometimes," I say.

"You guys aren't helping," Eugenia grumbles. "He goes to UDub! And yeah, I dumped him, but it hurt my feelings he slept with Eva."

"Which one is Eva?" Cami asks.

"The software engineering major," someone reminds her.

"What does your *heart* tell you?" I ask Eugenia, only halfway serious.

She considers for several long moments, her gaze lingering on the freckled boy in question over Camila's shoulder. At this point, everyone at our table, including the retail team, is waiting on her answer with bated breath.

"My heart tells me if it's meant to be, Andrew and I will find our way back to each other," she decides, and then nods once. "But right now, it's not a relationship I would describe as healthy. And we don't give our unconditional love to the things that hurt us."

We all stare in stunned silence.

"I can be wise sometimes," Eugenia says.

I find Derrick in the Revenant office, just as I predicted.

It's perfectly quiet up here, save for the soft tapping of his fingertips on his laptop keyboard. He's in his favorite conference room, the lights dimmed, his salt-and-pepper hair pushed away from his face, wire-rimmed glasses across the bridge of his nose.

When he spots me through the glass wall, he doesn't look surprised.

"What's that?" he asks when I open the door.

I set the six-pack of pilsner down on the table. "You weren't at the party, so I brought you some beer."

He gives me a half smile. "Crack them open."

I pull two cans out of the plastic and pop the tabs. "What are you doing?"

He gives me a look. "You first."

I set one of the beers down in front of him and take a seat.

I know this place so well that I know exactly which chair I'm sitting in. It's the one that has a tiny *squeak* when you swivel left.

"I'm really tired, Derrick."

When I glance at him, he's already nodding, like he knows what I mean. "I . . ." He drifts off, tapping on the screen of his phone. It lights up with a picture of his daughter Maggie. "I never told you this, Josie. But the day before you pitched me, Maggie had basically already convinced me to invest with you."

I tilt my head at him. "She did?"

"Maggie was your biggest advocate. Loved the brand. Respected your ethos. Don't get me wrong, you knocked your pitch out of the park, but I was biased in your favor coming into the room."

I smile at the table. "Tell Maggie I said thanks."

It's quiet for a moment.

"Just say it, Josephine."

The beer can between my hands starts to glisten as my vision blurs. "I don't know if I can do this anymore," I whisper.

In my head, Eugenia's words repeat on a loop: *We don't give our unconditional love to the things that hurt us.*

"I have loved this company with my whole heart, the whole time," I go on. "It has saved me, and healed me, and broken me in half. I've given the employees and the customers all I can. And now I just don't know if I have anything left to give."

I've spent seven years in a tunnel, focused on only this. Making this. Building this.

But six years later, Revenant has legs to stand on. It can weather a storm without me.

Probably, it can weather a storm *better* without me.

"I know, Josie," Derrick says.

When I look at him, his eyes are calm, unsurprised. "How?"

"Camila." He shrugs. "I knew if *she* had burned out, you weren't far behind."

"I didn't mean for this to happen," I tell him, sighing. "I loved my CEO classes. I love the people I work with, and I love the *work,* too. But lately, it hasn't been loving me, my body, my mind. I'm not showing up as my best self anymore."

Derrick leans forward onto his elbows. "I want to make you a deal."

I smirk. "Why does that not surprise me?"

"Because we've known each other a long time now," he says. A blip of humor crosses his face, and then he's back to business. The Derrick I know. "I hear you, Josie. And I see what you've been through. Not just that, but I'm starting to see what all women in executive positions have been through, dealt with, that men have never once had to entertain. I'm starting to understand. And I want to make you a deal."

A tiny smile steals over my face. "I'm listening."

"I take over for one year," Derrick says. "If one year goes by, and you don't want it back, then *together* we look for a new CEO."

I cock my head sideways in disbelief. "You could do that for an entire year? What about your other investments?"

"I have plenty of money," he says, "which means I have plenty of people who can handle the other investments. *This* is the one that means the most to Maggie." He shifts in his seat. "Frankly, *this* is the one that means the most to me. I'll move here temporarily to make it work."

We stare at each other for a few moments.

"What if I can't do it?" I ask. "What if a year passes and I still don't feel right about it?"

Derrick shrugs. "Then you become a board member. And you watch someone else pick up the torch."

In a trance, I nod. Somehow both unsure about and okay with this option.

I don't know what the future holds, and for the first time in a long time, it's better that way. Right now, I'm operating with one goal. He has blue eyes, dimples, a crooked smile. He takes my tired body and pulls it into his arms.

Today, this month, maybe all year, *he's* what I'm working toward. Not because I want to deserve him, but because I already do.

But when I leave the office a little while later, my hands skimming over the racks of sample clothes on my way out the door, it occurs to me this place and these people don't actually need *me* anymore.

Camila and I can *both* go, and Revenant will stay.

It's fucking freeing.

CHAPTER FORTY-ONE

Camila and David's wedding weekend is perfect.

It's *perfect*.

At the bridal brunch, we laugh until our stomachs are sore, retelling every story we remember from the bachelorette. At the rehearsal dinner, in my newly finished midnight dress, I give the speech my mom and I wrote, with practiced ease. David's best man comes up to the mic afterward and makes a joke about the unfairness of having to follow a CEO. Which doesn't make any sense considering I *did* have to pause three times to swallow my tears.

On wedding day, the weather is a balmy seventy degrees, the breeze light, the sun cascading through the trees and bathing the outdoor venue in an effervescent halo. Camila walks down the grassy, petal-laden aisle like a goddess, and she looks so damn happy watching David waiting for her that I marvel at how special it is to get to witness this kind of commitment.

We dance all night, and right before Camila and David make

their grand exit, David pulls me aside and thanks me for loving his wife just as much as he loves her.

Which basically just ruins me.

"Where's Will?" he asks after I stop blubbering over him.

"He had family in town," I say, making an excuse. He'd gotten a verbal invitation to the wedding but had texted me to say he was going to spend as much time with Zoe and his mom as possible while they were down here.

David nods. "Maybe we'll catch him again soon? When we get settled in New York."

"I hope so," I say.

"You're done now, J." David turns in the direction of the tunnel of people holding unlit sparklers outside the reception hall. Camila comes out of the side bathroom, running toward us with a big smile on her face, and her brand-new husband says to me, "You did a great job."

The very next morning, I text and ask if I can see him.

Will tells me he's at Lake Travis with his family, but I should come over at five o'clock after he drops them off at the airport.

We text all day to tide ourselves over. I tell him about Camila's wedding; Will sends me pictures of his canoe against the sparkling lake water.

Soft living aesthetic! I joke.

It's calling you, he replies.

I spend the afternoon getting ready. Like a nervous teenager headed off on her first date. Blush on my cheeks, a gentle curl in my hair, jean shorts and an oversized cotton button-down.

I knock on his front door with a tiny shake in my bones. Behind me, the sun is splashing across my neck and legs, but I can't help but shiver.

After thirty seconds, Will opens the door.

"I really love you," I say, the *moment* I catch his eye. "And I really mean it. I actually love the way you snore. It's like a noise machine that was designed to remind me you're there as I drift off to sleep. That you aren't made up. You're real, and you're breathing. You're *badly* breathing, but you're breathing near me. And I love that you've made mistakes, and that you shared them with me, so I don't feel alone with mine. I love that you remember, that you bought me fabric because *months* ago, I mentioned offhandedly that I might want it for when I was doing nothing. I love everything you ever DM'd to the Revenant account. I love how you held me in your arms the night I was sick even though I was still holding you at a distance."

Will's dimples pop out, familiar and perfect and adorable. His lips are pressed together but expressive all the same.

"We can spend some of our weekends on the couch, you watching sports and me doing something else nearby that doesn't require my participation in your hobby but is still respectful of it. And probably, on those days, something you're cooking is in the oven or on the stove. And maybe—not soon, but one day—we have a doodle. Because of your allergies, and because I just like them."

"Josie," he tries to say, his voice gentle.

"I'm almost done," I say. "I still have to get to the serious part."

I shuffle my feet and look down to calm my nerves before meeting his Blue Ridge Mountain eyes again. "The thing is, Will. The thing is, even if you *hadn't* come into my life this summer, Camila still would have left Revenant. Margaret Dwyer still wouldn't have done a very good job planning the pop-up. I'd still be working with that shitty consulting firm, and I still would have tried to become B Corp Certified on what I can now see is an absurdly condensed timeline. I probably still would have ignored Nora Lindberg, and she might still have published about me. All of that is true, even if we had never met, even if you'd never crashed your bike into my bumper that day. It would all still be true. Basically, what I'm saying is I was *always* going to burn out at the end of this summer. I was *always* going to fall apart."

I swipe at a salty tear on my cheek, recalling his words from Barcelona.

You're a revenant, Josephine. And if you fall apart again, you'll put yourself back together again. *Because you're strong.*

"But you told me you'd be there to hold my broken pieces," I go on. "And *that's* the difference. You lived up to your word. You never pressured me. You gave me space to make a tough decision on my own."

"I didn't go very far," Will says. His eyes are kind.

"I know, and that's special, too," I say. "I quit my job yesterday. Maybe it's anti-girl-bossified of me to say this, but part of me quit for you. Part of me quit for *me,* too, but the thing is, I love you, which means you're a factor in my decisions. Everything I think about is in reference to you."

"That's my line," Will says.

"Now it's *our* line."

Will tugs on my arm then, pulling me into a fierce hug. He smells like warm cinnamon in sunlight, feels like a safe place. His arms trail down my back and haul my waist against his, pushing our bodies flush.

"I've got no fucking clue if I'll go back to Revenant," I whisper to him. "No clue. I am made up of broken pieces right now. My best friend is leaving, and I don't know if I can have a healthy relationship with my company ever again, and my anxiety still spikes when I think about all the stuff being said about me online. But I can live with the fact that somebody in Wisconsin doesn't think I'm a good person if the people who *matter* to me do. If *you* do."

After a few beats of silence, Will says, "Now?"

I laugh, the sound garbled. "Sure, go ahead."

Will noses along my neck, and my skin sparks at his touch. His hands clutch onto my hips. "I missed you."

"That was too easy," I whisper.

"Because I'm only giving you a moment to breathe," Will whispers. "I have things to say to you, too."

"Okay."

He hugs me close, runs his hand through my hair. "Brooks and I are going to start a catering company."

I smile against his chest. "That's amazing. I happen to know someone with entrepreneurial experience, plenty of free time, and about a million favors to pay back who could help you."

"What does she charge?" he murmurs.

"I'll have to defer to my consultant on that."

We're delirious as our hands roam each other. Will pulls away just enough to meet my eyes and bends his head in my direction. The sunlight is making his eyes iridescent. "You're still a person with a meaningful existence, Josie, even now that you want to be different than you were. *Especially* now." His voice is low, his tone sure. "You're my favorite person. You've guided me in so many ways."

"It's mutual," I say. Which feels wholly insufficient and is also exactly what I mean.

Will shakes his head, biting his lip. He moves his hands up to my cheeks, holding each of them. "I've spent the last few days with my mom and my sister revisiting all our favorite places in Austin. Doing our favorite things. I used to think I couldn't be here for too long without it stinging because of the memories of Dad. But now, when I think of Austin, I think of you. Us. Here, together, in our home. For years now, I've been untethered, fighting my instincts, but looking for a feeling of peace. I found it the day I ran into your car. *You* are the good feeling."

I grab his wrists, drag his arms back around my waist. "In that case," I breathe, "I think we should just be together."

"Because we both fucking deserve it," Will adds. "Because I'm pretty sure everything in my life—everything I've done, every choice

I've made—has pointed me straight back to you. How I love you, why I love you, the way I love you."

I grip the back of his neck, feeling overwhelmed that I might possibly be this lucky.

"I didn't think this would ever happen to me," I admit, the words tripping off my tongue.

His lips graze mine, close but still resisting. "Being this much in love?"

"Being at peace," I explain, repeating his same sentiment. "That's why I get to love you. You helped me find it."

Will kisses me then, and our emotions pour back and forth between us—all of me feeling all of him, him understanding every part of me. The good, the bad, the messy, the broken. Carefully, slowly, Will scoops me into his arms and carries me upstairs to his bedroom.

And the only thing I want to make—now, and probably months from now—is this love. Which feels like a fate we deserve and a peace we earned.

EPILOGUE

Fall

We go apple picking at an orchard forty-five minutes outside the city and wind up with inside-out clothes and kiss-bruised lips when we make it back to the car.

I start an Etsy shop for custom ribbons and bridal sashes—because I'm me, and even when I'm doing nothing, I can't do *nothing*. When I'm not at my sewing machine, I'm helping Will and Brooks set up their business. Which mostly consists of recipe tasting (more aspiring than vegetarian) and "borrowing" the Revenant photographer to take photos for their new website. I repay Will in favors, finally feeling fair, even though I've accepted nothing is.

We visit New York in early November, stay with Cami and David close to Gramercy Park. I meet Zoe's boyfriend, Martin, a bespectacled Londoner who fits her so perfectly I see exactly what Will meant when he said he can't fault him.

Will and I return home to a warmer autumn in Austin and fall deeper in love.

Winter

I start therapy in December, the same week Will and Brooks do their first catering gig. My Etsy shop explodes over the holiday season, which keeps me busy on the nights he's working. I never re-download social media, but I do send Will a selfie per day, and in return, he shows me all the things he's DM'd my latest defunct account.

On the nights Will isn't working, we sometimes try a new restaurant on our ever-growing list, sip cocktails with fancy names, and then make drunk, messy, verbal love when we stumble back to his town house.

Other nights, we'll stay home—usually his place—and make slow, desperate, quiet love that lasts *hours* and folds time.

Christmas is in Nashville. Christmas Eve with my family, the morning after with his mom and Zoe. It snows, and I catch snowflakes on my tongue, and Will's cheeks go rosier the longer I make him stand outside.

Spring

We go on countless bike rides, plant flowers outside Will's house. He says nothing at all as more and more of my things accumulate there. My bike, my only phone charger, two out of four of my sewing machines. Will simply clears a space and makes me feel like he'd been patiently waiting for those things to arrive.

We visit New York again with Gio and Leonie, who insist on a three-hour expedition to the Times Square Margaritaville with the whole gang. Will keeps his hand on my knee in the sticky booth and moans with boyish grief every time a Jimmy Buffet song comes on. I laugh at him and swoon over him and love him.

"I never got to see him live," Will complains, slurping on his cocktail.

"At least we have Margaritaville," I say.

On the other side of the table, Camila and Zoe are exchanging phone numbers.

Summer

JOSEPHINE DAVIS HAS FOUND HER THIRD WIND
By Zoe Grant for *The New York Times*

You know the brand, and you know the name. Now it's time you knew the person.

Josephine Davis was eighteen years old when she left her hometown of Nashville behind and relocated to Austin, Texas—where she would spend her next four years of college, and another six years after that building her company.

Josie grew up sewing with her grandmother, she tells me on a sunny afternoon when I'm invited into her home for the purpose of gathering notes for this piece. She lives in a dated, unassuming house not far from the South Congress shops (where the first physical store of her beloved brand has been thriving for almost a year now). Josie's refrigerator is mostly empty, every available surface covered with patterns or scraps of fabric or a container of buttons. She points to an old sewing machine in a corner. "That one was Oma's favorite," she says. "It isn't very functional, but I love to have it around."

One thing Revenant's customers might be surprised to learn is Josie didn't set out to build her company the way it currently exists. "It was mostly one-off designs I'd sell via DM at first," she admits, adding a laugh. "The buyers would just Venmo me. But the demand got away from me in those early days, and I couldn't bear to tell anyone no. Eventually I came to the conclusion I was going to need to grow or let the following down. I chose to grow."

Between the early days of one-offs and the brand we know today came the dramatic exit of both Camila Sanchez and Davis from the company around this time last year—and the social media storm that surrounded it.

"Neither Camila nor I left because of the bad press," Josie assures me. "We're still best friends, and we still love the brand. But as coincidence would have it, it was time for each of us to take a step back and leave Revenant in Derrick Lovell's hands.

"I spent years putting all my worth into that company," she goes on, sipping a grapefruit-and-seltzer mocktail. "Its success or failure was literally tied to what I believed about myself as a human being. I left no room for error. I left no room for other priorities. With therapy and a life change, I'm in a much better place now where things can be different, but last year, it was nonnegotiable for me to take a break."

When I ask her what part of her life changed, she blushes.

Josie tells me she's spent the last year figuring out what she wants for the rest of her twenties, her thirties, her forties. In between, she made dresses that sold at auction for charities, took vacations, joined a local book club. She helped her boyfriend get his catering business off the ground and spent time with her niece and nephew in North Carolina.

"And now?" I ask her—the question you've all been waiting on, as rumors continue to circulate about whether Josephine Davis's "step back" from Revenant was temporary or not. "What are you planning to do now?"

Josie's eyes drift over to a U-Haul packing box in a corner of her living room; it's been halfway loaded with books, some of which I recommended to her myself.

She's headed for a new life phase, she explains, which starts with selling this house because "Will can't bear to part with his kitchen, and I want to leave my memories of this place just to me and Camila. I'm moving in with my boyfriend," she says. "We're getting a puppy."

"And Revenant?" I probe.

She takes a deep breath, and answers:

ACKNOWLEDGMENTS

I am *still* overwhelmed to be in this position—writing thank-you notes to the people who helped me build this book. Especially after debuting, I'm now aware of what a group effort it is to not only publish a novel, but have that novel reach its readership. And I just feel so lucky to be in this position.

To Sallie Lotz, my phenomenal editor: thank you for your guidance on this one. I'm always sort of enchanted by your feedback, which is openhanded, probing, heartfelt, and genius. I'm well aware I'm not the type of writer who can give you something near finished that I've done in a vacuum; but it's been an honor to reinvent these characters with you. I'm also insanely grateful for the other books you've worked on, which have been a joy to read, and, for one reason or another, almost always bring me to tears. The kinship I feel to those stories constantly reaffirms my trust in your instincts.

To Melissa Edwards, my agent extraordinaire: thank you for reading all my words with enthusiasm and unmatched speed and for believing so fiercely in my stories. You encourage me to take chances and then allow me the space to do so. It truly means the world to me.

To Olga Grlic and Petra Braun, who designed and illustrated this cover: what is there to say, really, other than *ohmygoditsperfect!!!*

To the team at St. Martin's Press who helped with either *Love Interest* or *Perfect Fit* (or both!): thank you! This includes anyone who helped with copyedits, page design, proofreading, production, marketing, and publicity. And possibly something else they keep secret from me. Those of you I've met have been wonderful, and those of you I haven't have been my sneaky helpers.

Thank you to the drivers who distribute my books to retailers or drop packages at customer doors. You don't get thanked very often, even though you sometimes get asked to dance for Ring cameras or TikTok, and anyway—I see you, I'm with you, and I'll keep doing my best to make your jobs a little easier. Thanks for helping my dreams come true.

Thank you to the seriously wonderful team at Parnassus Books, my hometown heroes.

A moment of appreciation for the girl bosses. Though problematic some of you certainly were (as people but also, like, as a concept), you were also groundbreaking, and hardworking, and inspiring. I'm grateful you existed. I hope you exist again, differently, and better, and permanently.

To the entire bookstagram community: God, I love you guys. You're it for me. Let's do this forever. Let's keep it this good always.

To Anna, who kept me sane in Knoxville while I drafted this: thank you beyond belief.

Hannah Bonam-Young: thanks for being the first to read about Josie and Will.

Endless, eternal, unrelenting love to my friends and family who showed up for me in countless ways during my debut month.

Including the chic and aesthetic launch party of my dreams! I will seriously never be over it.

Lastly, to my fiancé, Morgan—who was designing an engagement ring for me last October while I focused on launching my book, then proposed on Christmas Eve after the dust had settled, after the storm of debuting a novel had cleared—I love you quite a bit.

ABOUT THE AUTHOR

Kelsey Shea Photography

Clare Gilmore lives in Charlotte, North Carolina, with her fiancé and a rambunctious dog. She spends her moonlight hours cooking excessively elaborate meals and planning more vacations than she'll ever be able to take.